PSEUDEPIGRAPHIC PERSPECTIVES:
THE APOCRYPHA AND PSEUDEPIGRAPHA
IN LIGHT OF THE DEAD SEA SCROLLS

STUDIES ON THE TEXTS
OF THE DESERT OF JUDAH

EDITED BY

F. GARCÍA MARTÍNEZ
A. S. VAN DER WOUDE

VOLUME XXXI

PSEUDEPIGRAPHIC PERSPECTIVES:
THE APOCRYPHA AND PSEUDEPIGRAPHA
IN LIGHT OF THE DEAD SEA SCROLLS

*Proceedings of the International Symposium of the Orion Center for
the Study of the Dead Sea Scrolls and Associated Literature,
12-14 January, 1997*

EDITED BY

ESTHER G. CHAZON

AND

MICHAEL STONE

WITH THE COLLABORATION OF

AVITAL PINNICK

BRILL
LEIDEN · BOSTON · KÖLN
1999

This book is printed on acid-free paper.

Library of Congress Cataloging-in-Publication Data

Orion Center for the Study of the Dead Sea Scrolls and Associated
Literature. International Symposium (2nd : 1997)
   Pseudepigraphic perspectives : the apocrypha and pseudepigrapha in
light of the Dead Sea scrolls : proceedings of the International
Symposium of the Orion Center for the Study of the Dead Sea Scrolls
and Associated Literature, 12-14 January, 1997 / edited by Esther G.
Chazon and Michael Stone with collaboration of Avital Pinnick.
      p. cm. — (Studies on the texts of the desert of Judah, ISSN
0169-9962 ; v. 31)
   Includes bibliographical references and index.
   ISBN 9004111646 (hardcover : alk. paper)
   1. Apocryphal books (Old Testament)—Congresses.   2. Dead Sea
scrolls—Congresses.   I. Chazon, Esther G.   II. Stone, Michael E.,
1938- .   III. Pinnick, Avital.   IV. Title.   V. Series
BS1700.075   1998
299' .9106—dc21   98–34509
                                                                        CIP

ISSN 0169-9962
ISBN 90 04 11164 6

PRINTED IN THE NETHERLANDS

CONTENTS

PREFACE

This book is the second volume of symposium proceedings published by the Orion Center for the Study of the Dead Sea Scrolls and Associated Literature. The Orion Center was established in 1995 under the auspices of the Institute of Jewish Studies at the Hebrew University of Jerusalem. Its primary aim is to achieve a better understanding of the history of the Jewish people, its language, literature, thought and religion during the Second Temple period. To this end the Center fosters scholarly discussion and research which integrate the new data from the Dead Sea Scrolls with what was previously known about that formative period in the development of Judaism and early Christianity.

The Orion Center holds an international symposium each year which focuses on a central topic. The Second International Symposium reassessed the Apocrypha and Pseudepigrapha in light of the Dead Sea Scrolls. In addition to fine literary studies of pseudepigraphical writings preserved at Qumran, these proceedings treat fundamental issues in the study of pseudepigraphy and its social, cultural and historical matrices. Several papers isolate different types of pseudepigraphy in the Dead Sea Scrolls and in rabbinic literature, highlighting the uses of pseudonymity and anonymity and weighing their significance. Others explore the theological, social and historical implications of pseudepigraphy at Qumran in the context of the whole of pseudepigraphic literature. What is the consequence of assigning the origins of evil to Adam and Eve (humans) or to the generations of Enoch and Noah (demons)? Why is the revelation of secret knowledge assigned by some to God or to Moses the lawgiver, by others to Daniel the seer and by still others, to a pre-Sinaitic, pre-Abrahamic or prediluvian figure?

Dr. Avital Pinnick, Chief of Publications at the Orion Center, was responsible for the copy- and style-editing of this volume and the preparation of the indices. We are indebted to Dr. Pinnick for her meticulous work. Dr. Hans van der Meij of Brill Academic Publishers has been tremendously helpful and supportive throughout the various stages of publication and we extend our sincerest thanks to him.

The second International Symposium and the production of this volume were funded by the Orion Foundation and the Hebrew

University of Jerusalem. It is thanks to the ongoing support of these foundations and our home institution that the Orion Center continues to operate and flourish. Finally, we wish to thank our colleagues in Jerusalem and throughout the world who have encouraged us in this endeavor and given generously of their time and energies.

Dr. Esther G. Chazon
Prof. Michael E. Stone

Jerusalem, May 1998 — Iyyar 5758

PSEUDEPIGRAPHY IN THE QUMRAN SCROLLS: CATEGORIES AND FUNCTIONS*

MOSHE J. BERNSTEIN

Yeshiva University

I. INTRODUCTION

The purpose of this paper is to investigate the practice of pseudepigraphy in the scrolls found at Qumran. Two matters need to be clarified at the outset. The first, rather obvious, fact is that due to the diverse nature of the Qumran library, there is no assurance that we are studying a practice which was prevalent *at* Qumran. The second, more complex, issue relates to the term "pseudepigraphy," whose meaning needs to be clarified. First, I shall introduce its better known relative, "pseudepigrapha."

The perception of the importance of the body of writings generally referred to as the Pseudepigrapha has increased over the last half century, since the discovery of the Dead Sea Scrolls.[1] The term "pseudepigrapha," however, has been employed in two different ways in recent scholarship and a very important distinction must be made for the purpose of this paper. Originally, "pseudepigrapha" was used to describe texts falsely ascribed to an author (usually of great antiquity) in order to enhance their authority and validity. Gradually, the connotation of this word was expanded to include a collection of Jewish and Christian writings dating from the last centuries BCE to the first centuries CE which did not become part of the canon in either religion.[2] Although the term "apocrypha," which accompanies it in the

---

* *Effective collegial criticism is one of the most valuable aspects of scholarship. At the oral presentation of this paper in Jerusalem in January 1997, a variety of critical comments were voiced by Professors Albert Baumgarten, Devorah Dimant, Sara Japhet, George Nickelsburg and Emanuel Tov. Their remarks compelled me to rework some of my ideas in a more nuanced fashion and have been taken into consideration, to the best of my ability, in the preparation of the written form of this article. No doubt there remain areas where they fail(ed) to convince me as I fail(ed) to convince them. At a later stage of writing, the paper benefited from the criticism of Professors Alan Brill and Yaakov Elman and Ms. Shani Berrin and, from beginning to end as usual, from that of Ms. Judith C. Bernstein.*

[1] An excellent example of a broad treatment of the relationship between the Qumran texts and the Pseudepigrapha is M. E. Stone, "The Dead Sea Scrolls and the Pseudepigrapha," *DSD* 3 (1996) 270-95. See particularly 270-74, "Definitions of Scrolls and of Pseudepigrapha."

[2] Cf. Stone's remarks in "Dead Sea Scrolls and Pseudepigrapha," 270-71.

phrase "Apocrypha and Pseudepigrapha" (the pairing perhaps ultimately owes its existence to E. Kautzsch and R. H. Charles), can be
defined fairly narrowly as a particular group of deuterocanonical
works which appear, with some variation, in the Roman Catholic,
Greek, Slavonic and Ethiopic Bibles, the term "pseudepigrapha" has
lost much of its specificity. Indeed, the first volume of Charlesworth's
Old Testament Pseudepigrapha,[3] "Apocalyptic Literature and Related
Works," generally follows the narrow generic definition of pseudepigrapha, works ascribed falsely to an author of antiquity. The sec-
ond volume, with the unwieldy subtitle, "Expansions of the 'Old
Testament' and Legends, Wisdom and Philosophical Literature,
Prayers, Psalms and Odes, Fragments of Lost Judeo-Hellenistic
Works," demands the broader understanding of the classification.
There are in fact many more works in the second volume which are
not technically pseudepigraphic than there are in the first.

The relationship between the pseudepigrapha and the Qumran
scrolls has become increasingly significant in contemporary scholarship as it has become evident that these two corpora share certain
works, genres, and historical contexts. To begin with an obvious
though important fact, copies of works which belong to the narrow-
ly-defined pseudepigrapha, such as Jubilees, 1 Enoch and early
forms of the Testaments of Levi and Naphtali, have been discovered
in the Qumran caves. Less obvious, however, but perhaps more significant is the way in which the apocrypha and pseudepigrapha have
subtly influenced the manner in which we name, define and characterize fragmentary Qumran documents.

As the known Qumran corpus has grown in scope, we have been
introduced to the fragments of many heretofore unknown works
connected with the Hebrew Bible. Scrolls editors have sometimes re-
sorted to indicating the relationship to biblical texts by adding
"pseudo-" or "apocryphal" to the name of the appropriate biblical
text or figure. Thus we find Apocryphon of Moses, Pseudo-Moses,
Apocryphon of Samuel-Kings, Apocryphon of Jeremiah, Pseudo-
Ezekiel, Pseudo-Daniel, Pseudo-Jubilees, Apocryphal Psalms, Non-
Canonical Psalms, as well as the Apocrypha of Jacob, Judah, and
Joseph. In the naming of Qumran texts, the categories "apocryphal"
and "pseudepigraphical" have become virtually synonymous or
often overlapping terms. The salient feature of pseudepigraphy, the
false attribution of authorship, appears no longer to be relevant in
the categorization of works as "pseudo-X." I am convinced that the

---

[3] J. H. Charlesworth, ed., *Old Testament Pseudepigrapha* (2 volumes; Garden City:
Doubleday, 1983-85).

practice of using this terminology in naming Qumran texts has obscured their true nature in many instances. The term "apocryphal" should, *prima facie*, denote a relationship to a body of material which is canonical or non-apocryphal from the standpoint of the author or audience but this is not always the case. Although the term "pseudo-" sometimes implies that the ancient author is consciously writing pseudepigrapha, in other instances it means only that the work has some unexpressed relationship to a biblical or other work on the same theme. While we need a common set of references for these documents, our terminology should be more discriminating.

Thus I use the term "pseudepigraphy" rather than "pseudepigrapha." I am interested in studying the phenomenon, at Qumran, of composing texts or portions of texts which are placed into the mouth of ancient figures. I hope to distinguish between works which are "genuinely" pseudepigraphic (if that not be too harsh an oxymoron) and those to which, out of convenience or expedience, the term "pseudo-" was attached by their editors. In the course of this analysis, I shall introduce the following categories:

1. Authoritative pseudepigraphy,
2. Convenient pseudepigraphy,
3. Decorative pseudepigraphy.

Once we perceive the range of the use of pseudepigraphy in the Qumran texts, I shall focus on the classification and functions of pseudepigraphy.

I admit that I still have more questions than answers and that I do not have a ready alternative in each instance where I reject a title. It is, of course, easy to find fault with other scholars' work, particularly when it was done in the early, more naive, period of Qumran scholarship. I intend to highlight the problems and to offer some preliminary clarifications in the hope that others will take up the challenge and provide further solutions.

II. Pseudepigraphy "Before" Qumran

What is the nature of the pseudepigraphy in works which were known before the Qumran discoveries?[4] If we were to survey lists of Second Temple works which are technically pseudepigraphic, we would cer-

---

[4] The question of pseudepigraphy in the Bible itself is beyond the scope of this discussion but a salient difference between biblical and Second Temple literature must be noted. It is fairly clear that, unlike most of the biblical authors, the Second Temple authors were writing against the background of something "canonical," "authoritative," "official," "authorized," or "approved," i.e., the Bible. Which ver-

tainly find a common core of documents such as Jubilees, 1 Enoch, 4
Ezra, 2 Baruch, the Psalms of Solomon, the Prayer of Manasseh and,
allowing for some chronological freedom, perhaps the Testaments of
the Twelve Patriarchs. It is clear that during the later Second Temple
period the technique of pseudepigraphy was frequently employed.
Yet, we cannot be certain whether pseudepigraphy functioned as a
convention whose audience knew that the words were not those of the
ancient writer but of a contemporary or whether they were "fooled"
by the pseudonymous attribution into accepting the document as one
of genuine antiquity.[5] Perhaps at different times, in different places, in
different circles, pseudepigraphy had different implications. In instances where pseudepigraphy may have been an accepted method of
composition, the use of the term "pseudepigraphy" by modern scholars may nevertheless carry a pejorative overtone, since "pseudo-"
tends to mean "not genuine." This development reflects a modern attitude concerning the morality or appropriateness of writers adopting
the voices of others, despite the fact that no such stigma may have
been attached to the genre in antiquity.

The literary forms which employ pseudepigraphy are varied and
include rewritten Bible (both narrative and legal, such as in
Jubilees),[6] expansions of biblical stories in 1 Enoch and similar
books, testaments, prophetic visions, sapiential literature, prayer and
poetry. It is clear, however, that the phenomenon of pseudepigraphy
does not always operate the same way or to the same end. One of
our goals is to clarify its distribution and function.

After surveying literature from the last decades on pseudepigraphy, I have found that a great deal of the scholarship focuses on

---

sions, sections or texts, which authorities determined their status and the component
parts, if any, into which the "Bible" was to be divided are not germane to this point.
The fact that the Second Temple authors acknowledged the authority of the Bible
as a point of reference enables us to employ terms such as "apocryphal" and
"pseudepigraphical" in the context of their literary works.

[5] One perspective is adopted by J. H. Charlesworth, "Pseudepigrapha, OT,"
ABD 5.539b, who writes "Why did the authors of these writings attribute them falsely to other persons? These authors did not attempt to deceive the reader. They, like
the authors of the Psalms of David, the Proverbs of Solomon, the Wisdom of
Solomon, and the additions to Isaiah, attempted to write authoritatively in the
name of an influential biblical person. Many religious Jews attributed their works to
some biblical saint who lived before the cessation of prophecy and who had inspired
them." It must be noted, however, that the Second Temple authors, lacking the
perspicacity of modern biblical scholars, probably did not assume that any of those
biblical works was pseudepigraphical and therefore could not have employed them
as a model for their own work.

[6] We shall argue that the pseudepigraphy of Jubilees differs from that of most
other examples of rewritten Bible. This phenomenon relates to the apocalyptic and
legal aspects of the text and not to its recapitulation of biblical narrative.

the function of pseudepigraphy in the context of apocalyptic literature.[7] Several of the works and genres which I listed above belong,
to greater or lesser degrees, to that family. Once prophecy was believed to have come to an end, the cycle of history, visions of the future (especially eschatological rewards and punishments), the revelation of cosmic truths and the disclosure of long-hidden secret
doctrines were most effectively expressed through the mediation of a
sage or visionary whose words bore the mark of divine authority and
approval. Since everything prophesied before the time of the actual
author could be "foreseen" with great accuracy, greater weight was
given to future predictions. The authors of these works may have regarded themselves as heirs (or even *redivivi*) of the writers whose
names they borrowed, mediating and reproducing the message of
biblical figures in the post-biblical age.

The Enoch literature, 2 Baruch, 4 Ezra and the Testaments certainly belong to this category and Jubilees, because of its apocalyptic

---

[7] A representative selection of references:
- "The vision is not published under its writer's name, but is attributed to a
famous figure drawn from the past. This pseudepigraphy is typical of the
apocalypses...."; M. E. Stone, "Apocalyptic Literature," in *Jewish Writings of
the Second Temple Period* (ed. M. E. Stone; CRINT 2.2; Philadelphia: Fortress;
Assen: Van Gorcum, 1984) 383;
- "Pseudepigraphy as such is a common feature of very much of the literature, Jewish and pagan alike, of the Hellenistic-Roman age. In Jewish literature it is particularly widespread in this period, very few of the Apocrypha
and Pseudepigrapha being other than pseudepigraphic in attribution. Yet, it
can be claimed that the pseudepigraphy of the apocalypses forms a special
class in the Jewish writings because of the nature of the claims made for
their content and teaching" (*ibid.*, 427).
- "The *pseudepigraphic form* [emphasis in the original] necessarily became a firm
rule for Jewish apocalyptic, since the apocalyptists' unheard-of claim to revelation could only be maintained by reference to those who had been endowed with the spirit in ancient times"; M. Hengel, *Judaism and Hellenism:
Studies in Their Encounter in Palestine During the Early Hellenistic Period* (Philadelphia: Fortress, 1974) 1.205.
- "Generally speaking, it is true that Jewish apocalyptic is pseudonymous.
The several writers throw their prophecies into the remote past and write in
the name of some honoured figure of antiquity who, it is claimed, had received divine revelations which he recorded in a book and passed onto those
who succeeded him"; D. S. Russell, *The Method and Message of Jewish
Apocalyptic* (London: SCM Press, 1964) 127-28.
- "A much cherished literary genre was pseudepigraphic-apocalyptic prophecy, where exhortation is based on special revelations which the authors
claim to have received concerning the future destinies of Israel. Pseudepigraphy, i.e. the placing of the revelations in the mouths of the great men
of the past, endowed the admonitions and consolations with special prestige
and great authority"; E. Schürer, G. Vermes and F. Millar, *The History of the
Jewish People in the Time of Jesus Christ (175 B.C.-A.D. 135)* (Edinburgh: T. &
T. Clark, 1973-87) III.1.179.

perspective, probably does as well. The function of pseudepigraphy in these examples is to strengthen the work's authority. This phenomenon I term "strong" or "authoritative" pseudepigraphy. Prophecies are placed in the mouth of the ancient patriarch or prophet to make them more convincing. In the case of Jubilees, however, apart from its apocalyptic component, the author has adopted a pseudepigraphic stance to promulgate legal truths and a correct system of halakhah.[8] How better to verify that the halakhic interpretation of the Pentateuch which you are presenting is faithful to the original intent of its divine Author and human author, than by presenting it as the revelation by a high-ranking angel of what is found on heavenly tablets to recipient of the Mosaic Torah at the very time when he received that Torah? We shall observe that it is particularly prescriptive legal material and prophetic/apocalyptic predictions which are best suited to strong, authoritative pseudepigraphy.

In the case of the testamentary literature, what better way to inculcate morals and values in a society which needs chastisement than through the patriarchs of old?[9] The loosely authoritative, even prescriptive, nature of the pseudepigraphy remains, but the technique is adopted to convey a moral message. This "convenient" pseudepigraphy is a "lighter" or "weaker" form of authoritative pseudepigraphy. We shall see other examples of convenient pseudepigraphy where the authoritative dimension is lacking completely. The model of the Testaments is actually intermediate between the purely authoritative and the purely convenient techniques.

Sapiential works such as Ecclesiastes and the Wisdom of Solomon are ascribed to Solomon because he was the wise man, *par excellence*, of antiquity. Words of wisdom are placed in his mouth and adorned with his reputation and authority to enhance their acceptability. Authorial assertion is less critical for sapiential literature than for works, such as Enoch and Jubilees, which might have fallen on deaf ears without this claim. The Solomonic authorship of biblical wisdom books may have established a tradition to which later writers of sapiential literature felt they belonged, in contrast to the more artificial assumption of the prophetic mantle by the authors of Enoch or

---

[8] Cf. the remarks of M. de Jonge, *Outside the Old Testament* (Cambridge: Cambridge University Press, 1985) 2: "Moses and the angel are the authorities behind this view of Israel's earliest history and this particular interpretation of its *halakhah* (binding regulations)."

[9] Pseudepigraphy of this type may not seem as dissonant to the modern reader as the prophetic/apocalyptic's *post eventum* pronouncement of truths to buttress arguments about the future or the assertion that the correct legal interpretations of the Mosaic Pentateuch were written by Moses in Jubilees.

Jubilees. This is also a weaker form of authoritative pseudepigraphy.

In the Prayer of Manasseh, pseudepigraphy facilitates biblical interpretation or expansion. This work attempts to fill in the gap left by 2 Chron. 33:12 and it lacks even the lighter *Tendenz* characterized above. It seems to owe its existence to the biblical story, although there is no reference to Manasseh in the text itself.[10] But, based on its contents, it could have been just another extra-biblical poem of its genre. Similarly, the Psalms of Solomon apparently owe their attribution not to any internal "evidence" but to the similarity between the messianic Ps. Sol. 17 and the canonical Psalm 72 which is explicitly headed "To/of Solomon." It is not clear whether the Solomonic authorship would have affected the reader of these poems. The fact that these works are pseudepigraphic only "externally" (i.e., by title and not by content) is worth keeping in mind. The term which I suggest for this type is "decorative" pseudepigraphy.

This brief survey of pseudepigraphy outside Qumran is intended to establish a framework in which we can examine the issue at Qumran. In these texts we have seen what I call a range of degrees of "pseudepigraphicity," as well as its roles or functions. There is, however, a quality which is shared by most of these works and which is critical to the way that pseudepigraphy should be examined and evaluated: this is the fact that they are *externally* and *internally* wholly pseudepigraphic (the Prayer of Manasseh and the Psalms of Solomon are exceptions). Their "pseudepigraphicity" is an essential feature of the work and the pseudepigraphic stance is maintained throughout (some modification of the latter statement might be required in the case of 1 Enoch). These qualities furnish useful standards for comparison with the Qumran material.[11]

---

[10] M. Smith, "Pseudepigraphy in the Israelite Literary Tradition," in *Pseudepigrapha I* (ed. K. von Fritz; Entretiens sur l'antiquité classique; Vandoeuvres-Genève, 1972) 212, actually speaks of "the anonymous prayers attributed to Azariah and Manasseh and the anonymous psalms attributed to Solomon." G. W. E. Nickelsburg suggested at the oral presentation of this paper that it was worth considering whether the Prayer was created for an expanded account of Manasseh's life such as we find in the Didascalia. In that case, the pseudepigraphy would be more than what I shall term "decorative."

[11] Albert Baumgarten (electronic mail communication May 11, 1998) suggests a conceptual distinction between the terms "pseudonymity" and "pseudepigraphy" which might prove valuable in further study of this topic. In the former, any name from the past will do for the purported author, while in the latter there is a need for an authoritative figure who is brought back on the stage of history. Examples of pseudonymity would be the author of the Letter of Aristeas or Scriptores Historiae Augustae. The particular names chosen by the authors of both are not as significant as the choice of Enoch for 1 Enoch or the angel/Moses for Jubilees.

III. Pseudepigraphy at Qumran

A. *Introduction*

As I have already noted, we may be creating an artificial corpus by speaking of the "Qumran scrolls." Even a descriptive approach must be used with caution in light of the haphazard nature of the collection. With this point in mind, our first step is an acknowledgment of the obvious fact that Qumran literature is largely anonymous and not pseudonymous.[12] The major whole documents of the Dead Sea Scrolls, the Community Rule, the War Scroll, and the Zadokite fragments or Damascus Document do not indicate their authorship. Neither do the Thanksgiving Hymns, the Songs of the Sabbath Sacrifice, the pesharim or the document known as Miqṣat Maʿase ha-Torah, however we may classify it generically. Whether the Teacher of Righteousness or any other particular Qumran figure wrote these texts, whether a unique personal imprint exists in the Thanksgiving Hymns, whether the interpretations of the pesharim are divinely inspired, none of this is known because no names are found internally or externally.

Among the works found only at Qumran, what might be considered pseudepigraphic and by what definitions? Here I return to my earlier remarks on nomenclature to demonstrate the complexity of the endeavor. Having remarked on the varied and often unenlightening official names of some Qumran texts, we may add to that list other works which need to be evaluated in regard to pseudepigraphy, such as 4QReworked Pentateuch, testament-type works attributed to Levi, Naphtali, Qahat, and Amram, to mention but a few, the Apocryphon of Joshua (formerly Psalms of Joshua) and other scripturally-based texts such as the Genesis Apocryphon. Furthermore, on the dust jacket of a very recent English translation of the Dead Sea Scrolls, we find the following assertion: "Twelve texts not included in the Bible *that claim Moses as their author* [my emphasis]. New psalms attributed to King David and to Joshua."[13] These claims and the titles highlight the difficulty. Scholars have not yet examined carefully many of these texts and they certainly have not examined the entire corpus in detail to see just what *claim* is made by the texts themselves

---

[12] M. Smith, "Pseudepigraphy," 212: "The first two books of the *Maccabees* are not pseudepigrapha, but anonymous. So are the great majority of the works found at Qumran."

[13] M. Wise, M. G. Abegg, Jr. and E. Cook, *The Dead Sea Scrolls: A New Translation* (New York: Harper, 1996).

regarding authorship and speaking voice. The fact that terms like "apocryphal" are, at least in part, dependent on the existence of a canon makes our analysis even more complex.

Names are not attached explicitly, as far as we can tell, to most of the fragmentary legal texts found at Qumran, with the possible exception of the Ordinances where Moses' name seems to appear (4Q159 5 4, 7). Regardless of the fact that many of them[14] are written in an overtly biblical style or employ language which paraphrases or borrows from the Pentateuch, we do not sense that we are reading texts whose personal authorial voice is loud and clear. From the complete texts of the community rules as well as their fragments, and those of other, more Scripture-like legal texts, it appears that pseudepigraphy was superfluous for the writing of legal codes. If pseudepigraphy were ever *de rigeur* at Qumran as a literary device, it may have been used only in texts which were attempting to proclaim a legal or theological doctrine to the outside world and considered unnecessary in works intended for insiders. Otherwise, we would expect to find an authoritative figure such as Moses as the putative author of various legal texts at Qumran.[15]

B. *"Classic" Pseudepigraphic Texts at Qumran*

Of the presence of pseudepigraphic texts at Qumran there can be no doubt, since the "library" possessed multiple copies of Jubilees and 1 Enoch as well as testament-type works. It is important to note that neither of these works is claimed by scholars to be of Qumranic origin. Moreover, I believe that one could argue that fully-pseudepigraphic works such as these were not composed at Qumran. It might even be claimed, based on the authoritative status of Jubilees within other Qumran texts, that its pseudepigraphy was taken at face value, that is, that its ascription to Moses was accepted just as Second Temple authors generally accepted the Mosaic authorship of the Pentateuch.[16]

The Aramaic Levi Document, the Hebrew Testament of Naphtali and the Aramaic fragments of testament-like works assigned to Jacob, Judah and Joseph (very fragmentary) and Qahat and Amram

---

[14] We must remember that we are dealing with fragments in many instances.

[15] For further discussion of legal pseudepigraphy at Qumran, see L. H. Schiffman's essay, "The Temple Scroll and the Halakhic Pseudepigrapha of the Second Temple Period" in this volume, 121-32, and my remarks on the Temple Scroll and Moses pseudepigrapha below.

[16] Cf. CD 16:3 and 4Q228 1 i 2, 9.

(a bit more substantial) are indubitably also pseudepigraphic in the fullest sense. They are "autobiographical," as far as we can tell, containing exhortations for virtuous behavior to the descendants of the speaker and prophetic visions of the eschaton. ALD also includes prescriptive priestly halakhah which might have required strong pseudepigraphy for its authority. In all these texts, pseudepigraphy intersects with apocalyptic, and authoritative pseudepigraphy is characteristic of their composition.

These are the indisputable examples of pseudepigraphy at Qumran. Turning now to a group of substantially-preserved Qumran documents, we shall examine to what degree they are pseudepigraphic and how pseudepigraphy functions in them. We shall then scrutinize less well-preserved documents for any light that they may shed. Because a number of them belong to the category usually labeled "rewritten Bible," some remarks on the nature of pseudepigraphy within that genre need to be prefaced to the discussion.

C. Rewritten Bible

1. Introduction

Unlike prophecies or testaments, legal texts and narratives need not have an explicit author. A rewritten Bible text makes no claim to strong pseudepigraphy if the text does not speak in the first person, whether in the name of, or as a narrative about, an ancient figure. Likewise, narrative texts which retell a biblical story but make no explicit or implicit claim to be part of a canonical work also lay no claim to strong pseudepigraphy. Jubilees is thus the exception to the model of most rewritten Pentateuch texts because it claims the authorship of the angel/Moses. Unlike Jubilees, narratives which include first person speeches by characters in the story ought not be construed as authoritative pseudepigraphy but rather as convenient pseudepigraphy. The goal of convenient pseudepigraphy is, in this case, obvious. The retelling and expansion of the biblical story is accomplished more easily, and the narrative rendered more vivid, through the creation and insertion of speeches into the mouths of characters. At an early stage of biblical exegesis, before the development of the commentary form, rewriting offered one of the few literary options for interpretation. The rewriter/interpreter was able to put words into the mouths of characters to convey his reading without creating an authoritatively pseudepigraphic work since the work as a whole makes no claim to authority or to pseudepigraphy.

2. *Reworked Pentateuch*

The Reworked Pentateuch manuscripts published in DJD 13 remain very difficult to classify. Most of the text is quite literally rewritten Bible, wherein a passage from the Pentateuch has been adjusted by slight rearrangements, the addition of exegetical comments and occasional omissions. How do we assess, from the standpoint of pseudepigraphy, a text like 4QRP which rewrites pentateuchal material in a minimal fashion as if it were literally rewriting the Bible?[17] Assuming that the author of RP conceives of the Bible as the backdrop against which he is rewriting, shall we conclude that 4QRP has employed pseudepigraphy in the rearrangement and slight modification of pentateuchal material? (By that token, we might even have to speak of the Samaritan Pentateuch as pseudepigraphic!) If we take into consideration the possibility that the author intended to rewrite a *biblical* text and "improved" it by rearranging certain details, harmonizing contradictions and juxtaposing like material, then perhaps we should not think of this technique as pseudepigraphy. We could conclude instead that this is a form of editorial work which makes no claim to authorship.

Amid various minor adjustments and insertions, however, the author of RP has inserted some atypical passages which have received much public attention in advance of the publication of DJD 13. Such passages include 4Q364 3 ii, which contains a narrative addition to Gen. 28:6 in the form of a dialogue between Rebecca and Isaac; 4Q365 6a ii-c, the Song of Miriam; and 4Q365 23 4 ff., a completely extra-biblical legal addition inserted after Lev. 23:42-44 which details the wood festival, already presumed to be part of the Qumran calendar on the basis of the reconstruction of the Temple Scroll (columns 23-24 and 43).

The first two additions present us with a specific question: how are we to evaluate the larger adjustments made to a work which is fundamentally the Hebrew Bible, slightly enlarged and expanded? Herein lies one of the key distinctions between works which are wholly pseudepigraphic and those which can be described as containing "pseudepigraphic interpolations." From the perspective of the writer of Miriam's song or Rebecca's dialogue with Isaac about Jacob, this composition is an addition to the biblical text and, al-

---

[17] The analysis of 4QRP is still in its initial stages. There is currently a good deal of discussion concerning whether all the manuscripts identified as 4QRP belong to a single work. A question has also been raised whether one or more is to be considered a "real" biblical text, rather than a "reworked" one. This issue can complicate the question of the work's pseudepigraphy.

though written in the style of the biblical text, the author was not
trying to mislead the reader as to its authenticity. After all, that was
the conventional manner in which to retell the biblical story and to
include interpretive remarks. If Scripture said that Miriam sang a
song, then adding that song would be appropriate.

If we are to characterize this literary activity as pseudepigraphy, it
is of the type that I call convenient, rather than authoritative,
pseudepigraphy. It is simply a formal way to supplement the biblical
text and to introduce exegetical or interpretive remarks without
rewriting the whole in a non-pseudepigraphic style, an approach
which seems not to have been available as yet. This is the same kind
of convenient pseudepigraphy which we will find in the Genesis
Apocryphon, where it is less obvious because it is not surrounded by
biblical passages written in biblical style. I would suggest, therefore,
that convenient pseudepigraphy not be considered evidence of intent
to deceive on the author's part.

The legal passage regarding the wood festival, on the other hand,
cannot be categorized as convenient pseudepigraphy, for the author of
RP introduces the law with וידבר ה אל משה לאמר, "The Lord spoke to
Moses, saying." He attempts to give the force of Mosaic law to a practice which was apparently important to his group and its calendar and
which, furthermore, has scriptural precedent (Neh. 10:35; 13:31).[18] The
author of RP (or his source, if the final editor of 4QRP is not responsible for the composition of this passage) meant the reader to take it as a
divine imperative, to be obeyed like the remainder of the commandments in the Pentateuch. This phrase constitutes an internal claim to
pseudepigraphy in a way in which the above-mentioned additions to
Genesis and Exodus do not. It forces us to consider whether this work,
which we would not have defined as pseudepigraphic on the basis of
the rest of its contents, is actually a pseudepigraphon, with the pseudepigraphy being employed to give authority to halakhic rulings, as we
saw on a broader scale in Jubilees. This characterization is awkward,
however, since the passage is surrounded by the biblical text and does
not merely resemble it or build upon it, as Jubilees does. The alternative is to suppose that the composer of RP assumed that he had the authority to add to the biblical text in this fashion, and therefore did not
consider what he composed to be pseudepigraphic. From the perspective of the modern reader, however, this passage (but not the work as a
whole) must be considered pseudepigraphic in the strongest, authoritative, sense.

---

[18] Cf. Y. Yadin, ed., *The Temple Scroll* (Jerusalem: Israel Exploration Society,
1983) 1.122-24.

3. *4Q158 Biblical Paraphrase*

4Q158, published by Allegro under the title Biblical Paraphrase, is close enough to 4QRP for the editors of 4QRP, Emanuel Tov and Sidnie White Crawford, to have claimed that it is another copy of the same text.[19] Like 4QRP, large pieces of 4Q158 are pentateuchal. The supplementary material, however, is far more extensive and this phenomenon has led me to conclude that 4Q158 is not a copy of RP or even an example of the genre of minimally rewritten Bible.[20] I believe that the extrabiblical additions in 4Q158 are not pseudepigraphic in spirit. Rather, the attempt by its composer to clarify the biblical text through rearrangement and supplementation is a form of interpretation. Any pseudepigraphic qualities which the text possesses are "convenient" rather than "authoritative." Thus, while some aspects of the status of 4QRP as a biblical or pseudepigraphical text may be open to debate, 4Q158 should be considered an example of rewritten Bible with no functional pseudepigraphic overtones at all.

4. *The Temple Scroll*

Much better known than the "Reworked Pentateuch" texts and probably more significant for our discussion is 11QT, the Temple Scroll.[21] Here the arguments for "pseudepigraphicity" are more concrete but the situation is slightly more complex.[22] A large part of 11QT consists of large segments of rewritten Pentateuch.

> One of the most characteristic features of the scroll is the author's quoting of whole chapters as they appear in the Pentateuch—or in the version which he accepted—but changing their grammar to the first person to dispel any doubt that God is speaking. This type of change...is in fact one of the principal characteristics of certain pseudepigraphic works as well.[23]

Thus, whenever Deuteronomy says, "which the Lord your God...," 11QT reads "which I..." Furthermore, as Yadin pointed out, many

---

[19] J. M. Allegro, ed., *Qumrân Cave 4, I (4Q158-186)* (DJD 5; Oxford: Clarendon, 1968) 1-6; S. White Crawford and E. Tov, *Qumran Cave 4.VIII: Parabiblical Texts, Part 1* (ed. H. W. Attridge *et al.*; DJD 13; Oxford: Clarendon, 1994) 189-91.

[20] A view similar to mine will be argued by M. Segal in a forthcoming article in *Textus*.

[21] On 11QT, see especially Schiffman's essay in this volume, "The Temple Scroll and the Halakhic Pseudepigrapha," 121-32.

[22] Many scholars, for example, do not consider 11QT to be a product of the Qumran group and this may be important for the overall picture of pseudepigraphy at Qumran. For our limited purposes, however, I do not think that we can divorce it from the Qumran corpus as easily as we might Jubilees, for example.

[23] Yadin, *The Temple Scroll*, 1.71.

of the supplementary laws in 11QT are also phrased in the first person. Our initial impression is that the composer of 11QT wanted to present the laws of the deuteronomic portion of his Pentateuch as divine utterances, like the earlier sections of the Torah.

The composer of 11QT was not, however, composing a pseudepigraphon in the manner of Jubilees or creating a document which was completely "pseudo-God" in authorship, for in many columns God is referred to in the third person using the Tetragrammaton. Yadin believes that

> the author of the scroll converts the words of Moses from the Deuteronomic source into the words of God by transposing the text from the third to the first person, but that he leaves in the third person the words found in the priestly sources and transmitted from God's lips.[24]

This theory, however, attributes a great deal of sophisticated source criticism to the ancient composer. Is it not equally plausible that in the process of composing the Temple Scroll from various, not necessarily biblical, sources, the composer integrated texts which referred to God in different ways? Indeed, the text from which he borrowed the first person recasting of Deuteronomy may well deserve the title pseudepigraphon but the Temple Scroll *as a whole* may not be a pseudepigraphon. If the author intended to convince his audience that the Temple Scroll was the genuine word of God, he failed because he did not maintain the transformation to pseudepigraphon throughout. The portions of the Pentateuch which appear unedited in the Temple Scroll should perhaps be viewed as a copying of the Torah and not as a new Moses pseudepigraphon. If the author of the reworked portions intended his material to be taken as divine in origin, that is to say, if he were employing pseudepigraphy, then his juxtaposition of genuine pentateuchal material with his new composition would constitute a significant facet of his pretense. Although 11QT is internally pseudepigraphic, it is so only in part. In my view, the composer's failure to sustain his pretense precludes us from considering the entire work as a pseudepigraphon.

It is interesting that neither Yadin nor Wise considers the Temple Scroll to be pseudepigraphic but for different reasons. Responding to Moshe Goshen-Gottstein's characterization of the Temple Scroll as "a 'halakhic pseudepigraph'," Yadin writes,

> In my opinion there is no warrant for applying the modern concept 'pseudepigraph' to a work whose author believed himself to be presenting a true Law, revealed to him under unique circumstances, whether by authority of tradition or divine inspiration.

---

[21] *Ibid.*, 73.

He continues:

> I have not the slightest doubt that we must consider this problem from the exclusive point of the author and his readers, that is, if they *believed* that the scroll construed a true Law of the Lord. It is perhaps of interest that, contrary to some of the pseudepigraphical books which intentionally attribute their words to a particular historical personality and often mention geographical sites and historical persons, the scroll deliberately avoids this.[25]

Michael Wise chooses one of Yadin's options and writes,

> This man [the author of 11QT] conceived of himself as a new Moses; hence the Temple Scroll is, properly speaking, not a pseudepigraphon. The redactor was not writing in the name of a long-dead hero of the faith, claiming that he had discovered a lost writing which that hero had produced. Rather his claim was to the same relationship with God that Moses had.[26]

The focus of Yadin and Wise on authorial intent is important and leads me to ask the following question: From how many perspectives must the question of pseudepigraphy in a work such as 11QT be considered? 1) That of the ancient author who might have believed what Yadin or Wise think he did; or 2) that of the ancient audience who might have accepted the belief of that ancient author or, alternatively, might have accepted the notion of pseudepigraphy as a literary convention; or 3) that of the modern scholar, whose perspective is much more limited and best served by employing descriptive terminology?[27] The answer to this question is critical for establishing an agenda for the broad analysis of the phenomenon of pseudepigraphy.

5. *Genesis Apocryphon*

A substantial Qumran text with stronger claims to pseudepigraphy than most other examples of rewritten Bible is the Genesis Apocryphon of Cave 1. A first person narrative by a biblical persona must be considered more pseudepigraphical on the formal level than first person speeches embedded in a third person narrative. In the

---

[25] *Ibid.*, 391-92, n. 8. Goshen-Gottstein's classification of the scroll as a pseudepigraphon is meant to exclude the possibility that the author is writing what he believes to be Torah, while Yadin denies the work's pseudepigraphy by claiming that the author is writing what he believes to be Torah. Schiffman, in his article in this volume, sets the question, "Is the Temple Scroll a Moses pseudepigraphon or a divine pseudepigraphon?"; Schiffman, "The Temple Scroll and the Halakhic Pseudepigrapha," 125.

[26] M. O. Wise, *A Critical Study of the Temple Scroll from Qumran Cave 11* (SAOC 49; Chicago: The Oriental Institute, 1990) 200.

[27] From the standpoint of Yadin's reader, rather than his author, the Temple Scroll may be pseudepigraphy if he does not share the author's preconceptions.

Genesis Apocryphon, not only are the speeches pseudepigraphical
but so are large portions of the narrative. The Apocryphon has not
one but three speakers/narrators of this type. Lamech, Noah and
Abraham all narrate their own adventures but—this is a critical
point—not all of the text is first person narrative. The portions of the
Lamech segment where he is off-stage, as it were, while the action focuses on his father Enoch and grandfather Methuselah, are narrated
by an unnamed narrator. Some of the story of Noah's division of the
earth among his sons appears to refer to Noah in the third person
(16:12 חלק, "he divided"; 17:16, חולקא די פלג לה ויהב לה נוח אבוהי
"the portion which Noah his father apportioned to him and gave to
him") side-by-side with first-person narrative by Noah.[28] It is well
known that Abraham tells his own story from his initial appearance
in column 19 (= early in Genesis 12) to the middle of column 21 (=
end of Genesis 13). The Apocryphon moves to a third person narrative at the beginning of Genesis 14 and continues to Genesis 15,
whose equivalent is interrupted by the end of the manuscript (end of
column 22). All three of the extant sections of the Apocryphon employ both first and third person narration.

Whatever the reasons for the shifts from first person narrative to
third, the fact remains that the first person parts of the text show, at
first glance, an appearance of strong pseudepigraphy. In the case of
1QGenAp, unlike some examples of rewritten Bible, we can view
this problem from two perspectives, that of these sections of the work
and that of their likely hypothetical sources.[29] It is possible that some
sources of the Apocryphon may have been completely pseudepigraphic, both externally and internally, from a formal standpoint
and that the editor of the Apocryphon integrated their first person
form into his narrative. That is to say, these sources could have been
pseudepigraphic works which purported to speak in the voices of

---

[28] Examination of the recently published fragments of the Genesis Apocryphon
by J. C. Greenfield and E. Qimron. "The Genesis Apocryphon Col. XII," *Abr-
Nahrain Supp* 3 (1992) 70-77 and M. Morgenstern, E. Qimron and D. Sivan, "The
Hitherto Unpublished Columns of the Genesis Apocryphon," *Abr-Nahrain* 33 (1995)
30-52, indicates that the only clear-cut first-person reference to Noah in the passages about apportioning the earth is 16:7, ושם ברי וחולקה בין בנוהי "Shem *my* son
[di]vided it among his sons." Were it not for the suffix on ברי, it would be tempting
to suggest that the section of the Apocryphon about the division of the earth was
not treated as a first person speech by Noah, and the discussion of this section as
pseudepigraphy would be excluded.

[29] On the question of the sources of the Genesis Apocryphon, at least as far as
the Noah material, see most recently R. C. Steiner, "The Heading of the *Book of the
Words of Noah* on a Fragment of the Genesis Apocryphon," *DSD* 2 (1995) 66-71, and
my forthcoming "Noah and the Flood at Qumran," in *The Provo International
Conference on the Dead Sea Scrolls: New Texts, Reformulated Issues and Technological
Innovations* (ed. E. Ulrich and D. Parry; Leiden: E. J. Brill, 1998) 199-231.

Lamech, Noah and Abraham. But from the standpoint of the final author/composer of the Apocryphon (and possibly his sources, if they were not authoritatively, but conveniently, pseudepigraphic), this form of convenient pseudepigraphy should be recognized as another example of a technique employed by the earliest biblical interpreters.

In order to retell the story vividly and to rewrite in a fashion which commented on, but did not directly interfere with, the biblical text, some rewriters (going beyond the examples of rewritten Bible discussed above where only first person speeches are introduced) apparently chose to place their stories in the mouths of characters in the narrative who are clearly different from the biblical narrator. Moreover, the author of the Genesis Apocryphon avoided the appearance of forgery by writing in Aramaic.[30] Of course, the author of the Apocryphon in its final form makes no attempt to maintain the pseudepigraphic stance overall, probably for the same reason suggested above for the *disiecta membra*, the separate parts of the whole. When convenient, he employs strong (but not authorial) pseudepigraphy in the form of first person narrative but, where inappropriate, he readily lets the mask drop and reverts to the third person narrative with which we are familiar from the Bible.[31]

D. *11QPs^a* - *Psalms Scroll and Non-Canonical Psalms*

The Psalms Scroll, 11QPs^a, is another substantial text where the issue of pseudepigraphy may be raised from two different perspec-

---

[30] In this way, we can distinguish very strongly between the sort of rewritten Bible we find in the Genesis Apocryphon or Jubilees and that found in the so-called Reworked Pentateuch texts where the question of imitation, copying or forgery of the biblical original is of paramount importance.

[31] G. W. E. Nickelsburg, in a very interesting recent article, "Patriarchs Who Worry About Their Wives: *A Haggadic Tendency in the Genesis Apocryphon*," in *Biblical Perspectives: Early Use and Interpretation of the Bible in the Light of the Dead Sea Scrolls. Proceedings of the First International Symposium of the Orion Center for the Study of the Dead Sea Scrolls and Associated Literature, 12-14 May 1996* (eds. M. E. Stone and E. G. Chazon; STDJ 28; Leiden: E. J. Brill, 1998) 137-58, focuses on the issue of first person narrative in the Apocryphon (156-57) and suggests that this is one of the major contributions of the author of the Apocryphon. He distinguishes correctly between Jubilees and the Apocryphon and suggests that the Apocryphon "provides reliability for its narrative by placing it on the lips of the characters themselves." I am not certain whether the first person speeches and narratives are directed at asserting reliability or creating vividness. I hope that this essay responds in part to Nickelsburg's call for "further work...on the use of first person narration, its characteristics, the forms in which it occurs, its relationships to other types of 'rewritten Bible' and [especially] the broader phenomenon of pseudepigraphy..." (157).

tives. The narrow perspective, of course, is that of Psalm 151A and B, known prior to the Qumran discoveries as LXX Psalm 151. Unlikely to be historically Davidic, we might consider 151A pseud-epigraphic only in the sense that other psalms ascribed to David in MT, LXX or the Syriac tradition are pseudepigraphic. To David, the poet *par excellence*, was ascribed the authorship of later songs, just as his son Solomon, the wise man *par excellence*, became the author of later wisdom works. Such pseudepigraphy I term "decorative" be-cause it is even less functional than convenient pseudepigraphy; it is not organic to the text and often the supposed author is linked to the text only by the title. Psalm 151A, however, demonstrates a closer relationship with David than do other decoratively pseudepigraphic psalms. Not only is it associated with his life (other psalms are simi-larly associated, in their titles) but it even describes events in David's life autobiographically. The voice of the psalm is David's voice. This individual text is thus externally and internally completely pseudepi-graphic. The same was probably true of Psalm 151B when complete; however it breaks off in the middle at the end of the scroll. These psalms are poetic examples of strong pseudepigraphy which we might compare either to the prose rewritten Bible or, perhaps, to the testamentary genre.[32]

A larger pseudepigraphic question may be raised regarding the Psalms Scroll. In light of the prose passage listing David's composi-tions (11QPs[a] 27 2-11), are we to assume that the compiler of the scroll considered all of the texts Davidic? This matter is of course re-lated to the better known problem of whether the Psalms Scroll is a biblical or a liturgical document. Even granting that the text is to be considered biblical or canonical, was everything in it believed to be Davidic? The question can be taken back, theoretically, another step: Did the authors of those non-biblical texts included in the Psalms Scroll intend them to be taken as Davidic? We can mix and match the answers: the texts could be pseudepigraphic on both lev-els, on neither level or on either level, since there is nothing internal to them which makes them Davidic and nothing explicit in the doc-ument which asserts their Davidic authorship.

Among other poetic texts, we find pseudepigraphic attributions in the titles of four psalms published by Eileen Schuller in *Non-Canonical Psalms*. Two are named (Obadiah and Manasseh), while a third is connected to a "king of Judah" and a fourth to "the man of God."[33]

---

[32] I owe the suggestion of the testamentary analogy to my colleague Professor Yaakov Elman.

[33] E. M. Schuller, *Non-Canonical Psalms from Qumran: A Pseudepigraphic Collection*

She has discussed these attributions and their connection to the rest of the collection, asking the key question

> about the relationship between the psalm titles and the psalms themselves. Were the works in 4Q380 and 4Q381 in fact composed as pseudepigraphic psalms, i.e., as the utterances of a specific biblical figure, or do we have a collection of psalms in which the titles ascribing them to biblical characters were added secondarily?[34]

Schuller concludes on the basis of the limited evidence that "the attribution of these psalms to historical figures seems to be only secondary, and the principle of pseudepigraphy was probably not the guiding factor in their composition."[35] We thus have another instance of decorative pseudepigraphy which is unconnected with the body of the work.

E. *Other Moses Pseudepigrapha*

Beyond these large examples, there are many other texts about which the issue of pseudepigraphy may be raised. If we recall the remark on the dust jacket of Wise, Abegg and Cook's translation, concerning a dozen non-biblical texts found at Qumran which claim Moses as their author,[36] we wonder to which texts those translators are referring. The Temple Scroll is probably the best known but I question whether we should refer to it as "pseudo-Moses" or "pseudo-God" since, in its rewriting of the Pentateuch, God becomes the speaker of more of the text than before. I do not believe that we should refer to 4QRP in those terms since any pseudepigraphy which it contains is not only partial but minimal in its overall scope. 4Q374 is correctly seen by Newsom *not* to be a Moses apocryphon, despite its earlier classification as such. It is a pseudo-prophetic text but we cannot tell with whom to associate it.[37] Further, and more

---

(HSS 28; Atlanta: Scholars, 1986). 4Q381 33 8 reads "Prayer of Manasseh, King of Judah, when the King of Assyria imprisoned him" (151), and 4Q380 1 ii 8 "Tehillah of Obadiah" (251). The anonymous king of Judah appears in 4Q381 31 4 (128) and the man of God in 4Q381 24 4 (115). "The Pseudepigraphic Attribution of the Psalms" is discussed by Schuller in her Introduction, 27-32.

[34] Schuller, *Non-Canonical Psalms*, 30. She notes that the latter is the usual explanation for the titles in the canonical Psalter (as well as in LXX and the Talmud).

[35] Schuller, *Non-Canonical Psalms*, 32.

[36] Note 13, above.

[37] C. A. Newsom, "4QDiscourse on the Exodus/Conquest Tradition" in *Qumran Cave 4.XIV: Parabiblical Texts, Part 2* (ed. M. Broshi *et al.*, DJD 19; Oxford: Clarendon, 1995) 100, precludes its being a Moses pseudepigraphon and allows for the possibility that the speaker may be Joshua.

important for the current discussion, it is also not clear on what level pseudepigraphy functions in this text.

Some texts which have been seen as pseudo-Mosaic have no incontrovertible internal evidence that they are ascribed to Moses while others need to be examined further. 1Q22 (Dibre Moshe/Dires de Moïse) is a good example.[38] There is no doubt that it is a narrative about Moses in which he speaks, again raising the question of its being "pseudo-God," "pseudo-Moses" or neither, but this is not a text composed independently. Rather, it is constructed completely out of pentateuchal verses with supplementation. The revisions in this text are much more extensive than those in 4QRP and portions of biblical verses are even rearranged into new combinations. Since the text makes no claim to Mosaic authorship but appears to be an anonymous narrative, the pseudepigraphy is not authoritative but convenient, as in rewritten Bible. The laws which are included in 1Q22 are all found already in the Pentateuch, and therefore there is no question of legal pseudepigraphy, which might narrowly be a form of strong pseudepigraphy.

There are, however, several other texts which are likely to be Moses pseudepigrapha in which the function of the pseudepigraphy is stronger. These are the apparently legal texts 4Q375-376 and 1Q29, which overlaps with them. In 4Q375, the speaker addresses the people directly in biblical style (although not explicitly in the name of God).[39] Following pentateuchal material about the law of the false prophet, the speaker continues with additional regulations concerning the testing of this individual.[40] This constitutes the introduction of legal pseudepigraphic material into a larger context, similar in some ways to what we have seen earlier in 4QRP. Strugnell has argued that 4Q376 (which overlaps with 1Q29) is another copy of 4Q375 (with which it has no overlap), containing non-pentateuchal material on the use of the Urim and Tummim. According to

---

[38] D. Barthelemy and J. T. Milik, ed., *Qumran Cave I* (DJD 1; Oxford: Clarendon, 1955) 91-97.

[39] I am not certain that the distinction made by Strugnell ("4QApocryphon of Moses[a]," DJD 19.130) and approved of by Schiffman (128-29), between Moses speaking *ex parte sua* and Moses speaking *ex parte Domini*, is compelling. For a Jewish reader in the Second Temple period, if a text described Moses presenting legal material, the presumption would be that the source of the laws was God. It is only from a formal standpoint that we can discuss the purported author of the pseudepigraphy; practically, the function would have been the same. For a more thorough discussion of "pseudo-God" vs. "pseudo-Moses," see Schiffman, 124-25; for "Moses the pseudepigrapher" at Qumran, see Strugnell, 133-36.

[40] Text in DJD 19.113-15.

Strugnell, these three texts, and perhaps 1Q22 which has no clearly extra-pentateuchal material, are Moses apocrypha.[41]

Strugnell distinguishes these works from Jubilees and 11QT: in Jubilees the dictating angel is the pseudepigraphic author, while in 11QT it is apparently God. In both cases, then, "Moses functions only as an amanuensis."[42] I think that he is right to exclude Jubilees from the comparison but what the other texts, including the Moses pseudepigrapha and 11QT, have in common is the introduction of new legal material into what is fundamentally a biblical framework. We might compare the law of the king in 11QT with the law of the trial of the false prophet in 4Q375-376. It is strong legal pseudepigraphy and it is likely that in certain circles this form of composition was required in order to maintain the notion that all law has a divine/Mosaic source. Dimant, in differentiating these texts from 4Q390 (see below), writes that they

> have none of the literary features or the religious concerns characteristic of the known apocalyptic pseudepigrapha attributed to Moses, such as the Testament of Moses or Jubilees. The Qumran documents are rather a kind of rewritten-Torah pieces [sic], a rewriting of mainly legal materials. They can be labeled as Moses apocrypha only to the extent that they rewrite the Torah. In this respect, they resemble the Temple Scroll rather than the Moses-pseudepigrapha.[43]

Dimant's criteria for inclusion in Moses pseudepigrapha differ considerably from mine (and perhaps from Strugnell's). Although I agree with Dimant that perhaps we ought to distinguish between legal and apocalyptic Moses material, they may both be categorized by their technique as pseudepigraphy. In my classification, if it claims to be by Moses, it is Moses pseudepigrapha.

In this context, it is worth observing that many Qumran legal texts, including those whose style resembles biblical idiom like 4Q251 Halakha, make no pretense of pseudepigraphy and simply

---

[41] Strugnell suggests that "1Q22 would provide the dramatic and pseudepigraphic framework of 4Q375" (118). As we have seen, though, the laws which survive in 1Q22 are not pseudepigraphic and stand in sharp contrast to those of 4Q375-376.

[42] DJD 19.132. Strugnell classifies these texts as belonging "to the genre of 'proclamation of law' by Moses (who speaks in the first-person singular) to a 'thou' (which is Israel or sometimes Aaron, but not Moses), God being usually referred to in the third-person masculine singular." The model, of course, is the biblical book of Deuteronomy.

[43] D. Dimant, "New Light from Qumran on the Jewish Pseudepigrapha," in *The Madrid Qumran Congress: Proceedings of the International Congress on the Dead Sea Scrolls, Madrid 18-21 March 1991* (ed. J. Trebolle Barrera and L. Vegas Montaner; STDJ 11; Leiden: E. J. Brill, 1992), 2.410, n. 18. A similar comment is made by Stone, "Dead Sea Scrolls and Pseudepigrapha," 273, n. 9.

present lists of laws without specifying a source. There is no clear allusion in the surviving fragments to either God or Moses as the authoritative promulgator of the laws. It is tempting to refer to one
form of legal code as modeled on a scriptual paradigm and the other
as "proto-mishnaic", where laws are enumerated without scriptural
support. For now it must suffice to distinguish between pseudonymity and anonymity.

Regarding 4Q390 which, according to Dimant, is a Moses pseudepigraphon from Qumran, I remain ambivalent about the evidence
that it is pseudo-Mosaic, although it is certainly pseudo-prophetic. If
it is Mosaic, however, Dimant is correct to stress the difference between this Moses apocryphon, which is apocalyptic, and the ones
which are not (e.g., 1Q22, 1Q29 and 4Q375-376). [44] Although
Dimant suggests that we might compare 4Q390 with 2Q21, I think
that the latter text is not particularly different from 1Q22; it supplies
exegesis or extra-biblical supplementation to explain what Moses did
in the Tent of Meeting outside the camp. The difference between
2Q21 and 4Q390 is likely to be the difference between narrative
pseudepigraphy, which is convenient and where the text makes no
claim to authoritative pseudepigraphy, as is characteristic of most examples of rewritten Bible, and prophetic pseudepigraphy which is, by
its very nature, strong and authoritative. Dimant groups 4Q390 with
Jubilees, ALD, 11QT and non-Qumranic texts, arguing that it does
not derive from Qumran but from a related group. Regardless of the
pseudonymous author, whether Moses or a later prophet, Dimant's
conclusion coincides with my tentative hypothesis that pseudepigraphic apocalyptic was not written at Qumran.

F. *Prophetic Pseudepigraphy*

When we think of the "authors" of pseudepigrapha which were
known before the Qumran discoveries, the names which immediately come to mind are Moses, David, Solomon and Baruch. Qumran
adds Ezekiel to this group in the various representations of the text
called pseudo-Ezekiel (or Second Ezekiel) by Dimant. It appears to
be a pseudepigraphic interpolation into a prophetic text, similar to
several of the legal texts in which new laws were introduced into a
pre-existing framework and made to appear part of it. Thus pseudo-
Ezekiel contains pseudonymous autobiographical narrative (strong
or authoritative pseudepigraphy) side-by-side with visions which cor-

---

[44] Dimant, "New Light," 410 and n. 18.

respond to canonical Ezekiel. A fuller picture awaits Professor Dimant's publication of all of the texts she has assigned to this group.

Similarly, 4Q384 (4QpapApocryphon of Jeremiah B?) shares with the rest of the pseudo-Moses, pseudo-Ezekiel and pseudo-Jeremiah material the usual problems of the assignment of fragments, as well as the use of nomenclature and the presence of citation formulas.[45] Its editor, Mark Smith, underlines the issue of naming when he writes, "Originally designated by J. Strugnell as 'Pseudo-Jeremiah', D. Dimant labels this collection of manuscripts [a selection from 4Q385-390] as 'An Apocryphon of Jeremiah', which describes the prophet's life in third-person narrative."[46] He makes the further observation that some of the fragments appear to be pseudo-prophetic and should thus be assigned to "pseudo-Jeremiah" rather than "Apocryphon of Jeremiah." My reaction to his comment is that a non-biblical narrative about a prophet is not strong pseudepigraphy and that the term "apocryphon" may be applied (although I believe that it begs certain questions of canon and the author's intent). Non-biblical prophecy by a biblical prophet, on the other hand, constitutes strong pseudepigraphy. Only if 4Q384 is found to contain such material should we label it pseudepigraphy, although we cannot be certain whether the pseudepigraphy is authoritative or convenient. If we find "prophecies" which seem to be directed primarily at members of Jeremiah's generation and are linked to the narrative, the pseudepigraphy may still be labeled as convenient. If, however, it is clearly directed across the ages at the Jews of the Second Temple period, it is likely to be strong, authoritative pseudepigraphy.

The final group of non-pentateuchal texts on which I would like to comment are those presented by Emanuel Tov in the proceedings of the first Orion Symposium (4QapocrJosh[a,b,c, etc]).[47] He suggests that "paraphrase" would be a better term than "apocryphon" for these works, a sentiment with which I wholly agree, since it describes a sort of rewritten Bible.[48] If Tov has correctly integrated these texts, then we have another example of that common form of convenient pseudepigraphy which pervades all rewritten Bible texts containing speeches. The text as a whole is not pseudepigraphic but anonymous because there is no authorial voice. The function, or strength, of the pseudepigraphy of Joshua's speeches is thus attenuated. However I

---

[45] M. Smith, "4QpapApocryphon of Jeremiah B?" in DJD 19.137-52.
[46] DJD 19.137.
[47] E. Tov, "The Rewritten Book of Joshua as Found at Qumran and Masada," in *Biblical Perspectives: Early Use and Interpretation of the Bible in the Light of the Dead Sea Scrolls*, 233-56.
[48] Tov, "Rewritten Book of Joshua," 233.

do not agree with Tov's characterization of the paraphrase of Joshua as similar to "the Book of Jubilees, the second half of the Temple Scroll, 4QparaGen-Exod (4Q422) and several other fragmentary compositions."[49] Jubilees contains the strongest authoritative pseudepigraphy and the Temple Scroll, although not totally pseudepigraphic, contains elements of authoritative pseudepigraphy and gives an overall impression of pseudepigraphy which seems to add authority to its contents. 4Q422, on the other hand, like most Qumran narrative texts, is not pseudepigraphic at all, as far as I can tell. It makes no claim to speak in a voice other than its own. I would rather compare the Joshua Apocryphon material to 1Q22, 4Q377 (Moses Apocryphon C)[50] or to 4Q368, which integrates biblical text with non-biblical data and which bears the unproductive official title, "Pentateuchal Apocryphon."[51]

G. *Where Do We Not Find Pseudepigraphy at Qumran?*

It is worthwhile to observe where we do not find pseudepigraphy, although we might have expected it based on a comparison with other Second Temple literature. For example, to the best of my knowledge we do not find at Qumran sapiential literature attributed to Solomon or to any other sage of antiquity. Despite the tradition of the Solomonic authorship of Proverbs and Ecclesiastes (continued by the Wisdom of Solomon and other works), none of the sapiential texts published in DJD 20,[52] nor soon-to-be published copies of 4QInstruction A, nor the already known 4Q184, "Wiles of the Wicked Woman" and 4Q185 in praise of wisdom, nor the wisdom hymn found in 11QPs[a] and in Ben Sira, is attributed to anyone. All of these are anonymous, even when the author speaks in the first person. Although a pseudepigraphic incantation against demons is attributed to Solomon (11Q11 1) together with one to David (11Q11 4), a precursor of later magical tradition found in rabbinic literature and the Testament of Solomon, Solomon's absence from the wisdom texts should make us consider the larger picture.

---

[49] Tov, "Rewritten Book of Joshua," 248.

[50] This text is more likely, in my view, to be a piece of rewritten Pentateuch about Moses than a Moses pseudepigraphon.

[51] For the texts of 4Q368 and 4Q377, see, for the moment (based on a reconstruction of the original transcriptions of J. T. Milik and J. Strugnell), *A Preliminary Edition of the Unpublished Dead Sea Scrolls: The Hebrew and Aramaic Texts from Cave Four* (ed. B. Z. Wacholder and M. G. Abegg; Washington, DC: Biblical Archaeology Society, 1995) 3.135-39 and 164-66, respectively.

[52] *Qumran Cave 4.XV: Sapiential Texts, Part 1* (ed. T. Elgvin et al.; DJD 20; Oxford: Clarendon, 1997).

We also observe that the eschatological-apocalyptic War Scroll, 1QM, stands out by not having an ancient prophet or sage as its speaker. Frequently, in Second Temple literature, predictions of the "end of days" are put into the mouths of speakers such as Daniel, Enoch, Moses, Baruch, Ezra or the twelve patriarchs. Authoritative pseudepigraphy is thus quite common in this genre and we might have expected the War Scroll also to adopt this form of strong pseudepigraphy. Arguments from silence are extremely hazardous, to be sure, but these two observations, regarding Wisdom Literature and the War Scroll, taken together, tend to support a position to which I have alluded very tentatively, that the writings of the Qumran group avoid authoritative pseudepigraphy.

IV. Conclusions

My investigation into the topic of pseudepigraphy at Qumran, its levels, roles, and functions, is still in an initial phase. My conclusions, such as they are, must be considered tentative; perhaps at this stage it would be more appropriate to call them observations.

1 There are at least two major (and one minor) levels of pseudepigraphy in ancient literature:

   a Authoritative: the speaker of the work is purported to be a figure of antiquity.

   b Convenient: the work is anonymous and individual pseudepigraphic voices are heard within the work.

   c Decorative: the work is associated with an ancient name with regard neither for content, nor, more significantly, for effect.

Convenient pseudepigraphy is particularly important for the genre we call rewritten Bible, since much rewritten Bible is anonymous, like Scripture itself. Jubilees is an exception to that rule and its strong authoritative pseudepigraphy makes it stand out (in contrast to 4QRP, for example). The addition of pseudepigraphic speeches to rewritten biblical narrative creates a localized, weaker form of pseudepigraphy which is completely conventional and which functions to render the work more vivid.

2 We should distinguish between texts which are both internally and externally pseudepigraphic, and thus strongly pseudepigraphic, and those which are pseudepigraphic only internally, where the pseudepigraphy is convenient. Only the former can be said to function pseudepigraphically as a whole. Decorative pseudepigraphy is only external.

3 We should probably employ the term "pseudepigraphy" only for authoritatively pseudepigraphic works.

4 Works which are partially pseudepigraphic, either through interpolation of legal material or of speeches, should not be classified as pseudepigraphic *in toto*.

5 Prophetic literature is only to be considered pseudepigraphic if it is authoritative and if the prophecies are pseudepigraphic. Narratives about prophetic figures are the same as any other rewritten Bible.

6 The terms "apocryphal" and "pseudepigraphic" should be used very sparingly in characterizing the Qumran texts. The nature of the authorship should not generate the title of the work. In particular, the term "apocryphal" should be limited because of its implications regarding canon. Because their goal is to interpret and clarify the Bible, the works described as rewritten Bible should probably never be classified as apocrypha or pseudepigrapha.

7 There appear to be several kinds of legal texts at Qumran: pseudepigraphic and anonymous, biblically styled and non-biblically styled. Within the pseudepigraphic, some are pseudo-Moses and some are pseudo-God.

8 There appear to be no pseudepigraphic apocalyptic texts native to Qumran.

9 The absence of pseudepigraphy from certain genres at Qumran should be noted since this omission may mark a distinction between Qumranic and other Second Temple literature.

PSEUDEPIGRAPHY IN RABBINIC LITERATURE

Marc Bregman

Hebrew Union College

Pseudepigraphy in rabbinic literature[1] is a broad and complex subject, which, as we shall see, has stimulated considerable scholarly debate. Within the limited framework of this presentation, I shall try to
touch briefly on various elements of this issue that seem to me most
relevant to the broader subject of pseudepigraphy in the Second
Temple period and late antiquity.

First we should note that despite the dominant rabbinic belief in
divine revelation (תורה מן השמיים),[2] the Rabbis are well aware of
possible challenges to the notion of God's authorship of the Torah.
We find lively debate as to whether God wrote the entire Torah[3] or
whether it was Moses who actually wrote the Torah, albeit at divine
dictation. There is also discussion of the possibility that Moses may
have authored some parts of the Torah himself, such as the curses
expressed in the third person by Moses in the book of Deuteronomy
(for example, "God will smite," Deut. 28:22).[4] The Rabbis are also

---

[1] This essay began as a presentation given in 1987 in the seminar on "Pseud-
epigraphy: Problems in Research in Judaism of the Hellenistic-Roman Period," directed by Prof. Michael Stone and Dr. David Satran at the Hebrew University of
Jerusalem. The version published here reflects papers read at the Second
International Symposium of the Orion Center for the Study of the Dead Sea
Scrolls, The Hebrew University, Jerusalem, January 1997, and at the Colloquium
on Early Rabbinic Judaism of the European Association for Jewish Studies, Yarnton
Manor, Oxford, September 1997. My thanks to those who responded to these pre-
sentations for their comments and questions which stimulated many of the changes
in this significantly revised version.

[2] See A. J. Heschel, *Theology of Ancient Judaism* (3 vols.; London/New York: Son-
cino; Jerusalem: Jewish Theological Seminary of America, 1962-90) [Hebrew].

[3] See Heschel, *Theology of Ancient Judaism*, 2.353-56, especially 354 citing R.
Shimon ben Laqish's interpretation of "And I [God] will give you the tablets of
stone, and the law and the commandments, which I have written" (Exod. 24:12) to
include the Ten Commandments, Pentateuch, Prophets, Writings (b. Ber. 5a).
Compare Ibn Ezra to Exod. 24:12, as cited by Heschel, 354: God did not write the
Torah [except for the Ten Commandments]. According G. Vermes, "The Deca-
logue and the Minim," *BZAW* 103 (1968) 232-40, this was the position of the מינים,
who were more enlightened hellenistic Jews acquainted with Greek philosophical
thought.

[4] B. Meg. 31b; see Heschel, *Theology of Ancient Judaism*, 2.181-83. Compare b.
San. 99a: ואפילו אמר כל התורה כולה מן השמים חוץ מפסוק זה שלא אמרו הקב"ה אלא משה
מפי עצמו, זהו "כי דבר ה' בזה" (במ' טו:לא) "And even if one said the whole Torah is
from heaven apart from this [i.e. one] verse, for the Holy One, blessed be He did

well aware of the impossibility that Moses himself wrote down some parts תורת משה ("the Torah of Moses"), particularly those verses at the end of Deuteronomy which describe his own death and burial (Deut. 34:5-12). A tannaitic tradition imagines Moses' concern that the Israelites might have reason to say that he "counterfeited" Scripture (זייף משה את התורה) by instructing them to do things which he was not commanded by God.[5] The Rabbis occasionally portrayed non-Jews claiming that the Torah had been forged, falsified or fabricated in some way. The word used in these passages is, significantly, a Greek loan word פלסטון, πλαστόν.[6]

In light of rabbinic sensitivity to the issue of divine and Mosaic authorship of Scripture, it is interesting that the Rabbis themselves have no compunction about simply putting words into the mouth of God, Moses and other biblical figures. Most readers of rabbinic literature, ancient or modern, do not seem to find this particularly surprising.[7] It is a commonplace in rabbinic literature that God makes statements to biblical personalities that have little or no scriptural basis. For example, the expression אמר הקב"ה למשה ("The Holy One, blessed be He, said to Moses"), followed by a statement which

---

not say it, but rather it is from the mouth of Moses himself, this is [i.e. to such a person applies the verse], 'for he has despised the word of the Lord' (Num. 15:31)." See L. Jacobs, "Rabbinic Views on the Order and Authorship of the Biblical Books," *Structure and Form in the Babylonian Talmud* (Cambridge: Cambridge University Press, 1991) 36.

[5] Sifre on Deut. 3:23, sect. 26 (ed. Finkelstein, 36); Lev. Rab. 31:4 (ed. Margulies, 2.720) in the name of R. Judah. See Heschel, *Theology of Ancient Judaism*, 2.120-22, who sees this relatively early rabbinic tradition as a response to claims by "Ebionites" in the Pseudo-Clementine Homilies that parts of the Torah of Moses had been "falsified" by others. See further Heschel's long footnote, 121-22, n. 12, in which he cites the Pseudo-Clementine Homilies (3, 47) as evidence that the Torah was first written hundreds of years after the death of Moses and repeatedly forged by the Jews who each time added additional falsehoods. Heschel further cites the claim of the pagan philosopher, Porphyry, that it was not Moses but Ezra who wrote the Torah and similar views expressed by Mandeans, Samaritans and in Islam.

[6] Num. Rab. 8:4: אמר ר' חיא בר אבא בשם ר' יוחנן והיו אומות העולם, אומרים תורתן של אלו פלסטון היא "R. Ḥiyya bar Abba said in the name of R. Yoḥanan...and the nations of the world would say: Their Law is forged"; Yalqut Shimoni on Jer., sect. 321, citing "Yelammedenu": א"ר לוליינא שאל קרוטיס אחד את ר' יוסי מה שאני רואה את, תורתכם פלסטירין "R. Luliana said: a [Roman] judge [κριτής] asked R. Yosi: As far as I can see, your Law is a forgery." On פלסטון, פלסטיר (πλαστόν) meaning "forged," see D. Sperber, *A Dictionary of Greek and Latin Legal Terms in Rabbinic Literature* (Jerusalem: Bar-Ilan University Press, 1984) 147-49.

[7] The same phenomenon is found in early Jewish liturgical poetry. See E. Fleischer, *Hebrew Liturgical Poetry in the Middle Ages* (Jerusalem: Keter, 1975) 107-08 [Hebrew] on ציטטות מדומות, "imaginary quotations," who notes that such direct quotations are "surprising." In teaching, I have found that beginning students of rabbinic literature also find this phenomenon quite surprising.

is not in scripture, is found hundreds of times.[8] One might argue that because of the use of special rabbinic epithets for God, such as הקב״ה, "the Holy One, blessed be He," or המקום "the Omnipresent," there is no danger of confusing such rabbinic attributions of statements to God with biblical ones. However, in at least one genre of midrashic literature, the Tanḥuma-Yelammedenu midrashim (particularly in the early stratum of texts) the divine epithet is the biblical אלהים, "God," and we still regularly find the expression אמר האלהים, "God said," followed by non-biblical statements.[9] In one midrashic pattern, the eschatological peroration of the composite or "literary" homily,[10] this sort of divine speech is so common that it has been given the name *theophoron* by the one scholar who has written extensively about this subject.[11]

It is important to note that when the Rabbis attribute extra-biblical statements to God in this way, the statements are, for the most part, aggadic rather than halakhic. However, we sometimes find theophoric statements of this sort which do at least support established halakhic practices, for example, the reading of the scriptural

---

[8] At the Orion Symposium it was suggested that this phenomenon might be termed "pseudo-God" (M. J. Bernstein, "Pseudepigraphy in the Qumran Scrolls: Categories and Functions") or "divine pseudepigraphy" (L. H. Schiffman, "The Temple Scroll and the Halakhic Pseudepigrapha of the Second Temple Period"). Such attributions of extra-biblical statements to God are only occasionally marked by the use of the term, כביכול, "as it were" which, it might be argued, does occasionally suggest a certain reservation on the part of the rabbinic authors or editors of the text. See for example, Gen. Rab. 38:6 (ed. Theodor-Albeck, 355) [Num. Rab. 11:7], Lev. Rab. 30:13, Num. Rab. 4:2, 11:7, 12:7, 23:11, Lam. Rab. Proem 2, 1:51, Pesiqta Rabbati, ch. 29 (ed. Friedmann, 136b). However, see Cant. Rab. to Cant 5:2 and Exod. Rab. 2:5(1) (ed. Shinan, 111) where כביכול seems to have been added before a statement attributed to God which *is* found in Scripture: כביכול אמר הקב״ה עמו אנכי בצרה, "As it were, the Holy One, blessed be He, said: "I [will be] with him in trouble" (Ps. 91:15); compare the parallel in Pesiqta de-Rav Kahana, Ha-Ḥodesh Ha-Zeh 6 (ed. Mandelbaum, 88) and Pesiqta Rabbati, ch. 15 (ed. Friedmann, 70a) where כביכול is not found. The word כביכול by itself is used as an epithet for God in modern Hebrew literature, according to A. Even-Shoshan, המלון החדש (3 vols.; Jerusalem: Kiryath Sepher, 1975). 1.492, s.v. יכל. On the use of כביכול to indicate particularly mythological statements, see Michael Fishbane's forthcoming work on rabbinic mythology.

[9] See M. Bregman, *The Tanḥuma-Yelammedenu Literature: Studies in the Evolution of the Versions* (Ph.D. diss., The Hebrew University of Jerusalem, 1991) 176-77, 267-68, nn. 40-45 and the earlier bibliography cited there.

[10] See J. Heinemann, *Public Sermons in the Talmudic Period* (Jerusalem: Bialik Institute, 1970) 23-28 [Hebrew].

[11] E. Stein, "Die Homiletische Peroratio im Midrasch," *HUCA* 8-9 (1931-32) 353-71, esp. 359ff. On 367-68, Stein suggests that the use of such theophoric perorations, particularly characteristic of the Tanḥuma literature, shows a higher rhetorical style and may even go back to earlier patterns reflected in such authors as Philo.

lection [Exod. 19:1ff] describing the giving of the Law which is assigned to the holiday of Shavuot.[12]

> The Holy One, blessed be He, said to Israel: My children, read this section every year and I will consider you as if you are standing before Mount Sinai and receiving the Torah.[13] When? [and now quoting the actual verse which begins the scriptural lection] בחודש השלישי לצאת בני ישראל מארץ מצרים "In the third month of the exodus of the children of Israel from the land of Egypt" (Exod. 19:1).[14]

In this passage, God is depicted as commanding the biblical Israelites and, by extension, their descendants in rabbinic times, to read the scriptural lection assigned by the Rabbis to חג מתן תורה "the Festival of the Giving of the Torah/Shavuot," as a kind of ritual re-enactment of the Giving of the Torah at Sinai.

Apart from such statements to Israel in general,[15] God is generally not depicted by the Rabbis as speaking to specific persons who are not biblical personalities.[16] The sages seem, for the most part, to have at least limited such direct divine speech to the biblical period.[17] In

---

[12] T. Meg. 4:5; j. Meg. 3:6, b. Meg. 30b.

[13] Compare Pesiqta Rabbati, ch. 12 (ed. Friedmann, 53a): "The Holy One, blessed be He, said to them [Israel], My children you only need to read the Amalek section every year and I will consider you as if you are eradicating his name from the world"; Tanḥuma, Ki Tissa 3: "The Holy One, blessed be He, said [to Moses]...just as you are now standing and giving them *parashat sheqalim* (Exod. 30:11 *et seq.*) and your are lifting up their heads, so every year when they read it before Me...."

[14] Pesiqta de-Rav Kahana, Ba-Ḥodesh Ha-Shelishi [ch. 12], sect. 1, (ed. Mandelbaum, 204). On this passage, see M. Bregman, "Past and Present in Rabbinic Literature," *Hebrew Annual Review* 2 (1978) 47-49; L. Silberman, "The Rhetoric of Midrash," in *The Biblical Mosaic* (ed. R. Polzin and E. Rothman; Philadelphia: Fortress, 1982) 24.

[15] It is interesting that God also speaks to other nations, including מלכות רומי, "The Empire of Rome"; see for example b. 'Abod. Zar. 2a. My thanks to Prof. Ofra Meir, University of Haifa, for calling my attention to this.

[16] See O. Meir, *The Darshanic Story in Genesis Rabbah* (Tel Aviv: Hakibbutz Hameuchad, 1987) 29 [Hebrew], and *The Acting Characters in the Stories of the Talmud and Midrash* (Ph.D. diss., The Hebrew University of Jerusalem, 1977) 105-06 [Hebrew], who states that God does not talk to non-biblical figures. A unusual exception, cited by Meir, is found in b. Ber. 7a, where R. Yishmael ben Elisha relates that אכתריאל יה ה' צבאות, "Akatriel Yah, the Lord of Hosts," said to him: "Ishmael, my son, bless me." It should also be noted that in 'Abot R. Natan, Version A, ch. 38 (ed. Schechter, 114) אמר להן הקב"ה אין אתם גובין מהן אלא נפשות, God seems to be speaking to unnamed but apparently non-biblical persons who let an unnamed woman and her two sons die of hunger. Perhaps significantly, in a very early Genizah fragment of this passage, the reading is עליהם [הכ]תוב [אומר יה]וה יריב ריבם citing Prov. 22:23, see M. Bregman, "An Early Fragment of *Avot DeRabbi Natan* from a Scroll," *Tarbiz* 52 (1983) 215.

[17] See t. Soṭ. 13:3-4 (ed. Lieberman, 230-31 and the parallels listed there): "Since Haggai, Zechariah and Malachi, the last prophets, died, the Holy Spirit has ceased from Israel" and the continuation there about those rabbinic sages who were "worthy" (ראוי) of the Holy Spirit, but whose generation did not merit (זכא) it.

addition to attributing extra-biblical statements to God, the Rabbis have no hesitation about putting words in the mouths of various biblical characters which have little or no basis in scripture.[18] When extra-biblical statements and actions are attributed to God and biblical personalities in this way, the Rabbis seem to be engaging in what we would call "historical fiction." However, this approach might be anachronistic on our part, imputing to the sages of late antiquity notions of past and present,[19] history and fiction,[20] that are really part of our western, and particularly post-Enlightenment, intellectual culture.[21] It might be more fruitful for scholars of rabbinic literature to compare the way God and biblical personalities are made to speak in rabbinic legend to the way the classical gods and heroes are made to speak and act in Greco-Roman culture (itself a complex question)[22] and particularly to the way biblical personalities are made to speak in Second Temple period pseudepigrapha and Qumran literature.

Considering the fact that the Rabbis seem to have no qualms about putting words in the mouth of God and biblical characters, such as Moses,[23] it should perhaps come as no surprise that they

---

[18] See *Moreh Nevukhei Ha-Zeman*, ch. 14, in *The Writings of Nachman Krochmal* (ed. S. Rawidowicz; London: Ararat, 1961) 243, where Krochmal regards such non-biblical statements attributed to biblical figures in the aggadah as imaginative rhetoric designed to stimulate the audience, as noted by L. Jacobs, "How Much of the Babylonian Talmud is Pseudepigraphic?," *JJS* 28 (1977) 54 [reprinted in Jacob's *Structure and Form in the Babylonian Talmud*]. See I. Heinemann, *The Methodology of the Aggadah* [דרכי האגדה] (Givataim: Magnes and Masadah, 1970) 42 [Hebrew]: "in effect the heroes of the past serve only as a mouthpiece for the ideas of the sages of Israel." For an English précis of this seminal study of rabbinic thinking, see M. Bregman, "Isaak Heinemann's Classic Study of Aggadah and Midrash" (forthcoming in *Judaism*).

[19] See M. Bregman, "Past and Present in Midrashic Literature," *Hebrew Annual Review* 2 (1978) 45-58.

[20] See Y. H. Yerushalmi, *Zakhor: Jewish History and Jewish Memory* (Seattle: University of Washington, 1982), ch. 2, on the lack of "historical" writing in rabbinic literature.

[21] On pre-modern "organic thinking," see I. Heinemann, *Methodology of the Aggadah*, 8-9 and particularly 200, n. 90, where Heinemann mentions the difference between his use of the term and that of Max Kadushin, particularly in two of his major works, *Organic Thinking: A Study in Rabbinic Thought* (New York: The Jewish Theological Seminary of America, 1938) and *The Rabbinic Mind* (1952; New York: The Jewish Theological Seminar of America, 1965²). See also *Understanding the Rabbinic Mind: Essays on the Hermeneutic of Max Kadushin* (ed. P. Ochs; Atlanta: Scholars Press, 1990) and particularly the essay there by R. S. Sarason, "Kadushin's Study of Midrash" 54-55, n. 31, on the difference between Heinemann's and Kadushin's use of the term "organic."

[22] See for example, P. Veyne, *Did the Greeks Believe in their Myths: An Essay on the Constitutive Imagination* (Chicago: University of Chicago, 1988).

[23] Moses is often referred to by the Rabbis as משה רבנו, literally "Moses, our Rabbi."

might occasionally put words in the mouths of fellow rabbis. Nonetheless, the aspect of rabbinic pseudepigaphy which has elicited the most scholarly discussion is the sometimes unreliable ascription of statements and traditions to named rabbinic sages.[24]

First we should note that in the Mishnah, the ascription of a statement to a particular named sage (דברי ר' פלוני) marks that statement as a minority opinion.[25] Rulings cited as the opinion of "the sages" in general (חכמים אומרים) are more authoritative.[26] But rulings cited anonymously are understood to be the ruling of the Mishnah itself and are the most authoritative.[27] Thus, in the Mishnah, anonymity

---

[24] See L. Jacobs, "Are there Fictitious Baraitot in the Babylonian Talmud?," *HUCA* 42 (1971) 185-96; L. Jacobs, "How Much of the Babylonian Talmud is Pseudepigraphic?," *JJS* 28 (1977) 47-59 [reprinted and revised in his *Structure and Form in the Babylonian Talmud* (Cambridge: Cambridge University Press, 1991) 6-17; W. S. Green, "What's in a Name?–The Problematic of Rabbinic 'Biography'," in *Approaches to Ancient Judaism: Theory and Practice* (Missoula, MN: Scholars Press, 1978) 77-96; D. W. Halivni, "Doubtful Attributions in the Talmud," *PAAJR* 56-57 (1979-80) 67-83 [Hebrew]; J. Neusner, *In Search of Talmudic Biography: The Problem of the Attributed Saying* (Chico, CA: Scholars Press, 1984); J. Neusner, *Reading and Believing–Ancient Judaism and Contemporary Gullibility* (Chico, CA: Scholars Press, 1986); D. Kraemer, "On the Reliability of Attributions in the Babylonian Talmud," *HUCA* 50 (1989) 175-90; R. Kalmin, "Talmudic Portrayals of Relations between Rabbis: Amoraic or Pseudepigraphic?," *AJS Review* 17 (1992) 165-97; S. Stern, "Attribution and Authorship in the Babylonian Talmud," *JJS* 45 (1994) 28-51; S. Stern, "The Concept of Authorship in the Babylonian Talmud," *JJS* 46 (1995) 183-95.

[25] See m. 'Ed. 1:5-6; compare t. 'Ed. 1:4. On the pejorative implication of "naming" in British Parliamentary practice, see L. A. Abraham and S. C. Hawtrey, *Parliamentary Dictionary* (ed. S. C. Hawtrey and H. M. Barclay; London: Butterworths, 1970³) 130-31, s.v. "naming a member" and compare the pejorative connotation of "naming" someone in a lawsuit. On the religious dimensions of naming, see *The Encyclopedia of Religion* (ed. M. Eliade; New York and London: Macmillan, 1987) 10.300-07.

[26] According to the talmudic rule: יחיד ורבים הלכה כרבים, "[in a dispute between] an individual and a multitude, the law is in accordance with the multitude" (b. Ber. 9a and parallels).

[27] According to the talmudic rule cited in the name of R. Yoḥanan: הלכה כסתם משנה "the law is according to the anonymous mishnah" (b. Shab. 46a and parallels). On this mishnaic method of indicating relative authority of rulings, see D. W. Halivni, "Doubtful Attributions," 79-80 and D. W. Halivni, "The Reception Accorded to Rabbi Judah's Mishnah," in *Jewish and Christian Self-Definition* (ed. E. P. Sanders *et al.*; Philadelphia: Fortress, 1981) 2.209. Rabbi Judah, at least occasionally, seems to have recorded the opinion of a particular sage with whom he agreed, anonymously or as the opinion of "the sages," in order to give it authority. See b. Hul. 85a and M. Elon, *Jewish Law: History, Sources, Principles: HaMishpat Ha-Ivri* (Philadelphia: Jewish Publication Society, 1994) 3.1060, on the formulation of the halakhah in the Mishnah as an anonymous statement or as the opinion of "the sages." Conversely, anonymous statements (סתם) in the Mishnah and other tannaitic compilations are attributed to specific rabbinic sages (b. San. 86a); see Stern, "Authorship," 193. Compare this to the "aggadic method" that Heinemann, *Methodology of the Aggadah*, 275, termed "avoidance of anonymity" (בריחה מן האנונימיות).

confers authority, contrary to what we find in pseudepigraphy where false attribution to some specific, well-known and highly respected personality is generally used to increase the authority of a literary work, statement or idea.

This practice, though limited primarily to the Mishnah which seems to be a particularly apodictic work,[28] is curious in light of the generally high regard the sages express for the precise attribution of rabbinic statements. This is exemplified in sayings such as שכל האומר דבר בשם אומרו מביא גאולה לעולם "Whoever cites a statement in the name of the one who said it, brings redemption to the world" (m. 'Abot 6:6:) and כל האומר שמועה מפי אומרה יהא רואה בעל השמועה כאלו הוא עומד כנגדו "Whoever cites a tradition according to the one who said it, should imagine the "tradent" standing in front of him." (j. Shab. 1:2 [3a]). The actual practice of citing rulings in the presence of a sage to whom it was attributed could, however, lead to disagreement, as a passage from the Tosefta (t. Mak. 1:3) demonstrates:

> Concerning a document dated on a day that turns out to have been a Shabbat or the tenth of Tishre [Yom Kippur, when of course writing is prohibited], R. Yehudah rules that the document is valid and R. Yosi rules that the document is invalid. R. Yehudah said to him [to R. Yosi]. Such a case came before you in Sepphoris and you ruled that the document was valid [הכשרת]. Rabbi Yosi replied: "I did not rule it valid. But if I did, I did" [אני לא הכשרתי :ואם הכשרתי הכשרתי]

What is remarkable here, and elsewhere in rabbinic literature, is the candid way in which the sages discuss the problem of unreliable attribution.[29] For example, a passage in the Palestinian Talmud relates that when R. Abbahu wanted to teach his daughter Greek, he was accused of simply attributing to R. Yohanan a ruling that this practice was permitted. Despite R. Abbahu's disclaimer that he did indeed receive this teaching directly from R. Yohanan, there seems to have been doubt as to whether R. Yohanan made such a ruling.[30]

---

[28] D. W. Halivni, *Midrash, Mishnah, and Gemara: The Jewish Predilection for Justified Law* (Cambridge and London: Harvard, 1986).

[29] See Kalmin, "Talmudic Portrayals," 196-97, who cites seven instances in which Rav Ashi's opinions are rejected by the anonymous editors of the Babylonian Talmud with the expression בדותא (ברותא) היא, which seems to mean "false, forged, fictional, or untrue." See also the comment on the expression, בדותא היא in b. Pes. 11a (ed. Steinsaltz, 46 עיונים): "the intent is to say that Rav Ashi never said these statements, but that someone attributed them to him."

[30] J. Pe'ah 1:1 (15c), Shabb. 6:1 (7d), Sot. 9:15 (24c): עלי אם לא שמעתיה מר' יוחנן. הוא תלי לה ברבי יוחנן [שמע רבי אבהו ואמר] יבוא, "He [R. Abbahu] attributed it [the ruling] to R. Yohanan. [When R. Abbahu heard this, he replied]: May [punishment] befall me, if I did not hear it from R. Yohanan." In the same discussion in the Palestinian Talmud, R. Hiyya bar Abba relates that R. Yohanan prohibits the teaching of Greek "because of informers" (מפני המסורות). "If this be the reason,

Significantly, in at least one passage the practice of pseudepi-graphy actually seems to be recommended. Rabbi Akiba is reputed to have taught his disciple Rabbi Shimon bar Yohai: אם בקשת ליחנק היתלה באילן גדול, literally: "if you want to hang yourself, do it in a big tree." This rather cryptic statement has been understood to mean, "If you want a ruling or statement to be accepted, attribute it to a famous sage (i.e. even if he never said it)."[31]

Another phenomenon which has been noted by several scholars is the attribution of rulings or sayings to sages whose name seems to be a pun on the subject matter of that particular statement, as when Rabbi Abba bar Memel explains the meaning of the rare term ממל (memel, part of the crushing apparatus of an olive-press) in the Mishnah.[32] This phenomenon seems to be a talmudic example of what Moshe Bernstein has termed "decorative pseudepigraphy."[33]

Among scholars of rabbinic literature, there are those who seem in general to accept the reliability of attributions of statements to specific sages and the historical veracity of stories about rabbis.[34] At the other end of the spectrum, one scholar has gone so far as to as-sert that "attributions are simply not historically reliable data."[35] Most scholars fall somewhere in between these extremes. The gener-al scholarly consensus seems to be that the historical reliability of each statement or story needs to be examined on its own merits and in many cases may be impossible to determine definitively. A num-ber of detailed studies have shown that particularly in the Babylonian Talmud there are statements which are incorrectly and

---

there is, of course, no difference between teaching Greek to boys or girls"; see S. Lieberman, *Greek in Jewish Palestine* (New York: Jewish Theological Seminary, 1942) 24 and n. 56, where Lieberman cites a later source (Pirke deRabbi [ed. Grünhut], 58) as attributing to R. Yohanan the specific view that "a man may not teach his daughter Greek," contrary to the view attributed by R. Abbahu to R. Yohanan.

[31] B. Pes. 112a. See Jacobs, "How Much of the Babylonian Talmud is Pseudepigraphic?" 53, n. 17 (*Structure and Form*, 111). Note that in this passage, and in the passage quoted above (n. 30) from the Palestinian Talmud, the Hebrew/Aramaic verb תלה/תלי with the preposition -ב is apparently used to indi-cate "(false) attribution"; see also the expression כאדם שמקלל את עצמו ותולה קללתו באחרים "like a man who curses himself, but attributes his curse to others" (b. San. 106a).

[32] See b. B. B. 67b on m. B. B. 4:5. On this passage and the phenomenon in gen-eral, see Jacobs, "How Much of the Babylonian Talmud is Pseudepigraphic?" 56-57 (*Structure and Form*, 15) where he cites several other examples and previous scholarly discussion by Z. H. Chajes, J. D. Wynkoop, B. Epstein and R. Margaliouth.

[33] See his contribution to this volume, p. 18.

[34] Green, "What's in a Name," 85-87, cites M. D. Herr, E. E. Urbach, S. Safrai, J. Podro, L. Finkelstein, J. Goldin and "virtually every article on an early rabbinic figure in the recent *Encyclopedia Judaica*" as examples of this "uncritical approach."

[35] W. S. Towner, *The Rabbinic Enumeration of Scriptural Examples* (Leiden: E. J. Brill, 1973) 34.

probably even falsely attributed,[36] fictitious baraitot (i.e. tannaitic statements not found in the Mishnah)[37] and stories about sages that seem more legend than history.[38]

So how is it possible to reconcile the apparent paradox between the Rabbis' own insistence on correct attribution with the considerable amount and variety of pseudepigraphy in rabbinic literature noted by various scholars? William Scott Green argues that the association of statements and stories with the names of particular rabbis facilitates the discrimination of one tradition from another but no more.[39] The preservation of the names of individual masters gives rabbinic Judaism its traditional character, that is to say, it provides a tangible connective between the present and the past.[40] Richard Kalmin sees a more tendentious motive. "Perhaps schools founded by early rabbis persisted for several generations or even centuries, and late authors attacked rival schools by composing accounts which reflected poorly on the long-dead founders of these schools... In addition, later generations might compose accounts about early rabbis who possessed or were said to possess some outstanding characteristic which particularly suited the author's message."[41] Louis Jacobs argues that statements are attributed to the rabbi from which they were received "not on the grounds of accuracy but simply because to do otherwise, to suggest that a teacher's saying was one's own, was a form of theft. It is plagiarism that is condemned. But there seems to have been no objection at all to attributing sayings to teachers who were not, in fact, responsible for them!"[42] While according to David

---

[36] See Jacobs, "How much of the Babylonian Talmud is Pseudepigraphic?"

[37] See Jacobs, "Fictitious Baraitot" and "How Much of the Babylonian Talmud is Pseudepigraphic?," 49, n. 7 (*Structure and Form*, 110): "at least some of the anonymous *baraitot* quoted in the BT must have been invented for the purpose of elaborating on the Talmudic discussion."

[38] See Stemberger, *Introduction to the Talmud and Midrash*, 61; compare Kalmin, "Talmudic Portrayals of Relations between Rabbis: Amoraic or Pseudepigraphic?"

[39] Compare M. Foucault, "What Is an Author?," in *Textual Strategies: Perspectives in Post-Structuralist Criticism* (ed. J. V. Harari; London: Methuen, 1980) 149 (speaking of the "scientific" literature of the Middle Ages): "'Hippocrates said,' 'Pliny recounts,' were not really formulas of an argument based on authority; they were the markers inserted in discourses that were supposed to be received as statements of demonstrated truth."

[40] Green, "What's in a Name," 88-89. This might also be characterized as "decorative pseudepigraphy," according to Moshe Bernstein's classificatory system (see "The Degrees and Functions of Pseudepigraphy at Qumran," 3).

[41] "Talmudic Portrayals of Amoraic Relationships between Rabbis," 170. This might be characterized as "strong pseudepigraphy," according to Moshe Bernstein's classificatory system ("The Degrees and Functions of Pseudepigraphy at Qumran," 3)

[42] "How Much of the Babylonian Talmud is Pseudepigraphic?," 53 (*Structure and Form*, 12).

Halivni, "It appears that when it was not known who was the author of a particular tradition, it was not transmitted anonymously, but in the name of who brought it to the study house."[43] Recently, Sacha Stern has argued that "the typical phrase 'Rabbi x said' is not necessarily designed to indicate the author of the saying: it may refer to his disciple, to a later tradent, or even to some earlier authority."[44] Stern astutely distinguishes talmudic attributions from authorship in the commonly accepted sense of authorship in modern Western society, which is predicated on the perception of the individual as a highly autonomous, creative force. Rather, in rabbinic culture, attributed as well as unattributed sayings may have been perceived as deriving "from earlier, undateable and anonymous collective traditions.[45] ... It is within the context of this 'flexible,' collective view of authorship that Talmudic pseudepigraphy ... should be assessed." [46] Stern links the question of talmudic authorship to contemporary literary theory, as reflected in the work of Roland Barthes, who has raised serious questions about the status of the author in literary production.[47] Such a perception about the fundamental nature of rab-

---

[13] "Doubtful Attributions," 70. The approaches of Jacobs and Halivni might be characterized as "convenient pseudepigraphy," according to Moshe Bernstein's classificatory system ("The Degrees and Functions of Pseudepigraphy at Qumran," 3).

[14] "Attribution and Authorship in the Babylonian Talmud," 48. See also E. S. Rosenthal, "Tradition and Innovation in the *Halakha* of the Sages," *Tarbiz* 63 (1994) 321-74 [Hebrew with English abstract, xix-xx].

[15] This point was previously made by B. Bamberger, "Dating of Aggadic Material," *JBL* 68 (1949) 115-23. The notion that all specific rabbinic teachings derive from a collective tradition should, of course, be compared with the traditional view that all "torah" (written and oral) derives from the divine revelation given to Moses on Sinai and transmitted to subsequent generations, including the rabbinic sages, see m. 'Abot 1:1 and other statements such as: שֶׁכָּל הַתּוֹרָה הֲלָכָה לְמשֶׁה מִסִּינַי, "For the whole torah is a law given to Moses on Sinai" (b. Nid. 45a) and מִקְרָא, מִשְׁנָה, תַּלְמוּד, אַגָּדָה, וַאֲפִילוּ מַה שֶׁתַּלְמִיד וָתִיק עָתִיד לְהוֹרוֹת לִפְנֵי רַבּוֹ כְּבָר נֶאֱמַר לְמשֶׁה בְּסִינַי, "Bible, Mishnah, Talmud, Aggadah, and even what an advanced disciple will in the future teach before his teacher was already said to Moses on Sinai" (j. Pe'ah 2:6 [17a] and numerous parallels); see Heschel, *Theology of Ancient Judaism*, 2.229-38, esp. 236, n. 10.

[16] "Attribution," 51. For a fuller working out of this approach, see Stern, "The Concept of Authorship in the Babylonian Talmud," particularly 195: "The Bavli's dialectical oscillation between creativity and tradition, individual authorship and collective anonymity, reflects no doubt an ideological motivation: namely, to accommodate, if not reconcile, the rather contradictory notions of revealed, oral Torah from Sinai on the one hand, and the personal authority of individual rabbis on the other, upon both of which depends the legitimization of rabbinic Judaism."

[47] Stern ("Attribution," 49, "Authorship," 185, 195, n. 43) cites Barthes' famous essay "Death of the Author," in *Image, Music, Text* (London: Fontana, 1977) 142-48, esp. 142-43. See also R. Barthes, "From Work to Text," in *Textual Strategies: Perspectives in Post-Structuralist Criticism*, 73-81, and Foucault, "What is an Author?," 141-60. For subsequent discussion of the important questions about "authorship"

binic culture and tradition is just one of many reasons why there has been a shift in the last generation or so of scholarship toward viewing rabbinic texts less as historical reportage and more as literature.[48]

Stern's discussion of rabbinic authorship raises important questions about the larger nature of "rabbinic thinking." For example, in his discussion of what he terms "conjectural" or "inferential" attribution, Stern argues that the ubiquitous phrase "Rabbi X said" often means: it can be conjectured or inferred that Rabbi X thought or was of the following opinion, conveying not so much an historical fact or a direct quotation of what the said rabbi really said but rather a later interpretation of his thoughts and opinions.[49] I suggest that this talmudic approach to inferential interpretation of rabbinic statements can be profitably compared to the talmudic approach to the interpretation of Scripture. For the Rabbis, legal rulings that are regarded as "biblical" (דאורייתא) include not only what is specifically stated in Scripture but also what may be legitimately inferred from Scripture by means of interpretation (מדרש) and rational conjecture (סברא).[50] This is related to the rabbinic notion that the Torah was given in accordance with the rulings of the sages. The authority of the sages to make legally binding inferences and interpretations of the Divine Will was formulated in the following way: מה שיסכימו,

---

raised by Barthes and Foucault, see the essays collected in *What is an Author?* (ed. M. Biriotti and N. Miller; Manchester and New York: Manchester University Press, 1993). See also *Authorship: From Plato to the Postmodern* (ed. S. Burke; Edinburgh: Edinburgh University, 1995); A. J. Minnis, *Medieval Theory of Authorship* (London: Scolar, 1984). On the decentering of "authorial voice" in rabbinic literature and post-modern literary theory, see I. B. Siegumfeldt, "Old Ideas in a New Setting," *Nordisk Judaisk: Scandinavian Jewish Studies* 17 (1996) 109-17, esp. 113-14, and *The Judaization of Postmodern Theory* (Ph.D. diss., Odense Universitet, 1997, presently in preparation for publication) 219.

[48] See for example, *Midrash and Literature* (ed. G. H. Hartman and S. Budick; New Haven and London: Yale University Press, 1986); D. Boyarin, *Intertextuality and the Reading of Midrash* (Bloomington and Indianapolis: Indiana University Press, 1990); D. Stern, *Midrash and Theory: Ancient Exegesis and Contemporary Literary Studies* (Evanston: Northwestern University Press, 1996); D. Kraemer, *Reading the Rabbis: The Talmud as Literature* (New York and Oxford: Oxford University Press, 1996).

[49] Stern, "Attribution," 32-38. A possible objection to Stern's understanding of "Rabbi X said" as inferential attribution is the existence of more specific terminology (ר' פלוני לטעמיה דאמר/ר' פלוני דאמר) to express this particular sort of attribution. See the extensive discussion of this terminology by J. L. Rubenstein, "The Talmudic Expression 'Rabbi X Following his Reasoning Said'," *Sidra* 10 (1994) 111-29 [Hebrew with English abstract, ix-x].

[50] See Elon, *Jewish Law*, 2.988-89; *Encyclopedia Talmudica* (Jerusalem: Yad Harav Herzog, 1974) 2.433-34, s.v. אסור דאורייתא, Torah Interdictions. A similar approach is found in the interpretation of the Mishnah. One example is found in b. Yeb. 25b where Rav Ashi, asked whether a teaching he inferred from the Mishnah is גמרא או סברא ("received tradition or the product of his own reasoning"), replies מתניתין היא ("it is our Mishnah"); see Stern, "Authorship," 192.

[חכמי הדור] בדבר מדבריהם הוא מה שנצטווה משה מפי הגבורה, "Whatever the sages [of any generation] will agree upon is what Moses was
commanded by God."[51] This notion of rabbinic authority provides
legal warrant for attributing to God what has been arrived at by
human reason. In rabbinic thinking, the result of inference seems
more closely identified with the text or statement from which the inference is made than post-Enlightenment legal thinking would nor-
mally accept.[52] Ultimately, it may be that even halakhic statements
attributed to rabbinic sages are not so unlike aggadic statements attributed to God and biblical personalities[53]; both kinds of statements
may express what it is possible to infer or imagine the speaker to
have said.

The rabbinic attitude to attribution, which may seem rather paradoxical to contemporary sensibilities, can be better understood by
further comparison to the methodology of rabbinic aggadah. Any
discussion of pseudepigraphy must address the question of *dolus*,
whether the incorrect or false attribution has been undertaken in a
deceitful way, with the intention to mislead. This is one of the most
difficult things to determine about rabbinic pseudepigraphy.[54] Did
the sages intend to mislead us deliberately when they attributed
statements to authorities who were clearly not their true authors?
Isaak Heinemann, in his seminal study of the methodology of the aggadah, points out that an appreciation of "craftiness" is an element
of "organic thinking," typical of pre-Enlightenment thought in gen-

---

[51] Rabbenu Nissim ben Reuven Gerondi, *Derashot Ha-Ran* No. 7, cited by Elon,
Jewish Law, 1.245, n. 18; see there further, 243-47.
[52] This may be related to the closer identification, in rabbinic and other pre-
modern cultures, of "image," i.e. representation, with "presence," i.e. the object
represented. See Y. Loberbaum, *Imago Dei: Rabbinic Literature, Maimonides and
Nahmanides* (Ph.D. diss.; The Hebrew University of Jerusalem, 1997) 48-53 [He-
brew].
[53] See, for example, b. 'Erub. 13b: "For three years the House of Shammai and
the House of Hillel disputed, these saying, 'the halakhah is in accordance with us,'
and those saying, 'the halakhah is in accordance with us.' A heavenly voice rang out
and said: 'these and those are the words of the living God (אלו ואלו דברים אלהים
חיים); but the halakhah is in accordance with the House of Hillel'." And indeed, aggadic legends about God and Moses may be interwoven with stories about halakhic
texts and statements attributed to rabbinic sages; see Pesiqta de-Rav Kahana, Parah
'Adumah 7 (ed. Mandelbaum, 1.73, and parallels cited by M. Kasher, *Torah
Shelemah* on Exod. 18:4 (Jerusalem: Machon Torah Shelemah, 1973) 15.10, sect. 25,
for an aggadic tradition in which Moses, upon ascending to heaven to receive the
Torah, hears God reciting a halakhic statement in the name of R. Eliezer found in
the Mishnah (m. Parah 1:1). Compare the famous aggadic tradition in which Moses
does not recognize or understand a halakhic teaching which R. Akiba claims is a
"law given to Moses on Sinai" (b. Men. 29b).
[54] See Stern, "Attribution," particularly 39: "it is often difficult to assess the extent to which the attribution was *deliberately* falsified."

eral and rabbinic thinking in particular.[55] Heinemann cites the following example. When Jacob, at his mother's behest, enters the tent of Isaac to steal the birthright of his older brother, he poses as Esau by saying to his blind father, אנכי עשו בכורך, "I am Esau your first-born" (Gen. 27:19). A midrashic tradition on this verse says: "despite what you might think, Jacob did not really lie to his father" ואף על פי שאתם אומרים שיקר, יעקב לא שיקר,[56] for Jacob paused in mid-sentence in a rather crafty way: אנכי – עשו בכורך, which can now be read: "It is I (Jacob); (but) Esau is your first born."[57] For our discussion of rabbinic pseudepigraphy, this example is particularly instructive. The Bible seems surprisingly uncritical of Jacob's posing as Esau and indeed even speaking in his brother's name. The Rabbis, using the interpretive technique of midrash, transform this from an outright lie into an act of artfully deceptive speech. This deception is viewed in a positive light, to Jacob's credit, for the ultimate purpose is a good one, that Jacob our forefather should get his father's blessing and that the wicked, older brother Esau (who, for the Rabbis, symbolized Rome and later Christianity) should be denied the birthright. The Rabbis here seem to accept that Jacob acted with *dolus*, with the intent to deceive.[58] However, they view Jacob's behavior not as *dolus malus*, misrepresentation which is the ground for discrediting the action,[59] but rather as *dolus bonus*, artful deception. This

---

[55] *The Methodology of the Aggadah*, 119-20.

[56] Tanḥuma (ed. Buber), Toledot 10. But compare Tanḥuma (ed. Buber) Balaq 18: "I am Esau your first-born." Should not a liar be cursed? But not only [was Jacob not cursed], but he was blessed, as it says, 'moreover, he shall be blessed'" (Gen. 27:33):

אנכי עשו בכורך, המוציא בפיו שקר אינו ראו להתקלל!? ולא עוד אלא שנתברך (יעקב),
שנאמר גם ברוך יהיה (בר' כז:לג).

[57] Leqaḥ Tov on Gen. 27:19 (ed. Buber, 67a) and Rashi to Gen. 27:19. Compare Ibn Ezra, *ad. loc.*, who regards this midrash as "babble" (דברי רוח).

[58] Note that in Gen. 27:12, Jacob expresses the fear that if Isaac should discover that he is not Esau, והייתי בעיניו כמתעתע, "And I shall seem to him as a deceiver" (KJV and AV; compare the new JPS translation: "I shall appear to him as a trickster").

[59] Compare Philo, *Questions and Answers on Genesis* (trans. R. Marcus; Loeb Classical Library; Cambridge, MA: Harvard and London: Heinemann, 1971) 501, on Gen. 27:18-19: "'I am Esau, thy first born.' ... Again he will seem to be a deceiver, although he is not to be thought (to be connected) with any evil." In the previous comment, on Gen. 27:16 (499-500), Philo employs an analogy to acceptable deception in the theater and medical practice: "sometimes he [the physician] will speak falsehoods, not being a liar, and he will deceive, not being a deceiver." For the notion of the physician's use of acceptable deception, see Plato, *Republic* 382c, 389b, 459c; on Plato's notion of acceptable deception in general, I have benefited from H. Dietcher (Jerusalem), "The Platonic Lie and Jewish Bible Education" [unpublished paper].

form of deception is evidence of estimable sagacity, for it is deception employed for positive purpose.[60] I would like to suggest that the same kind of *dolus bonus*, "acceptable deception" employed for a positive purpose, may be at work in at least some cases of rabbinic pseudepigraphy.

In conclusion, let us return to Heinemann, who consistently emphasizes that rabbinic thinking is quintessentially creative.[61] The midrashic interpretation of letters, words and sentences is characterized by Heinemann as "creative philology"[62] while the rabbinic interpretation of biblical history is characterized as "creative historiography."[63] To better understand the Rabbis' perplexing penchant for pseudepigraphy, it might be useful to extend Heinemann's terminology to include the notion of "creative attribution."

The Rabbis believed that not only the written Torah but also the Oral Torah – rabbinic tradition – was given by God to Moses at Sinai and transmitted generation by generation to them. Considering their passionate belief in the literal truth of divine revelation, the Rabbis' freedom in creating inventive interpretations of Scripture sometimes seems paradoxical to the modern reader. A similar paradox seems to pertain to the Rabbis' attitude to attribu-

---

[60] On the history and use of these two concepts in Roman and European law, see A. Carcaterra, *Dolus Bonus/Dolus Malus* (Naples: Casa Editrice Dott. Eugenio Jovene, 1970); on *dolus bonus* in Greek philosophy, see 225-26, and on *dolus bonus* in patristic literature, see 156-60. See also H. C. Black, *Black's Law Dictionary* (St. Paul: West, 1990[6]), 483 s.v. *dolus bonus, dolus malus*; *Webster's Third New International Dictionary* (Springfield, MA: Merriam, 1971) 670, s.v. *dolus bonus, dolus malus*. Lieberman, *Greek in Jewish Palestine*, 8, notes that דולוס, δόλος, occurs frequently in rabbinic literature but not with the general meaning of deceit, only of admixture, adulteration of pure objects.

[61] *Methodology of the Aggadah*, 1-14, esp. 4-7 and 11 where Heinemann cites, as an illustration of rabbinic promotion of textual creativity, the parable of the king who gave wheat and flax to his servants, not simply to be preserved but so that they should make these raw materials into bread and cloth (Seder Eliyahu Zuta, ch. 2; ed. M. Friedmann, 171-72). In private conversation, Sasha Stern raised the important question, how do the talmudic sages express our notion of "creativity" (Heinemann uses the adjective [ח]יוצר, see below)? I think the word that comes closest in rabbinic terminology is "midrash." See for example t. Soṭ. 7:21 (ed. Lieberman, 199-200 and parallels): ובנית ביתך (משלי דכ:כז) זה מדרש ... דרוש וקבל שכר, "'and build your house' (Prov. 24:27), this refers to midrash ... make a midrash and receive reward."

[62] *Methodology of the Aggadah*, 96-164, "Book II: The Methodology of Creative Philology (הפילולוגיה היוצרת)."

[63] *Methodology of the Aggadah*, 15-95, "Book I: Creative Historiography (-ההיסטור יוגרפיה היוצרת)."

tion.[64] While stressing the need to attribute statements and stories correctly, the sages were sometimes quite creative in inventing rabbinic attributions, just as they were creative in attributing extra-biblical statements to God and biblical personalities. An appreciation of the remarkable blend of fact and fiction, history and creative writing is essential, I believe, for a nuanced understanding of rabbinic culture in general and rabbinic pseudepigraphy in particular.

---

[64] On the ubiquity of paradox in rabbinic culture, see the important study by A. J. Lelyveld, *The Unity of the Contraries: Paradox as a Characteristic of Normative Jewish Thought* (B. G. Rudolph Lectures in Judaic Studies; Syracuse, NY: Syracuse University Press, 1984).

PSEUDEPIGRAPHY AND GROUP FORMATION
IN SECOND TEMPLE JUDAISM

JOHN J. COLLINS

University of Chicago

The device of pseudepigraphy offered many advantages to writers of the hellenistic period, most obviously the prestige of antiquity.[1] In the pseudepigraphic writings found at Qumran, another factor is prominent. Several of them utilize the antiquity of the pseudonymous author to present a pseudo-prophecy that outlines a long expanse of history after the fact. Examples are found in the Apocalypse of Weeks and the Animal Apocalypse of 1 Enoch; in Daniel 10-12; in Jubilees 23; in 4Q390 (Pseudo-Moses) and in the Pseudo-Daniel fragments. This device of prophecy after the fact, authorized by a venerable pseudonym, is well known throughout the hellenistic world from Persia to Rome. On the one hand, it conveys a sense that history is pre-determined, since it could be predicted centuries in advance. On the other, it inspires confidence in the real prediction with which these prophecies typically conclude. There is another feature of these prophecies, on which I wish to focus here, which comes at or near the point of transition between prophecy after the fact and real prediction. This concerns the rise of an elect group which is foretold from ancient times and thereby legitimated. It is reasonable to suppose that the real authors of the works in question belonged to these elect groups.

Since the best known elect group to emerge in the second century BCE was the Dead Sea sect, the question of the relationship between these pseudepigraphic writings and that sect inevitably arises. Many scholars have argued that the books of Enoch and Jubilees derive from a parent movement of the Dead Sea sect, and Daniel is sometimes also included in the same broad movement.[2] In her contribution to the Madrid Qumran Congress, Devorah Dimant

---

[1] See the overviews by B. M. Metzger, "Literary Forgeries and Canonical Pseudepigrapha," *JBL* 91(1972) 3-24; W. Speyer, "Religiöse Pseudepigraphie und literarische Fälschung im Altertum," in *Frühes Christentum im antiken Strahlungsfeld* (Tübingen: Mohr, 1989) 21-58; W. Speyer, "Fälschung, pseudepigraphische freie Erfindung und 'echte religiöse Pseudepigraphie'," in *Frühes Christentum im antiken Strahlungsfeld*, 100-39.

claimed that the Pseudo-Moses text, 4Q390, "now provides for the
first time solid textual data for reconstructing different strands within
the growing corpus of works related to the Qumran community."[3]
While this claim, in my opinion, exaggerates the significance of the
Pseudo-Moses text, we do indeed have a complex body of data relevant to this issue. In this paper I wish to take up Dimant's challenge
by outlining some of the different strands in this literature and reflecting on the significance of the pseudepigraphic attributions.

The Enoch Apocalypses

The figure of Enoch is the subject of a few enigmatic verses in Genesis:
he lived 365 years; then he walked with אלהים and was no more, for
God took him.[4] It would seem that he was already associated with the
solar calendar in Genesis. His primary qualification as a pseudepigraphic author, however, lies in the claim that he walked with אלהים,
whether that word is understood to refer to God or to angels. Enoch's
journeys to the ends of the earth in the Book of the Watchers may be
understood as an attempt to spell out how he walked with אלהים.
Consequently, he was uniquely qualified to impart wisdom about the
mysteries of cosmos and history. The earliest Enochic writings, the
Book of the Watchers and the Astronomical Book, contain compendia
of cosmic revelations, including such matters as the movements of the
stars, the storehouses of the elements and the abodes of the dead.

The extant Enoch literature contains several hints that there was a
community in the hellenistic period that claimed to possess a wisdom
derived from Enoch. The clearest allusions to this community are
provided by the Apocalypse of Weeks in 1 Enoch 93:1-10; 91:11-17.
This apocalypse pays much less attention to cosmic revelations than
was the case in the Book of the Watchers and the Astronomical
Book. Instead, it presents a schematic outline of patriarchal and

---

[2] E.g. M. Hengel, *Judaism and Hellenism* (Philadelphia: Fortress, 1974) 1.175-80; D.
Dimant, "Qumran Sectarian Literature," in *Jewish Writings of the Second Temple Period*
(ed. M. E. Stone; Compendia Rerum Iudaicarum ad Novum Testamentum 2.2;
Philadelphia: Fortress, 1984) 542-47; F. García Martínez, "Qumran Origins and
Early History: A Groningen Hypothesis," *Folia Orientalia* 25(1989) 119; P. R. Davies,
Behind the Essenes (Atlanta: Scholars Press, 1987) 107-34. See now also G. Boccaccini,
Beyond the Essene Hypothesis: The Parting of the Ways between Qumran and Enochic Judaism
(Grand Rapids: Eerdmans, 1998).

[3] D. Dimant, "New Light from Qumran on the Jewish Pseudepigrapha—
4Q390," in *The Madrid Qumran Congress. Proceedings of the International Congress on the
Dead Sea Scrolls* (ed. J. Trebolle Barrera and L. Vegas Montaner; Studies on the
Texts of the Desert of Judah 2; Leiden: E. J. Brill, 1992) 2.447.

[4] On the figure of Enoch see most recently J. C. VanderKam, *Enoch. A Man for
All Generations* (Columbia, SC: University of South Carolina Press, 1995).

Israelite history that highlights a pattern of sin and salvation. In the second week, culminating in the Flood, great wickedness arises, but a man (Noah) is saved. After the Flood, iniquity grows again but at the end of the third week "a man will be chosen as the plant of righteous judgment and after him will come the plant of righteousness for ever." The pattern continues until the seventh week, which is dominated by an apostate generation, but "at its end the chosen righteous from the eternal plant of righteousness will be chosen, to whom will be given sevenfold teaching concerning his whole creation." At this point the course of history changes and sinners are destroyed by the sword. The sword continues to rage in the eighth generation and at the end the elect acquire houses because of their righteousness and "a house will be built for the great king in glory for ever." In the ninth "week" the world is written down for destruction and in the tenth the judgment of the Watchers takes place and the old heaven is replaced with a new one.

It is clear that the rise of the "chosen righteous" is a pivotal moment in this process and that one of the purposes of the apocalypse is to accredit this group as the elect of God. The author of the Apocalypse of Weeks most probably belonged to the number of the chosen righteous. We are not told much about this group, except that it is given "sevenfold teaching concerning the whole creation." Since the entire apocalypse is attributed to Enoch, it is reasonable to assume that this teaching is related to other books in the Enochic corpus, such as the Book of the Watchers and the Astronomical Book, both of which purport to describe "the whole creation." The Book of the Watchers uses the phrase "the plant of righteousness" to refer to the emergence of righteousness on earth after the Watchers are destroyed (1 Enoch 11:16). Books are important for this group. Enoch reads from books. But the righteous are not necessarily reclusive scholars. They are evidently willing to wield the sword by which the wicked are destroyed. It is arguable that the mention of the sword in the eighth week is a reference to the Maccabean revolt but the apocalypse is clearly written before the building of the "great house" at the end of that week. Even if the sword is part of the real prophecy, however, and is still in the future from the perspective of the real author, it is clear that the Apocalypse endorses the use of violence. We have, then, a group that is both learned, in its way, and militant, playing an active role in implementing the divine judgment.

If there is doubt as to whether the Apocalypse of Weeks is referring to the Maccabean revolt, there is no such doubt about the Animal Apocalypse. Here too there is an elect group, identified allegorically as "small lambs." The character of this group is even more

difficult to discern than was the case in the Apocalypse of Weeks because of the allegorical language. They are said to open their eyes
and to see, in contrast to the blindness of their contemporaries.
Whether their vision entailed "a sevenfold teaching about all creation," like the Apocalypse of Weeks, is not stated. When we are told
that "horns came upon those lambs," however, the symbolism is
clear, and when "a big horn grew on one of those sheep" the reference is unmistakably to Judas Maccabee. [5] Many scholars have identified the "lambs" with the Hasidim of the Maccabean books who
are described as "mighty warriors" (1 Macc. 2:42)[6] and whose leader
is said to be Judas Maccabee (2 Macc. 14:6). The Hasidim may also
have been, or at least included, scribes.[7] In 1 Macc. 7:12-13 the
statement that a group of scribes appeared before the High Priest
Alcimus is followed by a statement that the Hasidim were the first
among the Israelites to seek peace.

There is no apparent reason why a vision predicting the rise of a
militant group should be attributed to Enoch. If militancy were the
defining characteristic of the group, more suitable pseudonyms could
be found, such as Joshua or Elijah. Presumably the pseudonym was
chosen for other reasons and the author of this apocalypse comes
from the same circles that produced the other early Enochic writings, such as the Book of the Watchers and the Apocalypse of
Weeks. The Animal Apocalypse at least shows familiarity with the
myth of the Watchers. It seems reasonable to associate the lambs of
the Animal Apocalypse with the chosen righteous of the Apocalypse
of Weeks. If the lambs are the circle from which the author of this
Enochic apocalypse came, however, we should attribute to them a
range of interests in cosmic speculation that are otherwise unattested
for the Hasidim. Conversely, the Hasidim are represented in 1
Macc. 2:42 as devoted to the law rather than to esoteric wisdom.[8]
There may have been more than one group of militant scribes that
supported the Maccabean revolt.[9]

---

[5] See P. A. Tiller, *A Commentary on the Animal Apocalypse of 1 Enoch* (Atlanta:
Scholars Press, 1993) 355.

[6] Note, however, J. Kampen, *The Hasideans and the Origin of Pharisaism* (Atlanta:
Scholars Press, 1988) 95-107, who argues that the phrase could equally well be
translated as "leading citizens."

[7] V. A. Tcherikover, *Hellenistic Civilization and the Jews* (New York: Atheneum,
1970) 197-98; Tiller, *A Commentary*, 109; J. Sievers, *The Hasmoneans and their Supporters*
(Atlanta: Scholars Press, 1990) 39-40.

[8] Kampen, *The Hasideans*, 107-14.

[9] Cf. Tiller, *A Commentary*, 114-5, who argues that the *Animal Apocalypse* should
not be ascribed to the Hasidim.

If we include the Epistle of Enoch in the profile of the Enoch movement, then this group would seem to come from a socially underprivileged class, despite its literacy, since much of the criticism of the Epistle is directed against the rich. ("Woe to those who build their houses with sin, for from their whole foundation they will be thrown down, and by the sword they will fall; and those who acquire gold and silver will quickly be destroyed in the judgment. Woe to you, you rich, for you have trusted in your riches, but from your riches you will depart, for you did not remember the Most High in the days of your riches," 94:7-8). The Apocalypse of Weeks, also, hopes for "houses" for the righteous in the eschatological time. Again, there is no apparent reason why Enoch should be chosen as the mouthpiece of social criticism. Presumably he was the pseudonym of choice because of the wisdom revealed to him and because of the literate character of the group. The social criticism of the Epistle was incidental to the pseudonymity.

In her *Compendia* article of 1984 Devorah Dimant suggested that the "lambs" of the Animal Apocalypse correspond to the Dead Sea sect, which is described as a "plant root" in CD (the Damascus Document).[10] Her main argument is that the time of emergence appears to be the same in both documents. In Col. 1, as the passage is usually read, God causes a "plant root" to spring from Aaron and Israel 390 years after the destruction of Jerusalem by Nebuchadnezzar.[11] Dimant takes as her starting point 605 BCE, the date of the accession of Nebuchadnezzar, so that the plant root would emerge in 215 BCE and the Teacher of Righteousness in 195. She also calculates the chronology of the postexilic period in the Animal Apocalypse from 605 BCE and arrives at a date of 199 BCE for the emergence of the lambs. It is doubtful, however, whether the chronological data can be pressed in this way.[12] The 390 years of CD is a symbolic number and should not be taken precisely, and even if it were, the calculation should more reasonably begin from 586 BCE.

It is true that both the Enochic apocalypses and the Dead Sea sect regard the Second Temple as polluted. (This does not appear to be the case with the Hasidim).[13] According to the Apocalypse of Weeks,

---

[10] Dimant, "Qumran Sectarian Literature," 544.

[11] On the difficulties of reading CD 1, see P. R. Davies, *The Damascus Covenant* (Sheffield: JSOT, 1982) 61-72.

[12] J. J. Collins, "The Origin of the Qumran Community: A Review of the Evidence," in *To Touch the Text* (ed. M. P. Horgan and P. J. Kobelski; New York: Crossroad, 1989) 169-70 (= Collins, *Seers, Sibyls and Sages*, [Leiden: Brill, 1997] 250).

[13] Tiller, *A Commentary*, 104-05.

the Second Temple generation is apostate. According to the Animal Apocalypse, the bread offered in the Second Temple was unclean and impure (1 Enoch 90:73). Calendrical disputes, and specifically the solar calendar, figure prominently in both corpora, as does the metaphor of planting.[14] Nonetheless, the character of the "plant root" of CD appears to be quite different from that of the "lambs." The movement in CD is said to grope in blindness at first and then to recognize that they were guilty men. It is, in short, a penitential movement concerned with the observance of the Torah, as CD proceeds to make clear.[15] There is no hint of militancy and the movement does not arise in reaction against foreign rule. Conversely, the Torah of Moses receives scant attention in the Enochic apocalypses and there is no admission of guilt on the part of the "lambs," although they appear to have been in blindness before they began to see. The Torah is acknowledged in the Apocalypse of Weeks (93:6: "a law for all generations") and the Animal Apocalypse singles out Moses as a sheep that became a man (89:38) but the revelations of Enoch are not derived from or based on the Torah of Moses. Enoch came first and his revelations concern matters on which the Torah had little to say. Although the Enochic writings were preserved at Qumran and CD makes reference to the Watchers of heaven, it seems quite unlikely that these two groups should be identified with each other.

Daniel as a Pseudonym

The name of Daniel is also used to lend authority to a group or movement in the second century BCE. The biblical book of Daniel develops the identity of the protagonist in a collection of Aramaic stories about Jewish courtiers in Babylon. The second half of the book purports to report the visions of one of these sages, which point to climactic events in the hellenistic period. Daniel 11 builds up to a crisis when "the people who know their God stand firm and take action." The heroes of the story, however, are the משכילים, the wise among the people who give instruction to the common people. These are the ones who are singled out to shine like the stars at the resurrection. It is reasonable to suppose that the authors of the Book of Daniel belonged to the circles of these משכילים.[16] Like the elect in

---

[14] Davies, *Behind the Essenes*, 130-32.
[15] Compare 4Q306, "Men of the People who Err," the subject of a presentation by T. H. Lim at the annual SBL meeting in New Orleans, Nov. 24, 1996.
[16] See further J. J. Collins, *Daniel* (Hermeneia; Minneapolis: Fortress, 1993) 385-86.

the Apocalypse of Weeks, these people are distinguished by their wisdom; as Philip Davies has noted, books play a prominent role in Daniel, even more than in 1 Enoch.[17] Like the "lambs" of the Animal Apocalypse, the משכילים emerge in response to a political crisis. Unlike the lambs, however, they do not appear to take up arms. At most, they regard the Maccabees as "a little help" (11:34) and it is not clear that they regarded them as any help at all. While these משכילים bear some similarity to the group or groups described in the Enoch literature, they can not be simply identified with them. Neither can they be identified with the Torah-oriented tradents of Jubilees or CD, since Daniel barely refers to the Law of Moses.

The specific associations evoked by the choice of Daniel as a pseu-donym would seem to be two-fold. First, there is the claim to re-vealed wisdom, grounded in Daniel's reputation as an interpreter of dreams and mysterious signs. Second, there is the political context. Daniel functions as adviser and critic to kings and predicts the rise and fall of kingdoms. The apocalyptic predictions of Daniel 7-12 are similarly political in character. If we take the court tales in Daniel 1-6 as in some sense indicative of the social roles to which the משכילים aspired, we might cast them in the role of religious advisers in politi-cal affairs, not unlike some of the ancient prophets, but such a corre-lation of narrative and social roles is admittedly risky.[18]

The name Daniel occurs in three manuscripts found at Qumran which are not part of the Book of Daniel, 4Q243, 244 and 245, known respectively as Pseudo-Daniel a, b, and c.[19] 4Q243 and 244 overlap, and clearly belong to the same manuscript. Milik tentative-ly proposed that 4Q245 belonged to the same work,[20] but this now seems doubtful.[21] 4Q243-244 present a speech by Daniel in a royal court. His speech is an overview of history, beginning with Noah and the flood and continuing down to the hellenistic period. The document contained several personal names. Only one, Balakros, is preserved. This name was borne by several figures in the early hel-

---

[17] P. R. Davies, "Reading Daniel Sociologically," in *The Book of Daniel* (ed. A. S. van der Woude; Leuven: Leuven University Press, 1993) 352-55.

[18] Davies, "Reading Daniel Sociologically," 355, attributes to the משכילים a more direct political ambition.

[19] See the edition of these texts by J. J. Collins and P. W. Flint, "Pseudo-Daniel," in *Qumran Cave 4. XVII. Parabiblical Texts, Part 3* (ed. G. Brooke *et al.*; DJD 23; Oxford: Clarendon, 1996) 95-164. See also J. J. Collins, "Pseudo-Daniel Revisited," *RevQ* 17(1996) 111-35 and P. W. Flint, "4Qpseudo-Daniel ar^c and the Restoration of the Priesthood," *RevQ* 17(1996) 137-50.

[20] J. T. Milik, "'Prière de Nabonide' et autres écrits d'un cycle de Daniel," *RB* 63 (1956) 411-15.

[21] Collins, "Pseudo-Daniel Revisited," 112.

lenistic period. 4Q245 contains a long list of names. In part, this list gives the names of High Priests from the patriarchal period (Qahat) down to the hellenistic age (Onias, Simon). It then continues with a list of kings, including David, Solomon and Ahaziah. It is difficult to see how these lists could be integrated into the document preserved in 4Q243 and 244. The latter document views Israel in the context of universal history and is concerned with the problem of foreign domination. 4Q245 is focused on the internal history of Israel. The two documents may come from the same or related circles but their relationship seems to be one of complementarity rather than identity. The so-called "Son of God" text, 4Q246, is also often called "Pseudo-Daniel" and uses phrases that are also found in, and probably derived from, the biblical book. Since the name Daniel is not found in the extant fragments, however, we shall not consider it in the present discussion.

The text preserved in 4Q243 and 4Q244 is in a very fragmentary state. We have 40 fragments of 4Q243 and 14 fragments of 4Q244. Both manuscripts are written in Herodian script (late first century BCE). Milik found affinities between this text and the Book of Daniel in allusions to seventy years and a four kingdom schema, while he found a reference to resurrection in 4Q245. Neither the seventy years nor the four kingdom schema is actually found in the fragments. The reconstruction of "seventy years" seems more plausible than any alternative in 4Q243 fragment 16. The reference, however, is not necessarily to the Exile, as it is in Daniel 9. (4Q390, the Pseudo-Moses text, has two references to seventy years, neither of them in an exilic context). The four kingdom schema is inferred from the fourth line of the same fragment which reads היא מכלוחא קד[. Milik restored קדמיתא "first." This reconstruction is problematic on two counts. First, two lines earlier in the same fragment we read that "he will save them." It seems unlikely that an act of salvation would be followed immediately by the inauguration of the first of a series of Gentile kingdoms. Second, if Milik's interpretation were correct this would be the only case where the four kingdom sequence (familiar from the Book of Daniel and the fourth Sibylline Oracle) is inaugurated after deliverance from the Exile.[22] The first kingdom is always either Babylon or Assyria. Alternative reconstructions are possible. The phrase can be read as מכלוחא קדישתא "holy kingdom" and the passage may be located in the eschatological phase of the prophecy.

---

[22] On the four kingdom sequence see Collins, *Daniel*, 166-70.

4Q245 survives in four fragments, one of which contains the list of names already noted. The second fragment contains a passage reminiscent of CD 1, where some people are said to wander in blindness. There follows a statement that "these then will rise" (יקומון). Milik saw here a reference to resurrection and a parallel to Daniel 12, but the verb קום is not used in Daniel 12 and does not necessarily refer to resurrection. The following line says that some people "will return" (יתובון). There is, then, little evidence for direct literary dependence of these texts on the Book of Daniel. There is no mention of dreams or visions in either text. Each refers to a writing and this may have been expounded by Daniel. Both texts presuppose that Daniel is an authoritative source of historical revelations and, while this presupposition may derive from the biblical book, it could arguably be derived from part of the Daniel tradition, such as the stories preserved in Daniel 1-6, which circulated independently before the Maccabean era. The pseudo-Daniel texts do not necessarily derive from the same משכילים to whom we ascribed the Book of Daniel.

Both 4Q243-4 and 4Q245 appear to have had eschatological conclusions and to have spoken of elect groups in the eschatological time. 4Q243 frg. 24 speaks of the gathering of the elect and frg. 25 seems to imply an eschatological battle ("the land will be filled ... with decayed carcasses"). Pseudo-Daniel a-b shares several motifs with other quasi-prophetic pseudepigrapha of the time. Israel at large lives in error, due to the influence of demonic spirits. Eschatological restoration is the destiny of an elect group which walks in the way of truth, in contrast to the "error" of others. The eventual emergence of this elect group is surely one of the major themes of this work. In this respect it resembles such works as the Animal Apocalypse and the Apocalypse of Weeks which we have discussed above. Unfortunately little can be said about this group, however, because of the fragmentary state of the text. It seems clear enough that the elect are only a segment of Israel and that their emergence is set in the context of foreign oppression. It is not clear whether they constitute an organized community or are scattered individuals who adhere to the way of truth. There are distinct parallels between the Pseudo-Daniel text and CD in the account of the Exile as the giving of Israel into Nebuchadnezzar's hands, for the desolation of the land (cf. CD 1:12; 5:20. Cf. also 4Q390 1.7-8). Yet there is no mention of a יחד and no unambiguously sectarian language. Pseudo-Daniel's relation to the Dead Sea sect may be analogous to that of Jubilees or the Enoch literature, which were evidently treasured at Qumran but which derived from separate, older movements.

4Q245 also envisages a group that wanders in blindness and another group that "returns." The key to the provenance of this document, however, lies in the list of names. The priestly names include חוניה (Onias) and, in the following line, שמעון (Simeon). The name preceding Simeon ends in ן- and the trace of the preceding letter seems more like ה than נ. It is possible (though not certain) that the text refers to Jonathan and Simon Maccabee (especially since Onias is represented as חוניה, rather than יוחנן).[23] The final fragment of this text speaks of people wandering "in blindness and error" and envisages some eschatological reversal. It is not clear whether the "error" is due to the priests at the end of the list or to some other cause. Whether the list included the early Maccabees or not, I would suggest that the separate lists of kings and priests were meant to show that the two offices, the kingship and the high priesthood, had always been distinct (even Jonathan and Simon had not laid claim to kingship). In this case, the lists of priests and kings in 4Q245 may be setting up a critique of the combination of priesthood and kingship under the Hasmoneans. Such a critique would be highly compatible with the expectation of two messiahs, of Aaron and Israel, at Qumran.[24] While much of this cannot be proven, due to the fragmentary state of the text, it is certainly the case that the Danielic writings focus on political events and institutions, in contrast to the halachic focus of works like Jubilees and the Damascus Document. While they were evidently congenial to the Dead Sea sect, their focus and sphere of interest are somewhat different and we should hesitate to ascribe them to one and the same movement.

Moses as Pseudonym

The use of pseudonymity in connection with Moses is somewhat different from the cases of Enoch and Daniel. With the exception of the Testament or Assumption of Moses which is presented as the farewell speech of Moses to Joshua, Moses is not usually the speaker. In contrast, such works as 4Q390 and the Temple Scroll are presented as divine speech addressed to Moses. In Jubilees, the principal speaker is the angel of the presence but again Moses is the addressee. As we might expect, the Torah is of central importance in all these Mosaic writings and there is extensive influence of the Book of Deuteronomy. We will confine our attention here to the use of *ex*

---

[23] See Collins and Flint, "Pseudo-Daniel," 160.
[24] See further J. J. Collins, *The Scepter and the Star* (New York: Doubleday, 1995) 74-101.

eventu prophecy, especially as it relates to group formation.

The Book of Jubilees shares several areas of interest with the Enoch literature, notably the calendar and the origins of demonology. It differs from the Enoch literature, however, in one important respect: it has a pervasive interest in halachic rulings. The evils that later generations do are specifically related to transgression of the Sinai covenant (1:5), even though the halacha of Jubilees often differs from that of the Pentateuch.

The fate of future generations is most explicitly addressed in an *ex eventu* prophecy in Jubilees 23, although the historical allusions are not as transparent as in the Enochic books.[25] The passage refers to "an evil generation that transgresses on the earth and practices uncleanness and fornication and pollution and abominations" (23:14).[26] This generation is characterized by a decline in the human lifespan. It is marked by strife between the generations, and also by calendrical error (23:19). Moreover, some in that generation "will take their stand with bows and swords and other weapons of war to restore their kinsmen to the accustomed path, but they will not return until much blood has been shed on either side" (23:20). The deeds of that generation will bring retribution from God, who will "abandon them to the sword and to judgment and captivity" and "stir up against them the sinners of the Gentiles" (23:23). Most scholars have taken these verses as allusions to events of the Maccabean period.[27] The allusions, however, take on a mythical quality: "the heads of the children will be white with grey hair" (23:25).

In this context, as in the Enoch apocalypses, we find a decisive turning point towards final salvation. In this case the turning point comes when "the children will begin to study the laws, and to seek the commandments, and return to the paths of righteousness." It is not clear that the reference here is to a specific group. The point may be simply that the turning point will come when people begin to study the law. The "children" are not said to take up arms like the "lambs" of the Animal Apocalypse. The earlier reference to those who do take up arms is ambivalent at best, and may be read as disapproving. The "children" of Jubilees are closer to the "plant root" of CD than to the Enoch movement. While the calendar remains a

---

[25] See the cautionary comments of R. Doran, "The Non-dating of Jubilees: Jub 34-38; 23: 14-32 in Narrative Context," *JSJ* 20 (1989) 1-11.

[26] Jub. 23:10-13 is found at Qumran in 4Q221 (DJD 12.70-71) but the following passage is not.

[27] G. W. E. Nickelsburg, *Jewish Literature Between the Bible and the Mishnah* (Philadelphia: Fortress, 1981) 77.

common concern in all these books, the interest in the law indicates a closer link between Jubilees and CD.

The law is also of central importance in 4Q390. The problems that befall the people of Israel come about because "they will not walk [in] my w[ays], which I command you so that you may warn them" (4Q390 1.3). Like other pseudepigrapha that we have discussed, this one is critical of the Second Temple establishment: "the sons of Aaron will rule over them, and they will not walk [in] my w[ays]." A notable, and unique, exception is made for "the first to come up from the land of their captivity in order to build the temple" (4Q390 1.5) but this variation hardly alters the document's ideological stance. As Dimant has shown, the text is not only indebted to Deuteronomy but shows great affinity with Jubilees and CD.[28] The affinities with Jubilees include a division of history into jubilees and various stylistic and terminological parallels. Especially noteworthy is the reference to the Angels of Mastemoth, to whom the Israelites are given over in punishment. In Jubilees, the Satan figure is called Mastema, and he is called "Angel of Mastema" in CD 16:5 and 1QM 13:11.[29] The Pseudo-Moses text also refers, however, to "the rule of Belial." The name Belial, which occurs frequently in the Scrolls, is not found in Jubilees and may indicate that this text is closer than Jubilees to the cultural milieu of Qumran. This impression is strengthened by the numerous terminological parallels between 4Q390 and CD that have been pointed out by Dimant.[30]

Dimant has also suggested a correlation between the Angels of Mastemoth and the angelic shepherds to whom Israel is handed over in the Animal Apocalypse: "As a matter of fact, the Angels of Mastemoth play precisely the role assigned by the Animal Apocalypse to the shepherds. In both texts they serve as instruments for the punishment of Israel, in both the Israelites are unaware of the source of their distress. In addition, both works place the evil rule of these angels in a chronology of sabbatical years and jubilees."[31] While all this is true, there is also an important difference between the Angels and the Shepherds. The Shepherds are most satisfactorily explained as the patron angels of the nations, who also appear as the adversaries of Israel in Daniel 10.[32] In 4Q390, there is no such national correlation. The Angels of Mastemoth are functionally indistin-

---

[28] Dimant, "New Light on the Jewish Pseudepigrapha," 437-39, 444-45.
[29] 1QS 3 23 refers to the domain of the Angel of Darkness as ממשלת משטמתו.
[30] Dimant, "New Light on the Jewish Pseudepigrapha," 444-45.
[31] Dimant, "New Light on the Jewish Pseudepigrapha," 442.
[32] Tiller, A Commentary, 51-54.

guishable from Belial, and should be regarded as the agents of his reign. Here again, the Pseudo-Moses text is closer to the cultural milieu of Qumran than are the other pseudepigraphic apocalypses. The division that it envisages is not between Israel and the nations but between God and Belial, righteous and unrighteous. This division is not far removed from the dualism of light and darkness that we find in the Community Rule and the War Rule at Qumran.

By analogy with other examples of *ex eventu* prophecy, it is reasonable to suppose that 4Q390 predicts a decisive turn for the better in the eschatological time. Unfortunately, that part of the document is not extant. Consequently we do not know whether it speaks of an elect group or what language it might use to describe it. It should be noted that the Testament of Moses, which has a fully preserved *ex eventu* prophecy in the name of Moses and has many parallels with 4Q390, does not refer to an elect community within Israel, although it singles out the mysterious Taxo and his family for a special role. But neither does the Testament of Moses have significant parallels with the sectarian rule books from Qumran. What it shares with 4Q390 and CD is simply the heritage of Deuteronomy, which was available to all strands of ancient Judaism. 4Q390 is much more likely to have envisaged an elect community. One thing that we may safely infer is that if such a community was envisaged, it would be defined by its fidelity to the Torah of Moses, whatever halachic interpretations it might have.

The Absence of Pseudepigraphy in the Sectarian Scrolls

We have seen several texts which speak of the elect groups which will emerge in the eschatological time and establish the legitimacy of these groups by the authority of a famous ancient figure. I have argued that the groups in question should not be conflated. Rather we should postulate a multiplicity of groups in the early second century BCE, groups that were probably quite small and loosely structured. In a recent essay on the social location of Ben Sira, Benjamin Wright suggested that the Enoch books, Aramaic Levi and Ben Sira represent "competing groups/communities (and with Ben Sira and 1 Enoch competing notions of wisdom), who know about each other, who don't really like each other and who actively polemicize against each other, although not necessarily directly."[33] In the case of Ben

---

[33] B. G. Wright, "Putting the Puzzle Together: Some Suggestions Concerning the Social Location of the Wisdom of Ben Sira," *SBL Seminar Papers* (Atlanta: Scholars Press, 1996) 146.

Sira, the group or community consisted simply of a teacher and his pupils and the Enoch group may not have been much more complex. The various groups I have discussed in this paper, however, did not necessarily dislike each other, although they had different emphases. It may well be that they all came together eventually in the community of the new covenant which we know from the Scrolls but we should probably imagine them as distinct communities or schools, nonetheless.

None of the texts we have considered gives any indication of the social organization of the group in question and it remains unclear how far they were organized at all. The use of pseudepigraphy seems to coincide with low group definition. It may be that the pseudo-prophetic texts are intended to encourage the formation of the groups in question rather than reflect well-established entities.

CD 1 has served as a point of comparison for each of these texts mentioning the rise of an elect group. The Qumran text, however, is not pseudepigraphic and it does not use the device of *ex eventu* prophecy to provide legitimization for the group. The same can be said of all the major sectarian scrolls, such as the Community Rule, War Rule, or the pesharim. Those who were like blind men groping their way (CD 1:9) may well have found comfort in ostensibly ancient prophecies which spoke of blindness and error while predicting that the elect would prevail. Once "God raised up for them a Teacher of Righteousness," however, the revelations of Enoch and Daniel faded to secondary importance. The prophets of old were superseded. According to the pesher on Habakkuk, God made known to the Teacher all the mysteries of the words of his servants the prophets (1QpHab 7). New prophecies, in the names of ancient prophets, would still be in need of interpretation and would in turn be subordinated to the authority of the Teacher. While the sectarians evidently took an interest in the pseudepigraphic Enoch and Daniel writings, perhaps because they seemed to predict the rise of the sect, there is no clear case of a new pseudepigraphic prophecy composed to legitimate the rise of the Dead Sea sect itself, although the provenance of the pseudo-Daniel and pseudo-Moses texts remains uncertain.

Two reasons suggest themselves for the lack of pseudonymity in the sectarian scrolls. One is the new authority of the Teacher of Righteousness and the other is a new method of self-legitimization, through the exegesis of biblical prophecy. We might have expected that the Teacher himself would be depicted as the fulfillment of prophecy, as Jesus is in the New Testament, and to some degree this is so. The title "Teacher of Righteousness" implies that he is the fulfillment of Hos. 10:12. 1QpHab identifies the Teacher as "the one who runs" in Hab. 1:2. On the whole, however, there is remarkably little concern (or need) to justify the authority of the Teacher. Presumably he established his own authority by the charisma of his personality.

Yet, unlike Jesus in the Gospels, the Teacher does not teach in his own name. Rather he appears as the expositor of the traditional scriptures. He is the interpreter of prophecy, rather than its fulfillment. Primary authority is vested in the Torah and the prophetic books.

Interpretation of older scripture is not incompatible with pseudepigraphy, as can be seen from the case of Daniel 9. Yet exegesis plays only a minor role in the pseudepigrapha of Enoch and Daniel. One would scarcely infer the existence of a canonical or quasi-canonical scripture from the Enoch writings or pseudo-Daniel. The books that they expound are fictive writings, unavailable to the actual readers of the hellenistic period. The Mosaic pseudepigrapha are more similar to the sectarian scrolls but even Jubilees and the Temple Scroll are reformulations of the Torah rather than interpretations of it, thus demonstrating a different understanding of revelation than what we find in CD or the pesharim.[34]

The interpretation of scripture, no less than *ex eventu* prophecy, could also be used to establish the place of the sectarian community in the divine plan. CD expounds the "priests, Levites and sons of Zadok" of Ezek. 44:15 so that "the Priests are the converts of Israel who departed from the land of Judah, and (the Levites are) those who joined them. The sons of Zadok are the elect of Israel, the men called by name who shall stand at the end of days" (CD 4:2-4). Those who go out into the wilderness, according to 1QS 8:12-14, do so in order to fulfill the prophecy of Isa. 40:3. It seems to me then that the sectarian scrolls evidence a view of prophecy and legitimization that is quite different from what we find in the pseudepigraphic apocalypses.

In recent years we have had a growing appreciation of the diversity of traditions, and probably also of social groups, that went into the composition of the Dead Sea sect. What emerges from the evidence reviewed here, sketchy as it is, is a picture of several small parties or conventicles in the Maccabean era, with interests that overlapped in

---

[34] Cf. the argument of L. H. Schiffman, *Sectarian Law in the Dead Sea Scrolls* (Chico, CA: Scholars Press, 1983) 17, that the grounding of legal rulings in the Temple Scroll is fundamentally different from what we find in CD, since the rulings of the latter are derived by interpretation.

some respects and differed in others. It is a commonplace in the study of ancient Judaism that divergent biblical interpretation was a major factor in the rise of sectarianism.[35] The material we have reviewed here suggests that this is only half the picture. The incipient movements described in the pseudepigraphic apocalypses do not find their *raison d'être* in biblical interpretation but in the quest for esoteric wisdom. These movements surely played a part in the emergence of the Dead Sea sect.[36] But biblical interpretation was also a flourishing enterprise in the early second century, as we see from the veneration of the Torah in Ben Sira and from the new sapiential texts from Qumran.[37] The Teacher, whose authority prevailed at Qumran, was evidently more sage and interpreter than apocalyptic visionary. Under his tutelage, the Dead Sea sect dispensed with pseudepigraphy, but the pseudepigraphic prophecies retained an important place in the sectarian library.[38]

---

[35] See e.g. J. Blenkinsopp, "Interpretation and the Tendency to Sectarianism: An Aspect of Second Temple History," in *Jewish and Christian Self-definition. Aspects of Judaism in the Graeco-Roman Period* (ed. E. P. Sanders; Philadelphia: Fortress, 1981) 1-26.

[36] I have explored the continuities between the apocalypses and the scrolls in my book, *Apocalypticism in the Dead Sea Scrolls* (London: Routledge, 1997).

[37] The wisdom texts from Qumran are lucidly presented by D. J. Harrington, *Wisdom at Qumran* (London: Routledge, 1996).

[38] The first generation of the Christian movement also dispensed with pseudonymity, under the charismatic influence of Jesus and Paul, but pseudonymous writing flourished in the following century. See D. G. Meade, *Pseudonymity and Canon* (Tübingen: Mohr, 1986).

THE NAMING OF LEVI IN THE BOOK OF JUBILEES

BETSY HALPERN-AMARU

Vassar College

In the Genesis narrative neither the character Levi nor his name is associated with the priesthood. In the Book of Jubilees, on the other hand, not only is the third son of Jacob and Leah designated a priest, but the designation is associated with his name. The tradition of tracing priestly leadership back to the founding father of the tribe is not unique to Jubilees. It also appears in the Testament of Levi and in the Aramaic Levi Document.[1] However, only in Jubilees is Levi's appointment connected to his naming. It is that connection that I wish to explore here.

The naming of Levi is problematic in both Genesis and Jubilees. In the Genesis tradition, Jacob's wives, Leah and Rachel, name the children they bear, be it naturally or through the surrogates each presents to her husband. The names they choose reflect the particular meaning each newborn holds for its mother. For the unloved Leah, the choice frequently, and certainly in the case of Levi, is related to the pursuit of the love Jacob feels for Rachel. For the infertile Rachel, it is the pursuit of the many children which her sister has borne and she has not. Thus, the biblical narrative of the naming of Jacob's sons has a clear pattern: the woman conceives and bears a son; she describes the personal significance the birth holds for her and, accordingly, she assigns the child a name.

Maternal naming accompanied by personal, emotional rationales for the choice is not unusual in biblical literature. The name-giving of Leah and Rachel has analogues in Eve designating the name of Seth and Hannah, of Samuel. The problem lies not with the structure of the birth announcements, but with a break in its pattern when it comes to the naming of Levi. Still seeking Jacob's affections, Leah greets the birth of her third son with the words: "Now this time will my husband become attached to me for I have borne him three sons" (Gen. 29:34). According to the pattern, the rest of the verse should read: "Therefore she named him Levi." But instead, in this

---

[1] Strands of several accounts of how Levi came to be selected appear in all three texts. See J. Kugel, "Levi's Elevation to the Priesthood in Second Temple Writings," *HTR* 86:1 (1993), 1-64.

one case, the MT has a masculine form of the verb: "*he* (by implication, Jacob) named (קְרָא) him Levi."

The difficulty is, of course, easily remedied. One might, like the
LXX, Samaritan, and Syriac texts, emend the verb to a feminine
form. Alternatively, like almost all English translations, one might
understand the verb as impersonal and render the clause like the association of Esau with Edom in Gen. 25:30, "he was named."[2] It is
noteworthy that the author of Jubilees adopts none of these solutions
when he reworks the narrative and develops his version of the naming of Levi.

As John Endres notes in his study of the Jacob narratives,[3] a "fairly consistent" pattern is discernible in the Jubilees presentation of the
births: an act of intercourse (except in the cases of Rachel's pregnan-
cies),[4] conception, naming of the child, and a date of birth. In every
case the explanation for the choice of name is omitted. Most impor-
tantly, the mother is not necessarily the parent who names the child.

Although we are primarily interested in Levi, let us momentarily
broaden the focus and note how the name giving is distributed.
Jacob names the first four sons of Leah (Reuben, Simeon, Levi, and
Judah; 28:11, 13, 14, 15), and the first child by the surrogate Bilhah
(Dan; 28:18). In addition, he subsequently renames, as in Genesis,
the son Rachel bears on her deathbed (Benjamin; 32:33). Leah
names the two children borne by Zilpah (Gad, Asher; 28:20, 21), the
last two sons she herself bears (Issachar, Zebulun) along with her
daughter, Dinah, Zebulun's twin (28:22, 23). Rachel names the second child by Bilhah (Naphtali; 28:19), and the first child she conceives (Joseph; Gen. 28:24). Later, of course, she also designates a
name for the last child who is renamed by his father (Benjamin;
32:33).

Given the precision with which the author presents the births,
there surely is a pattern to the naming. But lest we, like Endres, "fail
to detect its tendency,"[5] we must add one more component to the

---

[2] Perhaps the most inventive solution is one cited by Rashi as from Deut. Rab.,
but not found in our texts. The angel Gabriel brought the newborn to God who
named him "Levi" in association with the twenty-four prerequisites of the priesthood that would accompany him. Rashi on Gen. 29:34.

[3] J. C. Endres, *Biblical Interpretation in the Book of Jubilees* (CBQMS 18; Washington, DC: Catholic Biblical Association of America, 1987) 106.

[4] The explicit description, "he went into her," is lacking in Zilpah's conception
of Gad. But the sexual act is implied: "she (Leah) gave her (Zilpah) to Jacob as a
wife" (28:20). In the case of Rachel, however, there is neither an explicit nor implicit reference to an act of intercourse preceding her conceptions of Joseph and
Benjamin.

[5] Endres, *Biblical Interpretation*, 107.

birth and naming narrative. Years after the births, when Jacob and his family return to Canaan, the patriarch takes Judah and Levi to Isaac and Rebekah in Hebron. On that occasion, Isaac confers blessings on the two sons. Midway through the extensive blessing of Levi we find the following:

> Your mother named you Levi, and she has given you the right name. You will become one who is joined to the Lord and a companion of all Jacob's sons. (31:16)

But, as we have seen, in the birth announcements it is *Jacob*, not Leah, who names Levi. Given the attention the author of Jubilees pays to detail throughout the work and the exegetical basis for a paternal naming of Levi in the MT (Gen. 29:34), it is highly unlikely that the attribution of the name to Leah in the blessing involves an inadvertent presentation of contradictory traditions or, as James Kugel has termed it, "overkill".[6] Thus, we must assume that the naming of Levi involves both of his parents. Just as Rachel and Jacob are both involved in the naming of Benjamin, so Leah and Jacob both participate in the naming of Levi. In the first case, the joint endeavor involves a renaming; in the second, the parents apparently choose, or agree to choose, the same name. Moreover, unlike those of the other sons, explanations are presented for the names Rachel and Leah choose for Benjamin and Levi (32:33; 31:16).[7]

The problems it poses aside, the doubled naming of Levi provides the logic that governs the naming of all the children. Both Leah and Rachel share the naming of their sons equally with Jacob. Leah, either personally or through her surrogate, bears eight sons. Of these eight, Jacob names four and Leah names four. Rachel, either personally or through her surrogate, bears four sons. Of the four, Jacob names two and Rachel names two. Lastly, each wife shares the naming of one son—Rachel that of Benjamin, Leah that of Levi—with her husband.

The obvious question is, why would the author of Jubilees go to the trouble of developing such an intricate formula? Everywhere else

---

[6] On the term "overkill," see J. Kugel, *In Potiphar's House* (San Francisco: Harper Collins, 1990) 38, 134, 146, 256-67. In "Levi's Elevation to the Priesthood in Second Temple Writings," Kugel applies the term to the multiple explanations of how Levi came to the priesthood in Jubilees. However, he does not relate it to the naming of Levi in Isaac's blessing. Indeed, in his close analysis of that blessing, he totally ignores the problematic reference to Leah.

[7] In the Genesis description of the naming of Benjamin an explanation is provided for Rachel's choice, but not for that of Jacob (Gen. 35:18).

in the work only fathers name children.[8] Since he had deleted the rationales for the name selections in the birth narrative, he could have
maintained that approach and had Jacob name all the sons.
Moreover, what is the significance of having Leah designated the
name giver in the blessing that prophesies Levi's elevation to the
priesthood? Within the context of his naming system, the author
could easily enough have inverted the order so that Leah named the
child in the birth announcement and Jacob did so in the context of
Isaac's blessing.

I believe the answer to both questions lies in the author's concern
with intermarriage, a concern that leads him to elevate the roles of
wives and portray the marriages of the founding parents as ideal
unions of co-partners. With each marriage, he reworks the biblical
narrative so that there is a demonstrable bond and a partnership relationship between the spouses. I offer a few examples.

In Genesis a frustrated Sarah, resigned to never conceiving a
child, expresses the hope, "Perhaps I shall be built up through her"
(Gen. 16:2), when she presents her husband with a surrogate. The
author of Jubilees portrays a very different Sarah. Linking the surrogacy tale to the revelation at Mamre that immediately precedes it,
he has a joyous Abraham tell "all of these things" to Sarah whom he
assumes will be the biological mother of the promised heir (14:21).
When she does not conceive, the matriarch, as in Genesis, offers
Hagar as a surrogate. But brought by the sharing of the revelation
into the covenant context that is exclusively Abraham's in the biblical text, this Sarah extends the offer with words that reflect concern
both for her husband and for fulfillment of the promise: "Perhaps I
will build up descendants *for you*[9] from her" (14:22).

The rewriting of the description of Sarah's death demonstrates
another aspect of the author's concern with spousal relationships. In
the biblical narrative, after the crisis of the *Akedah* Abraham resettles
in Be'er Sheva. Sarah, having completed one hundred and twenty-
seven years, dies in Kiryath Arba (Gen. 23:1-2). For reasons never
offered, the couple are obviously no longer living together. Such a
closure is clearly unsuitable for the ideal union that the author of
Jubilees wishes to portray. Consequently, he has Abraham go, not to

---

[8] In the antediluvian genealogies transmitted by the author, all the naming is
done by fathers. In Genesis Eve names Cain and Seth; Isaac and Rebekah together
name Esau. In Jubilees, Adam names Seth (4:7) and there are no naming announcements for Cain or Esau (4:1; 19:13).

[9] Emphasis mine.

Be'er Sheva, but to Kiryath Arba where patriarch and matriarch share fourteen years together before her death (19:1-2).

The biblical characterization of Rebekah and Isaac's marriage presents a different type of challenge. In this case there is no need for concern with the significance of the matriarchal role. It is the relationship between the matriarch and her husband that is problematic. The characterization of the early years of the marriage augurs a particularly close relationship. But when the couple become involved with their sons, the picture changes dramatically. Except for an editorial notation of their common distress over Esau's marriages to local Hittite women (Gen. 26:35), there is no indication of an emotional bond between Isaac and Rebekah. Isaac never speaks to Rebekah; and she speaks to Isaac only to manipulate him into delivering her favorite son from the hands of his angry brother (Gen. 27:46). Isaac does what his strong wife wishes without speaking to her; and Rebekah disappears from the narrative without the surviving spouse (or the narrator) noticing her death.

The task for Jubilees is to redevelop the narrative so that Isaac and Rebekah's personal relationship is not so overwhelmed by each parent's involvement with a favored child. The author does this by creating a family story that intersects with, but is independent of, the deception that empowers the third generation of the patriarchal line. In that story the author creates scenes that mitigate any impression of a family fractured by factionalism. Isaac and Rebekah join Abraham to celebrate the Feast of First Fruits and each contributes provisions for the ancient patriarch's meal (22:1-6). When the senior patriarch dies, they go together to find his body and to mourn his death (23:4). Isaac's preference for the older son has already been stated, indeed repeatedly (19:15, 19, 30), and the Jubilees version of Rebekah's intense involvement with the younger one has already been developed (19:16-31). Nonetheless, in these added scenes there is no tension between husband and wife. Indeed, even after the deception, the author develops a vignette that transforms Isaac from a father embittered into silence into a spouse who can comfort his bereaved wife, weeping over the separation from her beloved son (27:13b-18). The poignant passage effects a more appealing Isaac and a softer Rebekah. Its primary function, however, is to demonstrate that in spite of all that has happened, the emotional bond between the patriarch and matriarch endures.

With such examples in mind, let us turn back to the naming of Levi. The marriage of Jacob and Leah involves a state of insecurity and animus that ill befits the Jubilees notion of the unions of the matriarchs and patriarchs. However, recognizing that Jacob's lack of affection for Laban's elder daughter is inherent to the story line, the Jubilees writer waits until after Rachel's death to firmly convert that troubled union into an ideal spousal relationship (36:22-24). In the interim, he limits his reconstruction to enriching the quality of Jacob's affection for Rachel, minimizing the impact of his lack of love for Leah, and developing the partnership motif in both unions.

Jacob still loves Rachel and does not love Leah. But the contrast between the situations of the two sisters no longer dominates their story. The author deliberately constructs the narrative of the births of the children so that the two women experience common situations and common emotions. God opens Leah's womb when she gives birth to her first child and God opens Rachel's womb when she gives birth to hers (28:11; 28:24).[10] When her sister bears four sons, Rachel becomes "jealous of Leah, since she was not bearing children" (28:16) and offers her husband a surrogate. Thereafter, the situation reverses. The surrogate, Bilhah, bears two sons. Leah, having become "barren"[11] and "not bearing children," becomes "jealous of Rachel" (28:20) and in turn gives Jacob her handmaid as a surrogate.[12]

The rivalry between the women remains. But no longer is Leah pursuing her husband's affections and Rachel pursuing motherhood. Both women are motivated by same thing: the desire for children. The entire issue of Jacob's affections becomes subtext. The reader knows why Rachel's womb is closed and that Jacob cohabits irregularly with Leah (hence the notations of intercourse before each conception). But in the narrative of the births, neither woman expresses concern about the feelings of the common husband. Everything which brings that issue to the fore in the Genesis text is expunged. In its place stands the intricate pattern of birthing and naming that affirms the matriarchal equality of the two wives and establishes each of them in a partnership relationship with her husband.

There still remains the question of why the reference to a maternal naming in the blessing scene. Although only a single name is involved with Levi, one might argue that the two explanations that Isaac offers for Levi's name (31:16) parallel the two parental explanations for the names given to Rachel's youngest son. One rationale is that of the

---

[10] This is the only one of the similarities that appears in the Genesis version of the births (Gen. 29:31; 30:22).

[11] In the MT Leah "ceased bearing children" (Gen. 30:9). The Ge'ez mss. of Jubilees has *makanat*, "to be sterile, childless" (28:20).

[12] The biblical description of Leah's offer of Zilpah simply states that when Leah stopped bearing, she gave Jacob her maidservant as a concubine (Gen. 30:9).

mother, the other, the father. However much such an interpretation may solve the exegetical problem in the naming scene of the MT, it does not suit the naming in Jubilees. The author has too carefully placed Jacob's naming of Levi not only outside the blessing, but in a context where there are no explanations for the given names.

Leah is the only parent mentioned in the blessing scene and the singularity is telling. The name she is credited with giving her son has two rationales with the same etymological base: First, Levi will be one who is "joined" (יִלָּוֶה), (*niphal* form of לוה) to the Lord" (30:5). Second, he will be a companion to all of Jacob's sons, a play on the root לוה involving an interpretive reading of Gen. 29:34 that would have Levi "joined to," i.e., a companion to, his two older brothers and a reinterpretation of Num. 18:2, 4[13] where God designates the tribe of Levi to be "joined to," "associates with" (יִלָּוּו, נִלְווּ) the priestly line of Aaron, here transformed into the "kingdom of priests" (16:19) that will descend from the sons of Jacob.[14]

A comparable structure, that is, dual meanings developed from a single etymological base, appears in the naming of Samuel in 1 Sam. 1:20, 27-28. When he is born, his mother, names him Samuel, meaning, "I asked the Lord for him" (מֵה' שְׁאִלְתִּיו) (1 Sam. 1:20). When she brings him to God's service at Shiloh, the name takes on another meaning based on the same root: "I hereby lend him (הִשְׁאִלְתִּיהוּ) to the Lord. For as long as he lives, he is lent (שָׁאוּל) to the Lord" (1 Sam. 1:28).

I would suggest that the naming of Samuel serves as a subtext for Leah's presence in Isaac's blessing of Levi. The echo of that scenario in this one reinforces the judge and prophet role assigned to Levi's descendants earlier in the blessing ("They will be princes, judges, and leaders of all the descendants of Jacob's sons... They will tell my ways to Jacob and my paths to Israel" [31:15]) and creates a connection between Levi and the prophetic role of his descendant, Samuel.[15]

---

[13] You shall associate with yourself your kinsmen the tribe of Levi, your ancestral tribe, to be attached to you..."
(Num. 18:2)   וגם את אחיך מטה לוי שבט אביך הקרב אתך וילוו עליך...

"They shall be attached to you and discharge the duties of the Tent of Meeting..."
(Num. 18:4)   ונלוו עליך ושמרו את משמרת אהל מועד...

[14] None of the word play on Levi's name is carried over in the Ge'ez translation of the Hebrew original. *Lasaqa* is used for "joined" and *satuf*, for "companion."

[15] On Samuel as a Levite descending from the line of Kohath, see 1 Chron. 6:13. On the various roles of Levi, see J. C. VanderKam, "Jubilees and the Priestly Messiah of Qumran," *RevQ* 13 (1988) 353-65 and Kugel, "Levi's Elevation to the Priesthood in Second Temple Writings."

What is more important from the perspective of the question of Leah, Hannah's story invites a comparison (contrast as well as similarity) between the mothers. Leah and Hannah are both married to men who have two wives. Both women give birth to sons who are destined for future service with God. Each of them, Leah, intuitively, and Hannah, perhaps consciously, assigns to her son a name that is loaded with meaning related to his future.[16] Yet Hannah is the beloved wife with no children and Leah is the unloved wife with many children. The implications of the contrast are clear: (a) infertility is not the signature for maternity of a distinguished heir; (b) in a polygamous marriage, affection of the husband is not a necessary condition for giving birth to a son destined for distinction.

Significantly, neither connection is made in the Samuel narrative. That Peninah has children and Hannah does not is acknowledged without any reference to Hannah as עקרה, an infertile or barren woman. Moreover, Elkanah's love for Hannah is stated only over against the fact that God had closed her womb (1 Sam. 1:2, 5).

In contrast, the connection between infertility and giving birth to the distinguished heir is strongly implied in the Genesis narratives of the matriarchs. Sarah, mother of Isaac, Rebekah, mother of Isaac, and Rachel, mother of Joseph, are barren. Leah, on the other hand, is notably fertile. In Jubilees, however, Levi, son of Leah, not Joseph, son of Rachel, is the most distinguished of Jacob's sons. Consequently, in rewriting the matriarchal stories, the author deliberately undermines the connection between the matriarchs and barrenness. Sarah, Rebekah, and Rachel are never described as *makanat* "barren." In fact, the term is used only once, if the Ge'ez reading is correct,[17] and then it is applied to Leah after the birth of her first four sons (28:20).

---

[16] The intuitive nature of Leah's connection to Levi's significance is not insignificant. The author of Jubilees makes much of maternal instinct and intuition. The angels have told Sarah about the "kingdom of priests" that will descend through her son's heir (16:17-19), but it is "jealousy," not that knowledge, that initially motivates her concern with Abraham's bond with Ishmael (17:4). Moreover, the author deletes the prenatal vision in which Rebekah learns the future of her two sons and attributes her favoritism for Jacob to a maternal instinct that the patriarch Abraham recognizes and encourages (19:13, 16-19).

[17] See VanderKam's discussion of the term *makanat* in the note on 28:20.

In Jubilees, genealogy, not childbearing ability, is the noteworthy characteristic of the wife of a patriarch. As in Genesis, childlessness is an issue in the marriage of Abraham and Sarah. But here it ceases to be a motif particularly associated with matriarchy. No reference is made to the fact that the new wife is barren in the Jubilees announcement of the marriage of Abraham and Sarah (12:9).[18] When the fact of the absence of a child is acknowledged, the author deliberately avoids presenting the lack in terms peculiar to maternity. It is the patriarch who is "brokenhearted" when he separates from Lot "for *he*[19] had no children" (13:18). Moreover, the same neutral language is used to account for why Sarah offers Hagar as a surrogate, "she continued not to have a child" (14:21).[20] As for Rebekah, the biblical narrative of her difficulties with conception is totally omitted (19:13-14). Indeed, an announcement of the birth of the twin brothers almost immediately follows the notice of her marriage (19:10, 13-14).

The description of Rachel's barrenness in Genesis, "And the Lord saw that Leah was hated, and he opened her womb, but Rachel was barren" (Gen. 29:31), connects barrenness with the complex issues of two wives and spousal love. Rachel, the beloved wife, is barren; clearly, given the stories of Sarah and Rebekah, this is a forecast that she, like her predecessors, will give birth to the covenantal heir. Leah, on the other hand, lacks the primary signature of the other matriarchs specifically because her husband does not love her. Reworking the description, the author of Jubilees breaks apart the triad of associations, infertility, maternity to primary heir, and spousal love, that diminish Leah's status as a matriarch. He replaces "barren" with language that echoes the description of Hannah in 1 Sam. 1:5 and shifts the effect of Jacob's lack of love for Leah from the opening of her womb to the closure of Rachel's: "Now Rachel's womb was closed because the Lord saw that Leah was hated but Rachel was loved" (28:12). Leah's image as a matriarch is greatly enhanced. Her fertility no longer augurs poorly for the potential of her sons. Moreover, it no longer reflects the absence of her husband's love.

However, Leah's status as a matriarch is still deficient for her ma-

---

[18] In contrast, the Genesis announcement has, "Abram and Nahor took to themselves wives, the name of Abram's wife being Sarai and that of Nahor's wife Milcah, the daughter of Haran, the father of Milcah and Iscah. Now Sarai was barren, she had no child" (Gen. 11:29-30).

[19] Emphasis mine.

[20] "Sarai, Abram's wife, had borne him no children" introduces the surrogacy narrative in Genesis (Gen. 16:1).

triarchal function does not appear to extend beyond biological pro-
creation. Much as the author of Jubilees transforms the marriages of
the founding spouses into positive, loving relationships, so he also elevates the roles of the matriarchs by making them active participants
in covenant history. In the case of the mothers of the primary heirs,
the act involves somehow facilitating the futures of their elected sons.
The Genesis accounts of the expulsion of Hagar and Ishmael and of
the deception of Isaac provide frameworks for developing such roles
for Sarah and Rebekah. The author of Jubilees reworks those narratives so that each matriarch is aware of the covenantal promises and
of the place of her son within them. Sarah is informed by the angels
who do in fact return at Isaac's birth (16:18-19).[21] Rebekah receives
her knowledge from Abraham whose life is extended in Jubilees to
overlap with Jacob's (19:17-25).[22] Empowered by the knowledge,
each matriarch takes the initiative in guiding her husband in a way
that involves the destiny of the elected son. Aware that Ishmael's status has been elevated in Abraham's mind, Sarah insists that he and
his mother be sent away.[23] Knowing that Isaac is about to bestow
the patriarchal blessing on the wrong son, Rebekah orchestrates the
exchange of Jacob for Esau.[24]

Clearly a comparable role is necessary for Leah, mother of the
penultimate heir. Indeed, the various facets that comprise the elevated portraits of Sarah and Rebekah also appear in the Jubilees characterization.[25] Like the other matriarchs, she holds the love of her
husband. Like them, she has knowledge of the covenant and promis-

---

[21] The created scene fills in the lacuna left by the absence of a follow-up to the
visit the angels speak of in Gen. 18:9.

[22] Abraham's revelation of Jacob's future replaces the prenatal prophecy of Gen.
25:23.

[23] In Jubilees, the sight of "Ishmael, the son whom Hagar the Egyptian had
borne to Abraham" (Gen. 21:9) no longer introduces Sarah's demand. Instead, the
author describes a banquet table where "Ishmael, the son of Hagar the Egyptian"
sits "in his place in front of his father Abraham" (17:2). The patriarch, exulting in
his two sons, recalls "the message which He had told him on the day when Lot had
separated from him" and rejoices "because the Lord had given him descendants on
the earth to inherit the land" (17:3-4).

[24] The author adds a fifth blessing to the four part benediction of Genesis: "May
all the blessings with which the Lord has blessed me and blessed my father
Abraham belong to you and your descendants forever" (26:24).

[25] The author of Jubilees also elevates the stature of Rachel. But, since she is not
mother to a primary heir, her corrective role does not relate to any of her sons.

[26] In Genesis the content of the dream he shares relates back to the narrative of
Laban's schemes and to a command from God to return home which immediately
precedes the conversation with the wives (Gen. 31:10-13). None of that background
to the conversation is preserved in Jubilees. The reader is familiar only with the
statement that the patriarch "would return to his father's house," an assurance that
God gave to Jacob years earlier when He conveyed the promises of the covenant in

es of the future, for Jacob shares the dream vision he had at Bethel[26] with her and Rachel before their departure from Mesopotamia (19:3). Moreover, in guiding Jacob to love and respect her (36:22-24), she too assumes a corrective role in relationship to her husband. So, in assigning Levi a name that reflects his appointment as head of the priestly tribe, she also has a part in the covenanted future.

With Leah, however, the threads that connect the various motifs in the matriarchal portrait are broken. The components of the portrait, a loving partnership relationship with spouse; awareness of the covenant; and an active role in nurturing the future of that covenant, cannot be integrated for the timing is off. The love of her spouse comes long after her procreative years. Knowledge of the covenant is revealed to her not only before she receives that love but eight years after the birth of her most prestigious son.[27] Consequently, careful that his motifs not undermine one another, the author of Jubilees presents Leah's most significant role, the naming of Levi, in Isaac's blessing, a context related neither to marriage nor to maternity. There, discretely and subtly assisted by the mother of Samuel, she assumes her matriarchal place as an active participant in the workings of the covenant.

---

the dream vision at Bethel (27:22-24). Thus, the "everything in a dream" that Jacob reveals to his wives involves the revelation of the covenant and the future promised to him and his offspring.

[27] According to Jubilees, Levi was born in 2127 (28:14) and Jacob, his wives, and children returned to Gilead in 2135 (29:5).

LEVI IN ARAMAIC LEVI AND IN THE
TESTAMENT OF LEVI

Marinus de Jonge

Leiden University

1. Introduction

The subject of this paper is an investigation of the contribution of fragments of an Aramaic Levi Document (ALD) found at Qumran to the study of the Testaments of the Twelve Patriarchs in general and of the Testament of Levi (T. Levi) in particular.

The Testaments of the Twelve Patriarchs belong to the so-called Pseudepigrapha of the Old Testament transmitted to us by early and medieval Christianity. In their present form they form a clearly Christian writing addressing Christian concerns. Some scholars consider them basically Jewish, though more or less heavily interpolated and redacted by Christians. They still use them as evidence for ideas current in Judaism around the beginning of the present era. Others, like myself, are of the opinion that such a Jewish *Grundschrift*, if it existed at all, cannot possibly be reconstructed. The Testaments must be studied as a Christian composition which makes use of a surprising number of Jewish traditions, probably on the basis of acquaintance with written Jewish sources.[1]

For the study of the history, or rather the pre-history, of the Testaments of the Twelve Patriarchs, comparison with sources that are clearly not Christian is of great importance. In the beginning of the century Cairo Genizah fragments from the Cambridge University Library and the Bodleian Library in Oxford belonging to an Aramaic document dealing with Levi were published. R. H. Charles discovered that these partly overlapped with an addition found at T. Levi 18:2 in the eleventh century Greek manuscript

---

[1] Whichever solution is chosen, the Testaments of the Twelve Patriarchs raise interesting questions concerning the Christian circles which transmitted them and the relations of these circles with Jewish groups and individuals. For my latest statement on the question of the origin of the Testaments of the Twelve Patriarchs see my article "The Transmission of the Testaments of the Twelve Patriarchs by Christians," *VC* 47 (1993) 1-28. Compare also "The so-called Pseudepigrapha of the Old Testament and Early Christianity," in *The New Testament and Hellenistic Judaism* (ed. P. Borgen and S. Giversen; Aarhus: Aarhus University Press, 1995) 59-71.

Athos Koutloumous 39 (= MS *e*) of the Testaments of the Twelve Patriarchs.[2] After the initial publications of Aramaic Levi fragments found at Qumran by J. T. Milik under the siglum 1Q21[3] and the "Prayer of Levi" published by the same author in *Revue Biblique*,[4] it became clear that these fragments and those preserved in the Cairo Genizah represented one document. It was also obvious that yet another addition to MS *e*, the one at T. Levi 2:3, should be brought into play, in the same way as the addition to T. Levi 18:3 just mentioned.

For a long time very little happened, as Milik did not produce the volume of Levi-fragments which he had announced in 1976.[5] When further fragments were finally published in recent years,[6] initial conclusions were confirmed. We have a substantial number of Aramaic fragments from Qumran and from the Genizah, plus sizable parts of a Greek text preserved in MS Koutloumous 39, all representing one document which can shed light on the genesis of the Testament of Levi in the Testaments of the Twelve Patriarchs. Very recently Robert A. Kugler, in his *From Patriarch to Priest. The Levi-Priestly Tradition from Aramaic Levi to Testament of Levi*,[7] has tried to reconstruct this common document and to compare it to T. Levi. In doing

---

[2] H. L. Pass and J. Arendzen, "Fragment of an Aramaic Text of the Testament of Levi," *JQR* 12 (1900) 651-61, and A. Cowley and R. H. Charles, "An Early Source of the Testaments of the Twelve Patriarchs," *JQR* 19 (1907) 566-80. See also R. H. Charles, *The Greek Versions of the Testaments of the Twelve Patriarchs* (Oxford: Clarendon, 1908) Appendix III for a synopsis of the material; it also gives the text of a small Syriac fragment.

[3] D. Barthélemy and J. T. Milik, *Qumran Cave I* (DJD 1; Oxford: Clarendon, 1955) 87-92.

[4] "Le Testament de Lévi en araméen. Fragment de la grotte 4 de Qumrân," *RB* 62 (1955) 398-406. See also the small fragment published by him in *The Books of Enoch. Aramaic Fragments of Qumrân Cave 4* (Oxford: Clarendon, 1976) 23-24.

[5] In his article "Ecrits préesséniens de Qumran; d'Hénoch à Amram," in *Qumrân. Sa piété, sa théologie et son milieu* (ed. M. Delcor; BETL 46; Paris-Gembloux: Duculot; Leuven: Leuven University Press, 1978) 91-106, esp. 95.

[6] See in particular the publications by J. C. Greenfield and M. E. Stone. I mention here "Remarks on the Aramaic Testament of Levi from the Geniza," *RB* 86 (1979) 214-30; "Appendix III. The Aramaic and Greek Fragments of a Levi Document," in H. W. Hollander and M. de Jonge, *The Testaments of the Twelve Patriarchs. A Commentary* (SVTP 8; Leiden: E. J. Brill, 1985) 457-69; "The Prayer of Levi," *JBL* 112 (1993) 247-66; "The First Manuscript of *Aramaic Levi Document* from Qumran (4QLevi^a aram)," *Le Muséon* 107 (1994) 257-81; "The Second Manuscript of *Aramaic Levi Document* from Qumran (4QLevi^b aram)," *Le Muséon* 109 (1996) 1-14. M. E. Stone kindly put editions of 4Q Levi^c aram, 4QLevi^d aram, 4QLevi^e aram and 4QLevi^f aram at my disposal. All fragments can now be found *Qumran Cave 4. XVII: Parabiblical Texts, Part 3* (ed. G. J. Brooke et al., in consultation with J. C. VanderKam; DJD 22; Oxford: Clarendon, 1996) 1-72.

[7] SBLEJL 9, Atlanta: Scholars, 1996.

so he took into account the Levi-Priestly tradition in Jub. 30:1-32:9 and attempted to reconstruct a pre-Christian "Original T. Levi" in the stride. Kugler's treatment of the texts is thorough and interesting but his conclusions raise a number of questions.[8] That is why it may be useful to have another look at the matter at this occasion.[9]

I shall not deal here with many of the problems connected with the reconstruction, translation and interpretation of ALD but I shall make critical use of the results of others, while dealing with the question of the extent to which the recently published material sheds new light on the genesis of T. Levi. It should be clear that the new material at our disposal may help us to see things more clearly. Our knowledge, however, is still fragmentary and, as is so often the case, our arguments are like little pieces of string, each too short to reach our goal. We must tie the strings together in order to formulate an acceptable theory. Connecting the arguments within the framework of an overall theory remains a subjective activity.

2. THE TESTAMENT OF LEVI

2.1 The collection of farewell-discourses of the sons of Jacob that bears the title "Testaments of the Twelve Patriarchs", forms a unity. The opening and closing passages of the individual testaments are structured in the same way. In the body of each testament we usually find the description of one or more episodes of the patriarch's life. The biographical details serve as illustrations for the exhortations

---

[8] See my review of Kugler's book in *JSJ* 28 (1997) 115-17.

[9] I treated the question some 45 years ago when I prepared my dissertation where, incidentally, the comparison of T. Levi with the Genizah-fragments, plus the related Greek text, provided an important argument for regarding the Testaments of the Twelve Patriarchs as a Christian writing; see *The Testaments of the Twelve Patriarchs. A Study of their Text, Composition and Origin* (Assen: Van Gorcum, 1953; 1975²) 38-52. I took it up again in "Notes on Testament of Levi II-VII," in *Travels in the World of the Old Testament. Studies presented to Professor M. A. Beek* (ed. M. S. H. G. Heerma van Voss *et al.*; Assen: Van Gorcum & Comp, 1974) 132-46; reprinted in *Studies on the Testaments of the Twelve Patriarchs. Text and Interpretation* (ed. M. de Jonge; SVTP 3; Leiden: Brill, 1975) 247-60. Finally, in 1988, I wrote "The Testament of Levi and 'Aramaic Levi'," in F. García Martínez and E. Puech, *Mémorial Jean Carmignac, RQ* nos 49-52, vol. 13 (1988) 367-85; reprinted in M. de Jonge, *Jewish Eschatology, Early Christian Christology and the Testaments of the Twelve Patriarchs. Collected Essays* (ed. H. J. de Jonge; NovTSup 63; Leiden: Brill, 1991) 244-62. See also the relevant passages of the Introduction (17-25) and the Commentary (129-83) in Hollander and de Jonge, *The Testaments of the Twelve Patriarchs.* Now may be added: M. de Jonge and J. Tromp, "Jacob's Son Levi in the Pseudepigrapha of the Old Testament and Related Literature," in *Biblical Figures Outside the Bible* (ed. T. A. Bergren and M. E. Stone; Harrisburg: Trinity Press International, 1998) [forthcoming].

74 MARINUS DE JONGE

that follow. The exhortatory passages give a spectrum of virtues and vices, together with general admonitions to obey the law of God and the commandments of the individual patriarch. At the end of each testament we find a prediction or predictions of the future. There are many variations within this general framework, depending on the narrative material available (both biblical and non-biblical) and there is also great diversity in the predictions regarding the future.

This description also fits T. Levi. Compared to the other eleven testaments, however, this testament shows a relatively large number of individualistic elements. Many of these can be explained by comparing the testament with the available Aramaic and Greek fragments of the Levi-document under consideration. At the same time this comparison reveals a number of features that are peculiar to T. Levi. They are structural, rather than incidental, and cannot be disregarded as later interpolations. They reveal that the present T. Levi, although acquainted with the material found in the Levi-fragments and therefore different from the other testaments, looks at Levi, called to the priesthood by God himself, from a Christian point of view.

2.2   T. Levi focuses on Levi's priestly office and on that of his descendants. It is of central importance for Israel but it is limited in time. The Most High, seated on his throne of glory, says, "Levi, I have given you the blessing of the priesthood, until I come and sojourn in the midst of Israel" (5:2; cf. 4:4; 8:14). Repeatedly the future sins of the sons of Levi are described, especially those against Jesus Christ (4:4 and chs. 10; 14-15 and 16).[10] Chapter 17 describes the decline of the priesthood.

Chapter 18 announces the arrival of a new priest, sent by God, who will usher in a new era. Levi, predicting this arrival in very special terms, says that he will share in the joy over his coming, together with Abraham, Isaac and Jacob (T. Levi 18:14). He states, "His star will arise in heaven, as a king, lighting up the light of knowledge as by the sun of the day" (v. 3, cf. the description of his own office in 4:3), without mentioning that the new priest will be of his own tribe, whereas the corresponding passage in T. Jud. 24:1 predicts, "a man will arise from my seed like the sun of righteousness." In both cases Jesus, a descendant of Judah and often referred to as the "Son of David", is meant. In T. Levi 2:10-11 we hear that the one "who will

---

[10] One should note that T. Levi 1:1 announces that Levi's parting words to his sons are concerned with "all that they would do and that would befall them until the day of judgment."

redeem Israel," announced by Levi, will come from Levi and Judah. Levi and Judah are mentioned together in many other testaments, the one representing the priesthood and the other, kingship. Even Judah, in his testament (T. Jud. 21:1-6a), declares that the former is more important than the latter. A number of testaments connect the coming of a future deliverer with these two tribes, but with Judah in particular. This leads to a complex picture which I have analyzed elsewhere.[11]

In the Epistle to the Hebrews, Jesus is called priest and high priest, appointed by God as "a priest for ever, according to the order of Melchisedek" (Ps. 110:4, repeatedly referred to in Hebrews). He is superior to Levi and to the levitical priests (see especially Hebrews 7). The approach found in Hebrews did not encourage early Christians to emphasize connections between Jesus and Levi. But because Jesus was regarded as king and (high) priest the two could be linked as, for instance, in Hippolytus' commentary on Genesis 49 and Deuteronomy 33.[12]

2.3   Our oldest Greek manuscripts tell us that Levi's testament deals with "the priesthood and arrogance"[13] and that covers its contents pretty well. Its main biographical item concerns Levi's actions with Simeon at Shechem, the only story in the Bible in which Levi plays a significant role (Genesis 34). It is introduced in T. Levi 2:1-2 and recorded and commented upon in 6:3-7:4. It returns in the list of biographical details in chs. 11-12, where we read in 12:5, "I was eight years when I went to the land of Canaan, and eighteen years when I killed Shechem, and at nineteen years I became priest..." There is a close connection between the "zeal" displayed by Levi at Shechem and his call to the priesthood. The Shechem story is preceded by a complex vision in which Levi makes a heavenly journey, ending with an encounter with the Most High who appoints him priest (2:5-5:2). It is followed by an only slightly less complex vision in which seven men in white clothing carry out the actual investiture (8:1-17). The two visions are connected and corroborate each other. In 8:18-19 we read, "and when I awoke I understood that this (vi-

---

[11] See "Two Messiahs in the Testaments of the Twelve Patriarchs?," in *Tradition and Reinterpretation in Jewish and Early Christian Literature. Essays in Honour of Jürgen C. H. Lebram* (ed. J. W. van Henten *et al.*; SPB 36; Leiden: Brill, 1986) 150-62. Now in my *Collected Essays* (see note 9) 191-203.

[12] See "Hippolytus' 'Benedictions of Isaac, Jacob and Moses' and the Testaments of the Twelve Patriarchs," *Bijdragen* 46 (1985), 245-60. Now in *Collected Essays*, 204-19.

[13] See the title in *bldmef* διαθήκη Λευὶ περὶ ἱερωσύνης καὶ ὑπερηφανίας.

sion) was like the former. And I hid this also in my heart and I did not tell it to anybody on earth."

The first vision is preceded by a prayer of Levi in 2:3-4. Pasturing the flocks at Abelmaul, Levi "sees" the wickedness of men and asks God for salvation. The prayer is followed by an express command from the angel, who has accompanied Levi on his heavenly journey, to execute vengeance on Shechem because of Dinah. Levi is assured of the angel's assistance and receives a shield and sword (5:3-7). Levi takes this to heart (6:1-2) and acts accordingly (6:3-7:4).

After the second vision we hear that Levi, Judah and Jacob visit Isaac and that Isaac blesses Levi according to his visions (9:1-2). Jacob goes to Bethel (cf. Gen. 35:1-5), receives a vision concerning Levi's priesthood and brings tithes of everything through Levi (9:3-4). After the entire family has moved to Hebron, Isaac instructs Levi repeatedly in the law of the priesthood (9:5-14). Some rules are mentioned specifically; they form a very mixed set.

Chapter 10 deals, quite unexpectedly, with predictions of the future sins of Levi's sons, using the Sin-Exile-Return-pattern that is often found in the Testaments of the Twelve Patriarchs and that is, surprisingly, repeated in chs. 14-15 and 16.[14] This deliberate repetition of the SER-pattern shows how much importance was attached to the future sins of Levi's descendants and their punishment. Only 16:5 mentions future bliss in a clearly Christian phrase: "(among the Gentiles you will be for a curse and for dispersion) until he will again visit (you) and in pity receive you through faith and water."

Between the first SER-passage in ch. 10 and the second one in chs. 14-15 we find a list of biographical details concerning Levi, his children and grandchildren (chs. 11-12). A parenetical passage in ch. 13 follows, which emphasizes study of the law and obedience to it. "Wisdom in the fear of the Lord with diligence" cannot be taken from a person, even when he loses everything he possesses and goes into exile. The example of Joseph is expressly mentioned. Chapter 13 is the only straightforward exhortatory passage in T. Levi. It does not refer to Levi's priesthood or to that of his sons.

Chapter 17 describes the story of the priesthood according to jubilees. It is very brief and reads like a bad abstract from a larger text. It ends with a description of the seventh jubilee according to the SER-scheme, followed by a reference to new sins of the priests and

---

[14] For a detailed treatment of these chapters see my "Levi, the sons of Levi and the Law in *Testament Levi* X, XIV-XV and XVI," in *De la Tôrah au Messie. Mélanges H. Cazelles* (ed. J. Doré *et al.*; Paris-Tournai: Desclée & Cie, 1981) 513-23. Now in *Collected Essays* (see note 9) 180-90.

their punishment, the extinction of the priesthood and the arrival of a new priest (ch. 18).

T. Levi ends with the usual closing passage in which, remarkably, Levi's descendants are introduced as "we" (ch. 19). After Levi's summons to choose between darkness and light, the law of the Lord and the works of Beliar, we read, "And we answered our father saying: 'Before the Lord we will walk, according to his law'" (v. 2). One may note that Justin (Dialogue with Trypho 116:3) calls the Christian community "the true high-priestly race of God". Christians bring pure offerings to the Lord among all the nations, in accordance with Mal. 1:11.[15] Apparently the author expects his Christian readers to identify themselves with Levi's descendants.

3. THE ARAMAIC AND GREEK LEVI-FRAGMENTS

3.1. It is helpful to begin with some introductory remarks:

3.1.1 The Aramaic and Greek fragments dealing with Levi are of very diverse provenance. According to M. Beit-Arié the Genizah material was written before 1000 CE.[16] We have the text of ten columns, wholly or in part. On the basis of a close examination of the Bodleian and Cambridge material and a comparison with the Greek texts from Mount Athos, Kugler has recently concluded that originally there must have been three double leaves with a total of 24 columns.[17]

The fragments found at Qumran include those assigned to 1Q21, assembled by Milik, and the material from Cave 4 classified as 4Q213 and 4Q214, now divided over six manuscripts by J. C. Greenfield and M. E. Stone, all dated to about the middle of the first century BCE or slightly earlier. 4Q540 and 541 have been tentatively called 4QTestLevi[c,d] by E. Puech,[18] who came to that decision on

---

[15] See "The Testament of Levi and 'Aramaic Levi'," 383-85 (in *Collected Essays*, 260-62).

[16] This is mentioned in J. C. Greenfield and M. E. Stone, "Remarks on the Aramaic Testament of Levi from the Genizah," 216.

[17] See *From Patriarch to Priest*, 231-33: "Appendix 2. A Reconstruction of the Cairo Genizah Manuscript."

[18] "Fragments d'un apocryphe de Lévi et le personnage eschatologique. 4QTestLévi[cd](?) et 4QAJa," in *The Madrid Qumran Congress: Proceedings of the International Congress on the Dead Sea Scrolls, Madrid 18-21 March, 1991* (ed. J. Trebolle Barrera and L. Vegas Montaner; STDJ 11,2; Leiden: Brill, 1992) 2.449-501. He also mentions Milik's suggestion to link 4Q 548 with T. Levi 19:1 (see 491, n. 48). See also G. J. Brooke, "4Q Testament of Levi[d](?) and the Messianic Servant High Priest," in *From Jesus to John. Essays on Jesus and New Testament Christology in Honour of Marinus de Jonge* (ed. M. C. de Boer; JSNTSup 84; Sheffield: Sheffield Academic Press, 1993) 83-110.

the basis of supposed parallels between 4Q540 1 and T. Levi 17:6-10 and between 4Q541 9 and T. Levi 18:2-4. Kugler has rightly remarked that these proposals are based on what T. Levi contains and not on what is known to be part of Aramaic Levi, from unquestioned witnesses to it.[19] Moreover these parallels are not all that striking. Puech's hypothesis should, therefore, not be adopted.

The Greek texts are found in an eleventh century manuscript but the shape and the date of the *Vorlage* of these additions to the regular text of T. Levi cannot be determined. The first addition to *e*, at T. Levi 2:3, consists of a prayer of Levi with an introduction and a closing sentence. It forms a unity and is inserted just before a similar prayer in T. Levi 2:4. Did the scribe still know its original context? Does the same apply to the addition in *e* to T. Levi 5:2 which may also belong to the earlier Levi document? The last insertion, at T. Levi 18:2, has a proper beginning corresponding to T. Levi 9:1 but breaks off unexpectedly with the birth of Levi's son Merari (cf. T. Levi 11:7).

The small Syriac fragment published by R. H. Charles (British Library Add. MS. 17,913[20]) corresponds to part of the Cambridge Genizah fragment, col. d.

3.1.2 Notwithstanding this diversity of provenance these fragmentary texts are witnesses to one single underlying text. When arranged in parallel columns, they show numerous cases of overlap. There is clearly no direct literary dependence one way or the other between the existing witnesses. Yet they may be used to correct and to supplement each other and to reconstruct the underlying text, although there is likely to remain a considerable degree of doubt as to its original *Wortlaut*, due to the numerous orthographical and grammatical variants and differences in wording. The presence of a number of Aramaic fragments at Qumran makes it certain that the base text was not only non-Christian but pre-Christian. Most scholars date it to the third century BCE.[21] Some have argued in favour of the theory that the original language was Hebrew,[22] but this is difficult to prove conclusively.

---

[19] See *From Patriarch to Priest*, 51-52.

[20] See W. Wright, *Catalogue of Syriac Manuscripts* (London: British Museum, 1871) 2.997. The manuscript contains extracts of a great variety of writings and is dated 874 CE.

[21] See Kugler, *From Patriarch to Priest*, 131-35, for a survey of recent opinion.

[22] See, for instance, P. Grelot, "Notes sur le Testament de Lévi," *RB* 86 (1956) 391-406 and Greenfield and Stone, "Remarks on the Aramaic Testament of Levi," 228.

In view of all this one may call the underlying document Aramaic
Levi or, as Greenfield and Stone have suggested, the Aramaic Levi
Document (ALD). Because we do not have any remains of the beginning or the ending of the document it is difficult to determine its
literary genre. It is not advisable to use the word "testament" in the
title.[23]

3.1.3   Most scholars are of the opinion that T. Levi is directly or indirectly dependent on a written source identical or very similar to
ALD. The alternative, dependence of both documents on a common
source or oral tradition, has not much to recommend it.[24] In practice
this has meant that the order of the available fragments of ALD and
the structure of the document have been determined by comparison
with T. Levi. Kugler has recently protested against this procedure
and advocated a different structure as far as the first part of ALD is
concerned.

In principle the danger of circular reasoning indeed exists. It remains to be seen, however, whether there is any such danger in
practice and whether Kugler's alternative reconstruction is to be
preferred.

3.2   After these introductory remarks we may proceed to a survey
of the contents of ALD on the basis of the available fragments. Apart
from the very fragmentary text of columns a and b of the
Cambridge fragment (Shechem episode), the Cairo Genizah and
Athos material gives a continuous text, providing parallels for the
end of T. Levi 8 to the end of T. Levi 13, with the exception of T.

---

[23] ALD is related to 4QAmram and 4QQahat, also writings containing instruction (and visions) supposedly handed down in priestly circles from generation to
generation. 4QAmram is clearly a farewell discourse. It begins with the words, "A
copy of a book of words of visions of Amram, son of Qahat, son of Levi: Everything
that he made known to his sons and that he commanded them on the day of [his]
deat[h]." We may compare this with the end of the biographical section in ALD (v.
81, according to the numbering introduced by Charles): "and all the days of my life
were one hu[ndred thir]ty seven years and I saw my th[ird] generation before I
died." A strange remark, as it is not made by an author reporting the death of the
patriarch, but by the patriarch himself. Moreover, it is followed in v. 82 by an introduction to a speech given earlier by Levi, when his brother Joseph died. The text
of this speech is given *in extenso* in the following verses. It exhibits a number of testamentary features, but is clearly not a farewell speech. Was this second speech added
later? And how did the ending of ALD take up the information in v. 81? We simply
do not know. See also "The Testament of Levi and 'Aramaic Levi'," 370-73 (247-
50).
[24] For a review of current opinion see Kugler, *From Patriarch to Priest*, 28-33, 171-
74.

Levi 10. That is, they give the end of a vision, the journey to Isaac, to Bethel and again to Isaac, and Isaac's instructions to Levi (compared to those in T. Levi 9 these are extremely lengthy and detailed). This is followed by a biographical account concerning Levi and his descendants' fate, as we have already noted, ending with the typical verse 81. Levi's speech on the value of Wisdom, pronounced in the year his brother Joseph died, follows in vv. 82-95.[25]

Chapter 10, the first of the three SER-passages in T. Levi dealing with the sins of the sons of Levi, is a deliberate addition on the part of the author of this testament who wanted to stress that point, important in his picture of the levitical priesthood.

The new finds at Qumran have yielded additional material overlapping and supplementing the Genizah and Athos texts (with the exception of Cambridge cols. a and b), as Greenfield and Stone, as well as Kugler, have shown. Numerous details still remain to be discussed and close analysis, particularly of the speech on Wisdom for which there is relatively abundant new material, is called for. The point I want to make now is that there is still no reason to doubt that T. Levi and ALD run parallel here.

Some small fragments called 4Q Levi[a] ar 3-5 (so Greenfield and Stone) do not have anything in common with other known fragments but ever since Milik suggested[26] that they may correspond to the beginning of the second SER-passage in T. Levi 14, they have been put after the Wisdom speech.[27] Important elements in this text are the announcement of sins of the sons of the speaker and a supposed reference to Enoch (corresponding to that in T. Levi 14:1). I note, however, that Greenfield and Stone[28] are not at all sure that Milik's reading of that name is warranted. In that case the suggested place of these fragments is even more doubtful than it always has been.

---

[25] It is interesting to see how T. Levi avoids the awkward transition between v. 81 and v. 82. In 12:6-7 it reads: "And behold, my children, you are a third generation. Joseph died in (my) hundred and eighteenth year." In 13:1 the hortatory address follows as part of the present farewell speech. The mention of the year of Levi's death is found at the end, in 19:4, as part of the closing remarks of the author of the testament. We should note that the reference to the year of Joseph's death in 12:7 (still) comes unexpectedly; it would seem that this is a clear indication that T. Levi follows a *Vorlage* (at least) very similar to ALD.

[26] See *The Books of Enoch*, 23-24; cf. *HTR* 64 (1971) 344-45.

[27] It should be noted that Kugler, though more cautious in restoring the text resulting from the fragments than Milik, and adding another *caveat* about reconstructing Aramaic Levi on the basis of T. Levi, follows Milik at this point; *From Patriarch to Priest*, 53, 118-30.

[28] *Qumran Cave 4. XVII*, 22.

3.3   We now turn to the remaining texts, the Cambridge fragments dealing with the events at Shechem, the fragments containing the Prayer of Levi with an introduction to a vision (first edited by Milik and now called 4Q Levi[b] ar 1 and 2) and a piece of text dealing with a woman who has desecrated the name of her father, adding a blessing for the pious of the levitical line (4Q Levi[b] ar 3 and 4).

Although there is no direct link with other fragments of ALD or with T. Levi, the third piece of text seems to be connected with the story of Dinah and so will have to be placed somewhere after what remains of the narrative of the Shechem episode, in columns a and b of the Cambridge fragment. Greenfield and Stone,[29] as well as Kugler,[30] point to Jub. 30:5-17 which forbids intermarriage with Gentiles. This discourse comes immediately after a short account of what happened at Shechem; it is followed by vv. 18-20 which promise an eternal blessing for Levi and his descendants because of Levi's zeal for the law of the Lord.

Scholars have usually put 4Q Levi[b] ar 1-2, together with the corresponding Athos text, before the fragmentary Cambridge text on Shechem, assuming that ALD, like T. Levi, recounted two visions, one before and one after the events at Shechem. The first vision in T. Levi 2-5 is a very complicated one, with undoubtedly Christian elements, and its counterpart in ALD may have been much simpler. But given the agreement in order elsewhere there did not seem to be reason to doubt a parallel sequence here too.

There are positive indications: the reply of the angel in T. Levi 4:2-3, 5 seems to be addressed to Levi's prayer in ALD rather than to that in T. Levi 2:4. In T. Levi the vision is situated at Abelmaul while ALD speaks about Abel-main. There is one accompanying angel in both documents and in both cases the gates of heaven are opened. ALD unfortunately breaks off at this point but T. Levi describes a heavenly journey of the patriarch.

At the end of the vision recorded prior to the journey of Levi with Jacob's family to Bethel, we hear of seven angels both in T. Levi and in ALD (represented by Bodleian col. a 1-13 and supplemented with some small new fragments). Finally, in T. Levi 8:18-19, Levi says that he understands that this vision was like the former and that he will hide this also in his heart (cf. 6:2, at the end of the first vision). The corresponding passage in ALD has been translated, "The one vision is even as the other," following the (first ever) translation of Charles who, however, seems to have been influenced by the paral-

---

[29] *Qumran Cave 4. XVII*, 33-35.
[30] *From Patriarch to Priest*, 78-80, 83-85.

lel in T. Levi. Greenfield and Stone translate, "Then I said: 'this is a vision, and thus I am amazed that I should have a vision at all'."[31] The text continues, "And I hid this too in my heart," which may still implicitly refer to a first vision, as in T. Levi.

Greenfield and Stone[32] have questioned the usual view by pointing out that the prayer of Levi in ALD seems to suppose a situation at which Levi's children are present, befitting a farewell scene, but not the one presupposed in T. Levi 2. Next, the washing ceremony before the prayer is an action of levitical purification. This may mean that Levi's prayer followed his consecration. Greenfield and Stone do not, however, propose a specific order for this part of ALD.

Kugler's solution is a radical one.[33] He tries to prove that ALD had only one vision which took place after the Shechem incident and before the journey of Jacob and his family to Bethel. Neither the usual arguments for a two-vision theory nor the suggestions made by Greenfield and Stone convince him; at all points he offers alternative interpretations and translations. In favour of his hypothesis he cites[34] ALD vv. 78-79 (Cambridge col. d 15-18), "...and I was eighteen when I killed Shechem and destroyed the workers of violence. I was nineteen when I became a priest." He notes that this runs parallel to T. Levi 12:3 (already mentioned above), "...and (I was) eighteen years when I killed Shechem, and nineteen when I became priest." In Kugler's view the authors of T. Levi should have adjusted this statement, because according to the story the patriarch was already elevated to the priesthood before the incident at Shechem. But they did not, in my opinion, because for them it was the actual investiture in T. Levi 8 that counted. I fail to see why the author of ALD, too, could not have written the biographical note after recounting the two visions.

Another argument is supplied by Kugler's reconstruction of the Cairo Genizah document. It leads him to calculate an eight-column gap between the end of Cambridge a-b (with what remains of the Shechem narrative) and Bodleian a (the end of a vision). In that gap he situates Levi's prayer and one vision. The fragmentary text about

---

[31] See "Remarks on the Aramaic Testament of Levi," 219, and "The Aramaic and Greek fragments of a Levi Document," 461-62.

[32] "The Prayer of Levi," 248-55, and earlier "Two Notes on the Aramaic Levi Document," in *Of Scribes and Scrolls, Studies on the Hebrew Bible, Intertestamental Judaism and Christian Origins presented to John Strugnell* (ed. H. W. Attridge et al.; Lanham: University Press of America, 1990) 153-61.

[33] See *From Patriarch to Priest*, 47-50, 68-87.

[34] On this see especially *From Patriarch to Priest*, 52-59.

intermarriage, already tentatively situated after the Shechem incident, can well be explained as part of an angelic speech to Levi connected with the vision (cf. Jubilees 30).

This reconstruction is quite ingenious, as are Kugler's attempts to
disprove the arguments of those scholars who assume two visions.[35] I
want to suggest that Kugler, though cautious at every step he takes,
simply wants to prove too much. Given the fragmentary state of the
evidence we are unable to prove that the new non-Genizah evidence
has to be fitted in the gap just indicated (assuming that Kugler has
rightly assessed the size of the gap). It is still possible to put part of
the material before the Shechem episode and to assume that the
order of events in ALD and in T. Levi was similar, if not identical.
Definite proof one way or the other is not possible. In the meantime
there is something to be said in favour of proceeding on the assumption that, given the situation elsewhere, T. Levi and ALD run parallel here, too.

3.4 Our knowledge of ALD remains fragmentary like the document itself. Yet we may say a few things about its portrayal of Levi.[36]
Levi is a priest who receives very detailed instructions concerning
sacrifices (vv. 13-61), though not exactly those mentioned in the relevant sections of the Law of Moses. In the Prayer of Levi (vv. *6,
*18) and in the final passages of Isaac's instruction (vv. 48-50, 58-
61), his offspring join him in the priesthood and share in its eternal
blessing.

In the prayer, great emphasis is placed on Levi's holiness, purity,
wisdom and knowledge. He prays to be guarded from the unrighteous spirit, fornication and pride. He asks that God show him his
holy spirit and grant him counsel and wisdom, knowledge and
strength (vv. *7-*8). Further, Isaac's priestly instructions begin with
an exhortation to remain holy and to shun sexual impurity (vv. 16-
18). Levi's final prayer is, "Make me a participant in your words to

---

[35] I mention briefly that the "from Abel-main" in ALD would seem to indicate
that Levi received the vision elsewhere. The one angel mentioned at the beginning
may be the first of the seven mentioned at the end. The opening of the heavens may
be part of a dream on earth. In lines 12-13 of Bodleian col. a, one should not translate "I hid this also in my heart" but "I hid this very thing in my heart" (a strained
translation of the words אף דן in the text). The reference to Levi's sons in the Greek
text of the prayer is the result of mistranslation. The purification ceremony before
the prayer may be Levi's cleansing after his contamination by the corpses at
Shechem.

[36] Here I take up a number of points mentioned in "The Testament of Levi and
'Aramaic Levi'," 379-80.

do true judgment for all time, me and my children for all the generations of the ages" (v. *18). V. 59 in the priestly instructions ends
with "blessing will be pronounced by your seed upon the earth."

In the instructions pronounced by Levi in the year of Joseph's
death, the emphasis is on the reading, writing and teaching of wisdom. Here Joseph is the primary model for Levi's children (v. 82
and following verses). Warnings against the future sins of Levi's descendants would have accompanied the exhortations, although it is
difficult to determine their exact place in ALD.

ALD, as well as 4QQahat and 4QAmram, clearly originated in
priestly circles which stressed purity and the instructive role of the
priesthood (cf. Deut. 33:8-11; Mal. 2:4-9). Somehow there is a connection between Levi's calling to the priesthood and his exploits at
Shechem but, in view of the very fragmentary state of our evidence
at that point, it is difficult to make out the exact nature of that connection. Some scholars[37] have found indications that royal preroga-
tives are connected with Levi (Bodl. col. a, 1-7 together with 1Q21;
ALD v. 67 in the Greek and Aramaic; perhaps also a few phrases in
the newly discovered part of the Wisdom speech, now numbered v.
99 by Kugler). This would be in accordance with the picture of Levi
as a zealous fighter for the Lord at Shechem, after the manner of the
Levites in Exod. 32:26-29 and Phinehas in Numbers 25. Kugler
protests that this connection is present in T. Levi 5-6 where Levi,
after his calling to the priesthood, receives the explicit command to
execute vengeance on Shechem. According to him, it is not found in
ALD, which mentions Levi's appointment only after his exploits at
Shechem. "The first and foremost evident theme is Levi's suitability
for the priestly office owing to his passion for his own purity and that
of the community."[38] I do not accept Kugler's reconstruction as
proven at this point; we shall return to this in the next section.

4. LEVI IN ALD AND T. LEVI

4.1 It is now time to return to the portrait of Levi in T. Levi and to
ask again to what extent it was influenced by the version given in
ALD. As I indicated in section 2, although the present T. Levi is
"structurally" Christian, it does acknowledge the special position of
Levi and his tribe as (high) priests, judges, scribes and teachers of the
Law, in the time preceding the arrival of Jesus Christ. Its description

[37] Kugler mentions P. Grelot, Greenfield and Stone and K. Beyer; for details see
From Patriarch to Priest, 131-34. I also defended this view in the article just mentioned.
[38] *From Patriarch to Priest*, 135-37, quotation from 135.

of the role played by Levi and his descendants is, without any doubt, closely related to that found in the Aramaic and Greek fragments discussed in section 3.

The question then arises, how do we explain those differences between T. Levi and ALD that are more likely to go back to the *Vorlage* from which the Christian authors of T. Levi worked than to these authors themselves?[39] If we put the question this way we realize how little we know about that *Vorlage*. First, we do not know exactly what ALD contained or how it was structured. Second, the authors of T. Levi may have had ALD before them in a form that differed from the one we are trying to reconstruct on the basis of the existing fragments. Let us look, for instance, at the Greek fragments in MS *e* for a moment. We know next to nothing about the *Vorlage* from which they were taken. But if these fragments survived until the eleventh century, there is a chance that a much fuller Greek document could have been used by those responsible for the Testaments of the Twelve Patriarchs at the end of the second century. Such a document may have had its own development separate from and independent of that represented by the other witnesses to ALD.[40]

Kugler has come up with another solution by positing an intermediary Original Testament of Levi between ALD and T. Levi[41] and trying to determine its place in what he calls "The Levi-Priestly Tradition from *Aramaic Levi* to *Testament of Levi*." Although he proceeds cautiously and only wants to gain a sense of Original T. Levi's outline, not to determine its exact contents,[42] he is so enthusiastic about the result of his reconstruction and so confident of having found the "original" testament that he forgets to deal with the form of the Levi-priestly tradition in the T. Levi found in the Testaments of the Twelve Patriarchs. I am as skeptical about his reconstruction as about all previous attempts by other scholars. Kugler, of course, regards my position as too conservative. Yet we do well to bear in mind that it is the present Christian T. Levi that lies before us, not the supposed "original" one.

---

[39] For a full picture we would have to analyse Jub. 30-32 as well. This analysis cannot be undertaken here.

[40] We should note that there are two quotations from a Levi document in Greek in the letters of the Egyptian monk Ammonas (second half of the fourth century CE). There is some similarity in subject matter with the Prayer of Levi as found in MS *e* of the Testaments of the Twelve Patriarchs. Whether Ammonas quotes from a divergent Greek version of ALD or from a related Levi document must remain open. For details see J. Tromp, "Two References to a Levi Document in an Epistle of Ammonas," *NovT* 39 (1997) 235-47.

[41] *From Patriarch to Priest*, ch. 5 "The Levi-Priestly Tradition in Testament of Levi," 171-220.

[42] *From Patriarch to Priest*, 177-78.

4.2 In the present context there is no place for a detailed discussion of Kugler's analysis of T. Levi and his arguments for the reconstruction of the so-called original version. I want, however, to discuss some passages of T. Levi in order to illustrate how complicated the matter really is.

Let us begin with the first vision, T. Levi 2-5, without any doubt a composite passage.[43] It may be divided into two or three sections, preceded by an introduction which mentions a prayer of Levi and a subsequent sleep and vision (2:3-5). In 2:6-4:1 we have a very complex description of seven heavens, an announcement of Levi's future task and a prediction of judgment. In 4:2-6 we hear of the answer to Levi's prayer, directly followed by the account of a meeting of Levi with the Most High, his calling to the priesthood and a command by the angel to execute vengeance on Shechem because of Dinah (5:1-6:2). It ends with Levi's awakening; he blesses the Most High and the angel and returns to his father.

In both sections we find clearly Christian elements. Kugler tacitly omits those in 4:2-6:2, which he regards as part of Original T. Levi, together with 2:3-5. The first section, 2:6-4:1 he assigns to a later redactional stage. This seems to be too simple a solution but he is right in emphasizing that 5:1-6:2 link up with 6:3-7:4, which describes Levi's role in the events at Shechem, a section he regards as basically representative of what appeared in Original T. Levi.

In T. Levi, Levi is clearly depicted as a warrior-priest who executes God's judgment on Shechem (5:3-4, after vv. 1-2; 6:8). In this respect it deviates from the ALD reconstructed by Kugler. For Kugler, this is a clear sign that Original T. Levi represents a different stage in the development of the Jewish Levi-priestly tradition. Kugler thinks, however, that Original T. Levi used elements of the single post-Shechem vision in ALD as basic building blocks for the pre-Shechem vision in his work.

This is a very complicated theory. There is certainly no reason to assume that the Christian authors of T. Levi would have dwelt at such length on Levi's role at Shechem, both in 5:1-6:2 and in 6:3-7:4, if this had not been in their *Vorlage*. Because what they found went back to the biblical account in Gen. 34 and clearly formed part of the tradition concerning Levi's activities, they saw no reason to

---

[43] See my "Notes on Testament of Levi II-VII" and the relevant section in Hollander's and de Jonge's *Commentary*. For Kugler's views, see *From Patriarch to Priest*, 179-83, 199-201.

change the narrative as it stood.[44] But is it really evident that we should assume an intermediate Original T. Levi because this *Vorlage* does not agree with the supposed contents of a form of ALD? The situation is complex but Kugler makes it even more complicated, and unnecessarily so.

We now turn to Isaac's instructions to Levi about the priesthood (T. Levi 9:6-14, corresponding to vv. 14-61 in ALD).[45] There is no doubt that this part of T. Levi gives some sort of extract of the very detailed instructions in ALD, although it abbreviates so much that we cannot be certain it knew them exactly in that form. After "the law of the Lord" in general, Isaac teaches Levi "the law of the priesthood" in particular. Five types of offerings are mentioned (vv. 6-7), followed by a section which emphasizes purity (vv. 9-11) but says very little about sacrificing (vv. 12-14). In fact, Levi is warned against "the spirit of impurity (πορνεία)" which, in due time, "will defile the holy things by your seed" (we should remember that a SER-passage denouncing the sins of Levi's offspring follows in ch. 10). As a priest Levi will have to take for himself a wife who "has no blemish, and has not been defiled, and is not of a race of strangers and gentiles" (v. 10).

It would seem to me that the present text of T. Levi can be explained as the result of abbreviation and redaction of a text like that in ALD by its Christian authors and that there is no need to assume an intermediary Original T. Levi. Of course the authors of T. Levi acknowledged that the priest Levi had cultic functions, and that priests were subject to strict marriage laws. They did not go into details with regard to the rules concerning sacrifices, no longer relevant for their audience. They did emphasize the danger of πορνεία, however, a sin repeatedly denounced in the Testaments of the Twelve Patriarchs, especially in T. Reuben and T. Judah.

Next, a few remarks about T. Levi 13, a chapter with general exhortations, parallel to ALD vv. 81-95 (plus some text in new fragments).[46] Again there is general agreement that the former knew the latter, but abbreviated and redacted it heavily. The most striking feature is that ALD stresses "truth" and "wisdom", whereas in T. Levi the law of God and wisdom (subordinate to it) occupy a central

---

[44] See, however, the Christian phrase in 5:2b, already noted in section 2.2, and the parallel between 6:11 and 1 Thess. 2:16, too close to be coincidental; see my "Light on Paul from the Testaments of the Twelve Patriarchs?," in *The Social World of the First Christians. Essays in Honor of Wayne A. Meeks* (ed. L. M. White and O. L. Yarbrough; Minneapolis, Fortress Press, 1995) 100-15, esp. 112-13.

[45] See Kugler, *From Patriarch to Priest*, 186, 207-09.

[46] See Kugler, *From Patriarch to Priest*, 211-12.

position. In both cases the exhortations are general rather than specific and relevant for any audience, Jewish, Christian or even pagan.

How do we explain the emphasis on the Law in T. Levi 13 (vv. 1,
3, 4, cf. 19:1; 9:6)? Is this an indication of a Jewish *Vorlage* of the present T. Levi, different from the ALD-text we know? This is a not unlikely supposition.[47] As Greenfield and Stone have remarked, "it is
difficult to imagine a context in which a Christian translator would
have replaced 'wisdom' with 'Law'."[48] They are right. Yet the
Christian authors of T. Levi maintained the word νόμος. For them
the patriarchs belonged to the period before Moses and had observed God's law in their lives, before Moses had been ordered to
issue commandments especially for the Jewish people. These patriarchs had the necessary authority to exhort Israelites and Gentiles to
live in true obedience to God, even after the coming of Jesus Christ,
the new lawgiver who had summed up all that is righteous and pious
in the two great commandments to love God and to love one's
neighbour.[49]

Finally, as we have seen, it is very difficult to say anything with
certainty about the relationship between T. Levi and ALD after T.
Levi 13. In this point, Kugler and I agree.[50] There are very few specific similarities between 4Q Levi[a] ar 3-5 and T. Levi 14-15.
Moreover, T. Levi applies the SER-pattern, often used in the
Testaments of the Twelve Patriarchs. It is likely that T. Levi (16:1)
17:1-11 gives extracts from a larger story of the priesthood according
to jubilees and weeks, but that story is changed so drastically that reconstruction of the *Vorlage* is impossible—and 4Q540 1 is of little
help here. I see, again, no reason to assume that T. Levi goes back
here to Original T. Levi which already added such a passage to
ALD at this point. Nor do I think that we have any evidence that
this contained the Jewish *Vorlage* of the much discussed chapter, T.
Levi 18. Here, 4Q541 9 i 2-4, speaking about a new priest, says a
number of things about him that are parallel to T. Levi 18:2-4 but
the similarities are few and of a general nature (see the use of the imagery of light and darkness). As elsewhere, the Christian phrases in

---

[47] Again it is unnecessary to posit an intermediary Original T. Levi.
[48] "The First Manuscript of *Aramaic Levi Document* from Qumran," 259, n. 7.
[49] See my "The Pre-Mosaic Servants of God in the Testaments of the Twelve
Patriarchs and in the Writings of Justin and Irenaeus," *VC* 39 (1985) 157-70 =
Collected Essays, 263-76 and also "Die Paränese in den Schriften des Neuen
Testaments und in den Testamenten der Zwölf Patriarchen. Einige Bemerkungen,"
in *Neues Testament und Ethik* (ed. H. Merklein; R. Schackenburg Festschrift;
Freiburg/Basel/Wien: Herder, 1989) 538-50 = *Collected Essays*, 277-89.
[50] For Kugler's views see *From Patriarch to Priest*, 187-90, 213-16.

T. Levi 18 are found in strategic places. Efforts to reconstruct a pre-Christian version of this chapter have proven a challenge to many scholars,[51] but it should first of all be read in light of chs. 2-3, 4 and 8 and in the context of Levi's overall view on the levitical priesthood, as outlined in section 2. To suppose that Original T. Levi already composed this chapter, using themes and phrases already developed elsewhere in this work, is unnecessary.

5. Some Conclusions

a   The Levi-fragments found at Qumran form a welcome addition to the medieval Aramaic material from the Cairo Genizah already known to us and to the Greek text fragments preserved in two additions in the Greek MS *e*.

b   Eventually all available texts go back to one document (ALD), although they display a number of divergencies where they overlap.

c   Thanks to the fact that we now have fragments from Qumran, we may be certain that this material represents a text current before the beginning of the common era.

d   Our evidence still remains fragmentary, and differences will remain with regard to the reconstruction of the oldest accessible form of text and its structure. On the whole it seems advisable to let T. Levi help determine the order of the fragments.

e   The particular features of T. Levi within the Testaments of the Twelve Patriarchs can best be explained by assuming that it used, beside other (written) traditions, the text represented by the various fragments in some form, perhaps Greek. Its exact *Vorlage* cannot be determined.

f   There is no reason to posit a Jewish intermediate stage between ALD and T. Levi.

g   The redactional activity of the Christian author(s) of the Testaments of the Twelve Patriarchs in general and T. Levi in particular was at the same time conservative and drastic. A number of elements in the *Vorlage* were preserved, others were heavily redacted; all were fitted into a specific Christian framework. Levi's appointment as priest was acknowledged, but the failing of the levitical priesthood received much attention. The priest expected to introduce a new era would not be a son of Levi.[52]

---

[51] See the list in Kugler, *From Patriarch to Priest*, 215, n. 155.

[52] I thank Dr. J. Tromp for helpful comments on an earlier draft of this essay.

THE NATURE AND FUNCTION OF REVELATION IN 1 ENOCH, JUBILEES, AND SOME QUMRANIC DOCUMENTS

GEORGE W. E. NICKELSBURG

University of Iowa

INTRODUCTION

A conference on the pseudepigrapha and the Dead Sea Scrolls naturally invites a discussion of the issue of revelation. For several reasons this creates something of a conundrum: (1) revelation is central and critical in some of the pseudepigrapha, and the Qumran caves have yielded multiple copies of several such apocalyptic writings, including parts of 1 Enoch, the Book of Jubilees, Daniel, the Aramaic Levi Document; (2) this interest in the apocalyptic writings notwithstanding, there is no clear evidence that the Qumranites themselves authored pseudepigraphic apocalypses;[1] (3) nonetheless, some Qumranic sectarian documents make significant and substantial claims to revelation.

This paper does not address the question of genre: did the Qumranites compose apocalypses or didn't they? Nor does it discuss the function of the pseudepigraphic apocalypses at Qumran. Rather, it compares the content, form, function and social setting of revelation in two pseudepigraphic revelatory texts found at Qumran (1 Enoch and Jubilees) and a selection of Qumran "sectarian" documents. I shall argue that, although there are significant differences in the *forms* in which revelation is presented, the *content* of revelation is similar, comprising ethical or legal matters, eschatology, and sometimes cosmology. Moreover, I shall argue that revelation functions to constitute and shape what is considered to be the eschatological "community" of the chosen and that it often serves polemically to distinguish this community from others that are perceived to be unenlightened or the purveyors of bogus and deceptive revelation. Finally, I shall suggest that these findings indicate important points of continuity and discontinuity between these various types of revela-

---

[1] See, however, F. García Martínez, *Qumran and Apocalyptic: Studies on the Aramaic Texts from Qumran* (STDJ 9; Leiden: E. J. Brill, 1992).

tion and their predecessors in the Israelite prophetic and sapiential traditions, as well as their successors in early Christian communities.

1. 1 ENOCH

That 1 Enoch is properly called an apocalyptic writing is widely agreed. The Society of Biblical Literature taskforce on genres includes large sections of this work in its typology of apocalypses[2]: the Book of the Watchers (1-36); the Book of Parables (37-71); the Book of Luminaries (72-82); and the Dream Visions (85-90). In addition, I have argued that the Epistle of Enoch (92-105) bases its message on the revelations recorded in the Book of the Watchers[3] and, indeed, that 1 Enoch as a whole reflects an apocalyptic world view.[4]

1.1. *Revealed Torah*

1.1.1. *The Calendar*
1.1.1.1. *The Book of the Luminaries (72-82)*   Central to 1 Enoch's revelation is the Book of the Luminaries (72-82), an extensive compilation of texts about the structure of the cosmos and the functioning of the celestial bodies. Although much of the information in this text comports well with empirical observation, its author claims that Enoch obtained its contents while he was on a tour of the heavens in the company of Uriel the angel. This claim documents the validity of a solar, or luni-solar, calendar of 364 days. The importance of this calendar is evident in a passage that polemicizes against "sinners," who employ a different calendar and thus get the seasons out of line with cosmic reality (80:4-8; cf. 75:2).

1.1.1.2. *The Introductory Oracle (1-5)*   The introduction to the Enochic corpus (1-5) seems to allude to wrong calendrical teaching. Sandwiched between two pieces of poetry that imitate biblical prophetic oracles (1:1-9 and 5:4-9) is a piece of prose sapiential teaching about the structure of the universe. In heaven, the luminaries do not change their orbits or transgress their appointed order and, on earth, the seasons proceed in order and the trees shed or do

---

[2] J. J. Collins, "The Jewish Apocalypses," *Semeia* 14 (1979) 21-59.

[3] G. W. E. Nickelsburg, "The Apocalyptic Message of 1 Enoch 92-105," *CBQ* 39 (1977) 309-28.

[4] *Ibid.*, "The Apocalyptic Construction of Reality of 1 Enoch," in *Mysteries and Revelations: Apocalyptic Studies since the Uppsala Colloquium* (ed. J. J. Collins and J. H. Charlesworth; JSP Supp. 9; Sheffield: Sheffield Academic Press, 1991) 51-64.

not shed their leaves, as God has commanded them (2:1-5:3). This orderly obedience is contrasted with humans, who have turned aside from the right path and spoken harsh words against God's majesty. The contrasting metaphors of change and stability, obedience to the path and turning aside, suggest that, in part, the calendar is at issue.

1.1.2. Other Issues Relating to Torah

1.1.2.1. *The Epistle of Enoch (92-105)*   The imagery of sin as perversion returns in the Epistle of Enoch, in a section directed against certain false teachers whom the author threatens with damnation (98:9-99:10).[5] Central are three Woes.

> Woe to you who annul the words of the righteous;
>   you will have no hope of salvation. (98:14)

Here the author criticizes his opponents for nullifying (*akuroun*) the halakhah of the righteous. They will not be saved.

> Woe to those who write lying words and words of error;
>   they write and lead many astray with their lies when they hear them.
> You yourselves err;
>   and you will have peace, but will quickly perish. (98:15-16)

The opponents write down their false teaching, which is read publicly and "leads many astray." These teachers will perish in the coming judgment.

> Woe to you who change the true words
>   and pervert the eternal covenant
>   and consider themselves to be without sin[6];
> they will be swallowed up in the earth. (99:2)

This teaching perverts the "the eternal covenant." The fact that these people do not think they are sinning indicates that they are not callous sinners, but persons who interpret the law differently from the Enochic writer. This difference is sufficient to damn them.

This section of the Epistle is framed by an antithetical Woe and Beatitude which make the same point:

---

[5] G. W. E. Nickelsburg, "The Epistle of Enoch and the Qumran Literature," *JJS* 33 (1982 = *Essays in Honour of Yigael Yadin*) 334-43. My translations presume comparative textual criticism between the Greek and Ethiopic texts, on which see G. W. E. Nickelsburg, "Enoch 97-104: A Study of the Greek and Ethiopic Texts," in *Armenian and Biblical Studies* (ed. M. E. Stone; Suppl. Vol. to *Sion* 1; Jerusalem: St. James, 1976) 90-156.

[6] *Ibid.*, 94, n. 23.

Woe to you, fools;
   for you will be destroyed because of your folly;
And you do not listen to the wise;
   and good things will not happen to you,
   but evils will surround you. (98:9)

Then blessed will be all who listen to the words of the wise,
   and learn to do the commandments of the Most High;
and walk in the paths of his righteousness,
   and do not err with the erring;
for they will be saved. (99:10)

In opposition to the false teachers are "the wise," who also read out their teaching, which is, by definition, the commandments of the Most High that constitute the path of righteousness. One's salvation or damnation depends upon whether or not one listens to "the words of the wise."

Precisely what Torah is comprised by the words of the wise and the commandments of the Most High is not explicit. Surely, it includes Enoch's astronomical Torah.[7] In one other passage the author accuses his opponents of consuming blood :

Woe to you, stiff-necked and hard of heart,
   who do evil and consume blood.
Whence do you have good things to eat and drink and be satisfied?
   from all the good things that the Lord, the Most High, has abun-
     dantly provided upon the earth.
You will have no peace. (98:11)

The author may be criticizing the wrong slaughtering of meat or he may be advocating vegetarianism.[8] In either case, the violation of God's commandment is the issue.

In summary: the author of the Epistle criticizes his opponents for teaching and practicing wrong Torah and threatens them with damnation. As we shall see later, his authority is the revelation received by Enoch.

1.1.2.2. *The Animal Vision (85-90)* This comprehensive vision summarizes the historical content of the Bible from Genesis to Ezra-Nehemiah and then carries the story up to the author's time in the early second century BCE. The account of Israel's history has two emphases: Israel's victimization by the nations, recounted in the metaphor of the sheep and wild beasts found in Ezekiel 34; and

---

[7] Such an application of 99:10 appears in 82:4.
[8] For a passage that may suggest the notion of vegetarianism here, cf. Ps. 104:10ff.

Israel's apostasy, described as the blindness of the sheep. Especially
noteworthy is the claim that when Israel returned from exile,

> They began again to build as before, and they raised up that tower
> [*sc.* the temple] and it was called the high tower. And they began
> again to place a table before the tower, but all the bread on it was pol-
> luted and not pure. And besides all these things, the eyes of the sheep
> were blind, and they did not see... (89:73-74).

The allusion to Mal. 1:7 is clear. What is striking is the author's view
that the apostate blindness of the sheep continues into the hellenistic
period, until some of the lambs born of the sheep begin to open their
eyes and rebuke their elders who, however, remain deaf and blind
(90:6).

In summary, this author believes that the temple cult is polluted
and claims that this insight is the result of a revelation granted in his
own time, which stands on the brink of the eschaton.

1.1.2.3. *The Apocalypse of Weeks (93:1-10 + 91:11-17)*   This analysis
of Israel's situation is more radical than the Animal Vision. The
exile and the burning of the Temple in the sixth week are God's
punishment on a people who have become blind and have strayed
from wisdom (93:8). However, the postexilic seventh week is marked
by the rise of a totally perverse generation. Although the sanctuary is
in focus throughout that Apocalypse (the tabernacle, 93:6; the construction and burning of the Temple, 93:7, 8; the eschatological
temple, 91:13), the building of the Second Temple is ignored (unless
91:11 alludes to it metaphorically). Before the eschatological temple
can be built, the elect of the end-time must be chosen and invested
with seven-fold wisdom (93:10). While this appears to be a comprehensive wisdom that includes eschatology and cosmology, its function as an antidote to Israel's blindness and perversity, as well as to
their violence and deceit, indicates that this wisdom includes revealed instruction about the right life, i.e., Torah and ethics.

1.1.3. *Summary*
Although the Enochic corpus is generally recognized to comprise
revelations about the end-time and the structure of the cosmos, the
Book of the Watchers, the Book of the Luminaries, the Animal
Vision, and the Epistle (including the Apocalypse of Weeks) are all
concerned with right conduct and practice and they posit revelation,
traced back to Enoch, as the authority for this viewpoint.

1.2. *Eschatological Revelations*

1 Enoch's eschatological revelations are tied to the book's concern with Torah and right conduct. The coming judgment, which is the collection's central focus, is the event by which God will reward or punish human obedience or disobedience of the divine law, as this is spelled out in the Enochic corpus or presumed by it. The imminence of this judgment is clear from the timetables in the Animal Vision and the Apocalypse of Weeks. Although the Book of the Watchers contains no such timetables, the claim that this text is a revelation about the judgment intended for the chosen of the end-time (1:1-3; cf. 37:2-3) indicates that, in the view of this author, the final judgment is near. Even the Book of the Luminaries provides an eschatological perspective for its detailed account of celestial mechanics; this cosmology will be in place "until the new creation is accomplished, which endures until eternity" (72:1).

The revealed character of 1 Enoch's eschatology is evident in several ways. The Animal Vision is a revelatory dream through which God made known all the deeds of humanity until eternity (90:39-41). The Apocalypse of Weeks purports to summarize the deeds of humanity, which Enoch had read in the heavenly tablets (93:2; cf. 81:1-4). The Book of the Watchers, with its variegated eschatological message, is based on Enoch's cosmic journeys in the company of interpreting angels (1:2) and the eschatological message of the Epistle is based on the visions recounted in the Book of the Watchers. A claim to revelation is also implicit in the forms in which Enoch presents his message: a prophetic oracle (1-5); an account of a prophetic call (14-16)[9]; the long strings of Woes in the Epistle; and the use of dream visions.[10]

1.3. *Cosmological Revelations*

An important feature of 1 Enoch, virtually unique among the apocalypses, is the heavy preponderance of cosmological lore. The Book of the Luminaries is an obvious case in point, and we have already noted its revelatory form. In addition, the second half of the Book of the Watchers is a detailed account of the seer's journeys through the cosmos. Other blocks of cosmological material appear in the Book of Parables (41:3-44:1; 52:1-56:4; 59:1-60:16) and the Epistle occasion-

---

[9] On the form of this text, see H. L. Jansen, *Die Henochgestalt: Eine vergleichende religionsgeschichtliche Untersuchung* (Oslo: Dybwad, 1939) 114-17.

[10] See Nickelsburg, "Apocalyptic Message," 315-18.

ally refers to it (93:11-14; 100:10-101:9). As Stone has observed, these authors were familiar with a broad range of "scientific" knowledge that was the possession of contemporary sages.[11]

This preponderance of cosmological material is not presented for its own sake, however. The Book of the Luminaries supports calendrical practice. In the Book of the Watchers and the Book of Parables, cosmology undergirds eschatology. Enoch's first journey, to the west, climaxes in his visions of the places of punishment, and ch. 17 logs the landmarks that document his journey to these places. In his second journey, from the far West to the East, several new places of eschatological import for human beings are added and, again, chapters 32-34 document his journey to paradise.[12] Important parts of the cosmology in the Book of Parables also include visions of the places of punishment. The revealed nature of Enoch's cosmology is indicated by the angelic interpretations of the phenomena that he sees on his journeys.

1.4. Enoch's Primordial Wisdom: Constitutive of the Eschatological Community

1 Enoch purports to present or to imply a comprehensive system of wisdom revealed to the patriarch in primordial antiquity and committed to writing by him before his translation to heaven. Its character as the written deposit of heavenly wisdom is emphasized in 81:5-10,[13] where the angels who have escorted him through the cosmos command him to write down his commands and teaching and to transmit these as a testimony to his sons, notably Methuselah. Methuselah, in turn, is to preserve these writings and to see to it that this life-giving wisdom is transmitted to "the generations of eternity" (82:1-5). A further step in this process of transmission will occur in the end-time, when Enoch's books are given to the righteous and pious and wise, to instruct them in the paths of truth (104:12-13). They, in turn, will testify to/against the sons of earth (105:1-2).[14]

---

[11] M. E. Stone, "The Book of Enoch and Judaism in the Third Century B.C.E.," *CBQ* 40 (1978) 479-92.

[12] Here the Paradise of Righteousness is the place of the tree of wisdom.

[13] On the relation of this passage to other parts of 1 Enoch, see G. W. E. Nickelsburg, *Jewish Literature Between the Bible and the Mishnah* (Philadelphia: Fortress, 1981) 150-51, and R. A. Argall, *1 Enoch and Sirach: A Comparative Literary and Conceptual Analysis of the Themes of Revelation, Creation, and Judgment* (SBLEJL 8; Atlanta: Scholars Press, 1995) 257-65.

[14] Nickelsburg, "The Epistle of Enoch, 343-45.

Additional references to the eschatological proliferation of Enoch's wisdom are scattered throughout the book.

Then wisdom will be given to all the chosen;
    and they will all live,
And they will sin no more through godlessness or pride.

In the enlightened man there will be light,
    and in the wise man, understanding,
    and they will transgress no more,
    nor will they sin all the days of their life. (5:8)[15]

And at its (the seventh week's) conclusion, the elect will be chosen,
    as witnesses of righteousness from the eternal plant of righteousness,
    to whom will be given sevenfold wisdom and knowledge.
And they will uproot the foundations of violence,
    and the structure of deceit in it,
    to execute judgment. (93:10; 91:11)

And after this there will be a ninth week,
    in which righteous law[16] will be revealed to all the sons of the whole earth;
    and all the <deeds>[17] of wickedness will vanish from the whole earth and descend to the eternal pit,
and all humanity will look to the path of eternal righteousness. (91:14)

And the wise among men will see the truth,
    and the sons of men will contemplate these words of this epistle,
    and they will recognize that their wealth cannot save them when iniquity collapses. (100:6)

Finally, we note again the Animal Vision's reference to revelation in the end-time. The younger generation in the hellenistic period have their eyes opened to the apostasy that has pervaded the operation of the Temple cult and they exhort their elders to turn from their apostasy.

The Enochic corpus, then, is the sacred Scripture that constitutes the eschatological community of the chosen.[18] It does so in two ways.

---

[15] Translation is based on the Greek text of 5:8.

[16] For this translation of דין קשוט, see F. Dexinger, *Henochs Zehnwochenapokalypse und offene Probleme der Apokalyptikforschung* (SPB 29; Leiden: E. J. Brill, 1977) 141.

[17] J. T. Milik, *The Books of Enoch* (Oxford: Clarendon Press, 1976) 266, 269, fills the lacuna in 4QEn^g 1 4:20 to read "doers." I follow the Ethiopic text, albeit reading plural rather than singular.

[18] On 1 Enoch as scripture, see G. W. E. Nickelsburg, "Scripture in 1 Enoch and 1 Enoch as Scripture," in *Texts and Contexts: Biblical Texts in their Textual and Situational Contexts, Essays in Honor of Lars Hartman* (ed. T. Fornberg and D. Hellholm; Oslo: Scandinavian University Press, 1995) 333-54. On 1 Enoch as revealed, saving wisdom, see G. W. E. Nickelsburg, "Revealed Wisdom as a Criterion for Inclusion and Exclusion: From Jewish Sectarianism to Early Christianity," in *To See Ourselves as Others See Us* (ed. J. Neusner and E. S. Frerichs; Atlanta: Scholars Press, 1985) 73-91.

Its Torah instructs them in the path of righteousness. Its announcement of the judgment admonishes them to remain on the right path
and encourages them in the midst of persecution to remain confident of God's ultimate vindication of their righteousness. This corpus of revealed wisdom has a secondary function. The community of
the righteous is to testify to outsiders (the sons of the whole earth),
admonishing them to turn to the right path in order that they may
be saved from the judgment.

To what extent it is appropriate to refer to an identifiable Enochic
community, with structure and organization, is difficult to say. 1
Enoch is not a Rule of the Community. Nonetheless, the distinctive
Torah explicit in the Book of Luminaries and implicit in the Epistle's
criticism of false teachers who pervert the eternal covenant seems to
reflect a distinctive community ethos that encourages and facilitates
progress along the paths of righteousness.

1.5. *Social Setting: Roles and the Forms and Processes of Revelation*
Within this community there existed the latter day, real-life counterparts of primordial Enoch. The existence of such leaders and teachers is implied by the existence of the corpus itself. Someone wrote it.
The identity of these leaders and teachers is explicit in the Epistle's
references to "the wise." Their words, written down and read aloud,
express the commandments of the Most High and constitute the
path of righteousness. The term "the wise" may be the counterpart
of the title "maskil(im)," which refers in Dan. 12:3 to those "who
cause many to be righteous" and in 1 QS 3:13, to the one who instructs in the two ways. The title "Scribe," applied three times to
Enoch (12:4; 15:1; 92:1), may also point to a concrete social role,
while the title "Scribe of Righteousness/Truth" is also reminiscent of
the Qumran sobriquet, מורה-הצדק. The implications of the title
"scribe" are further attested in the content of 1 Enoch. Taken together, the authors of the Enochic corpus knew virtually every book
of the Tanakh and could speak the idiom of prophecy and the sapiential tradition.[19] They were concerned with the commandments of
the Torah. In addition, they were learned in the cosmological sci-
ences and could employ and transform motifs in pagan mythology.
In short, they did all the things that Ben Sira ascribes to the scribes
of his time (Sir. 39:1-4).

---

[19] Nickelsburg, "Scripture in 1 Enoch, " 335-42.

The identification of the figure of Enoch with leaders and teachers in the hellenistic period requires us to think about the forms of revelation. Much of the content of 1 Enoch is said to have been acquired through dream visions. This is true, not only of the symbolic dreams in chapters 83-84 and 85-90. To judge from 13:4-10, Enoch's ascent to the heavenly throne room, as well as his journeys through the cosmos, all took place in a dream vision.[20] His admonitions and Woes in the Epistle are based on these visions, in turn.

Should we think of all of this as literary fiction? The thoroughgoing literary character and sophisticated prosody of the material seem to indicate artifice and a contrived poetic process.[21] Be this as it may, it need not exclude the possibility that an unnamed figure in the hellenistic period had a genuine experience of a throne vision, however he may have elaborated his expression of it in traditional language. Thus 1 Enoch may well attest the ongoing life of the visionary tradition familiar from the pre-exilic, exilic, and postexilic prophets. Similarly, however elaborated they may be, the reports of dream visions like 1 Enoch 83-84 and 85-90 may attest the kind of mantic wisdom described in the Joseph cycle of Genesis and in the early chapters of Daniel.

Why the authors of Enoch, and Daniel for that matter, chose to adopt a pseudepigraphic manner of presentation is a complex question. With respect to 1 Enoch, I make a couple of observations. First, one should not confuse two things: 1) the likelihood that many of the contemporaries of the Enochic authors did not accept the prophetic credentials and genuine religious experience of these authors; 2) the prophetic self-consciousness that is expressed in the texts. To judge from the canonical texts, Michaiah ben Imlah (2 Kgs 22:5-28), Jeremiah, Amos, and others also experienced opposition to their prophetic self-consciousness.

Secondly, there may well be something to Russell's theory that pseudepigraphy implies an identification between the writer and his ancient patron and counterpart.[22] The figure of Enoch can be connected, albeit loosely, with the time of the Deluge or can be seen as living before the terrible evils that polluted the earth and required

---

[20] At the end of chapter 16, Enoch is in the presence of the angels in the heavenly throne room, where he has ascended in a dream vision. The beginning of Enoch's journeys in 17:1 indicates that his journeys began at that point. Cf., 81:5, however, which suggests a physical return to his house.

[21] On this issue, see M. Himmelfarb, *Ascent to Heaven in Jewish and Christian Apocalypses* (New York: Oxford University Press, 1993) 110-14.

[22] D. S. Russell, *The Method and Message of Jewish Apocalyptic* (Philadelphia: Westminster, 1964) 132-39.

the cleansing of the Flood (cf. 1 En. 93:3). Thus, he can interact with Noah and speak about a judgment that will have a latter day, final counterpart. Moreover, because he preceded Abraham and the division of humanity into Israel and the nations, his message has universal relevance. Whether, in addition, some of the Enochic authors spoke out of a mystic experience that brought them, they thought, into the orbit of the glorified Enoch (much as Christian prophets spoke in the name of the glorified Lord) is a question that may be worth posing.[23]

Thirdly, it is noteworthy that the authors of 1 Enoch do not simply attribute their writings to a pre-Mosaic author. They also present them in a manner that devalues the Mosaic pentateuch. The initial oracle in chapters 1-5 is a paraphrase of part of Deut. 33,[24] and some of the content and testamentary language is chapter 91 is reminiscent of Moses' farewell discourse in Deut. 29-32.[25] In effect, this casts Moses into the role of a "me-too." In addition, the account of the events at Mount Sinai in the Animal Vision, while it allows Moses an important role as a leader of Israel and even grants him a vision of the Deity, never states that he received the Torah on Mount Sinai (89:29-34). Revelation came to Israel at Marah (89:28; cf. Exod 15:25-26). Thus, 1 Enoch leapfrogs the Mosaic Torah and assumes for itself a prophetic authority that precedes Moses.

Finally, 1 Enoch claims revelatory authority for material that may well have been created through more "normal" processes. The Book of the Luminaries seems to reflect empirical observation. Similarly, the decisive interpretations of the Torah that are implied in the Epistle may well have developed through the kind of exegesis suggested by Ben Sira. That the Enochic authors knew most of the Tanakh is clear. Of course, their use of biblical material, not through citation, but by appeal to ancient (really new) revelation, is a corollary of the fictitious date of the writing. However, it also makes a theological point. This is revelation.

---

[23] On the possible connection between Enoch's account of his ascent and the later mystical texts, see briefly G. W. E. Nickelsburg, "Enoch, Levi, and Peter, Recipients of Revelation in Upper Galilee," *JBL* 100 (1981) 581-82.

[24] L. Hartman, *Asking for a Meaning: A Study of 1 Enoch 1-5* (ConBib NT Series 12; Lund: Gleerup, 1979) 22-26.

[25] Cf. esp. 91:1 with Deut. 31:28; 91:3 with Deut. 31:19, 21, 26 and 32:1; 91:8, 11 with Deut. 29:18, 20.

2. THE BOOK OF JUBILEES

Although the Book of Jubilees is not generally classified as an apocalypse,[26] it contains all the features that have led scholars to define
large parts of 1 Enoch as apocalyptic. It is a text with a narrative
framework in which an otherworldly being transmits secret information to a human agent who is identified as a figure of the past. To
make the comparison with 1 Enoch more precise, the author of
Jubilees claims for his writing the same status that 1 En. 81:5-82:4
claims for the Enochic corpus: it is the transcript of a heavenly revelation that provides the instruction that will grant to those who heed
it the reward of eternal life. Like 1 Enoch the instruction in Jubilees
relates to both Torah and eschatology and takes for granted the
Enochic cosmology that underlies a solar calendar.

2.1. *Literary Structure*

Taken as a whole, Jubilees is a rewritten version of Genesis and the
first half of Exodus, presented as a transcript of the divine account of
the events from Creation to the Exodus. It is set at the foot of Mount
Sinai with God summoning Moses in order to give him the two
tablets of the Torah (1:1). He then commands Moses to write what
he is told by the angel of presence who is reading from the heavenly
tablets (1:26-29). The angelic account (2:1ff.) follows the order and
general content of the narrative in Genesis and Exodus, albeit with
significant additions and revisions and some omissions.[27] The additions and revisions are of three kinds. First, the whole narrative is set
within an explicit chronological framework that dates events according to the solar calendar that God revealed to Enoch. Second, some
parts of the account are elaborated with narrative detail, substantial
haggadic additions, and even the insertion of new episodes. Finally,
and most significantly, the author uses the patriarchal narratives as a
source from which to derive specific laws and halakhot and he presents these as immutable laws, which are often said to be inscribed
on the heavenly tablets (3:31; 4:32; 16:29).

---

[26] Only Jub. 23 is included in Collins, "Jewish Apocalypses," 32-33.
[27] G. W. E. Nickelsburg, "The Bible Rewritten and Expanded," in *Jewish Writings
of the Second Temple Period* (ed. M. E. Stone; Compendia Rerum Iudaicarum ad
Novum Testamentum 2:2; Assen: Van Gorcum; Philadelphia: Fortress, 1983) 2.97-
101.

2.2. *Content*

Jubilees' modifications of its Genesis-Exodus prototype include material that corresponds roughly to the emphases in 1 Enoch mentioned above, although each has its own nuances and emphases.

2.2.1. *Law and Ethics*

Most clearly and emphatically, Jubilees is a book of law. This is most obvious in the many halakhic additions to the biblical narrative, which are usually introduced with formulae that delineate their status as eternal law and underscore the dire consequences for those who do not observe these laws (15:25-34; 16:30; 30:22; 33:10-14). Notable examples of the author's concerns include the solar calendar, the rite of circumcision, always performed on the eighth day (15:25-34), idolatry (22:16-18), the consuming of blood (7:27-33), nakedness (3:31), intermarriage with gentiles (ch. 30), incest (ch. 33), and the proper performing of sacrificial rituals (32:1-16). Although some of these issues are of concern to the Enochic authors, Jubilees is noteworthy for its formal articulation of laws and commandments. Conversely, it uses only sparingly the wisdom metaphor of the two ways that recurs frequently in the Epistle of Enoch.

Nonetheless, a counterpart to the sapiential viewpoint and its expression occurs in the haggadic elaborations that demonstrate right conduct through narrative example. In particular, the stories about Abraham depict him as a gentile who seeks the true God and then rejects idolatry and astrological prognostication (chs. 11-12). The account of the Akedah, moreover, epitomizes his faithfulness to God, which is exemplified in his right response to a series of ten trials (17:15-19:9). These stories, and others like them, focus less on specific commandments—though some are mentioned—and more on exemplary or non-exemplary behavior and its consequences.

2.2.2. *Eschatology*

A second, less prominent feature of Jubilees' narrative is its interest in eschatology. The chronological framework of the text stretches from creation to the new creation and is calculated in terms of solar jubilees (1:29). The events that are about to occur at Mount Sinai and the book's account of Israel's past history are prefaced by a look toward the future (ch. 1). Employing the scheme of Deut. 30-32, the divine revelation given at another mountain, God predicts that Israel will violate his Torah and suffer the consequences until they repent. A more finely tuned version of this eschatological scenario appears in 23:12-31, where it is an integral part of Abraham's testament to

Isaac. Another brief allusion to eschatology appears in the summary of Enoch's revelations in the Animal Vision and the Apocalypse of Weeks (4:18-19).

2.2.3. *Cosmology*

This author is much less interested in emphasizing cosmology than the Enochic authors. This is doubtless because he presupposes the Enochic, first, in his reference to Enoch's Book of the Luminaries, which forms the foundation for his chronological structures based on a solar calendar (4:17). They also appear in the interpolations in the Flood account, which are the springboard for his dualistic view of the universe. According to this world view, human sins and the experience of evil are functions of a demonic realm that was generated through the sin of the Watchers (ch. 5; 7:21-24; 10:4-12).

2.3. *Jubilees as a Revelatory Text*

The revelatory character of the Jubilees narrative is indicated by several factors. First, in contrast to the anonymous narrative of Genesis and Exodus, this account is ascribed to the prophet Moses and, in the idiom of apocalyptic writings, Moses' source of information is explicitly a revealer figure, God (1:26), and then the angel of the presence (1:27-2:1), whose voice recurs at various points throughout the narrative (23:32; 18:9; 48:4, 11-19). Second, the angel states that the narrative he rehearses and the laws that he recites are derived from the heavenly tablets, which also contain the names of the righteous (19:9). Third, this angelic narrator also refers to hidden things, namely, the origin, existence, and activity and punishment of the demonic offspring of the Watchers (see above). Finally, the narrator appeals to the revelations that Enoch had received from his angelic informants and cites them as authentic testimony to the human race (4:17-19).

Thus, Jubilees as a whole purports to be special revelation received and written down in ancient times and now presented for the edification and salvation of Israel, which stands at the threshold of the eschaton.

2.4. *Revelation as Constitutive of the Community of the End-Time*

This eschatological focus is especially evident in 23:12-31. Moreover, these verses provide a window into the real-life processes that generated the revelation which is the substance of the book. Employing the Deuteronomic scheme of sin-punishment-repentance-salvation, the author spells out the desperate situation of contemporary Israel whose disobedience has brought on the curses of the covenant, described as gentile oppression, short lives, and the failure of crops. The solution to this problem is similar to the passages quoted above from the Animal Vision and the Apocalypse of Weeks. There is a bitter dispute in which the younger generation accuse their elders of sin. The process by which this judgment is made and its consequences are spelled in detail.

As human lives are severely shortened,

> In those days the children will begin to study the laws
> and seek the commandments
> and return to the path of righteousness.
> And the days will begin to grow many and increase among those
> children of men,
> till their days approach one thousand years,
> and to a greater number of years than (before) was the number of
> days (23:26-27).

The return of blessing is catalyzed by the study of the Torah, the identification of right halakhah, which facilitates true obedience and leads to divine blessing, the salvation of Israel from its enemies and, ultimately, the ascent of the spirits of the righteous into the joy of God's presence (23:31).

This eschatological vignette reveals the process by which the author of Jubilees has arrived at the Torah that permeates his account. The study of Torah, the study of the laws and searching of the commandments (Eth. *hašaša* = דרש and perhaps בקש), leads to revelation, the right understanding of the commandments and laws that are inscribed on the heavenly tablets. In contrast to 1 Enoch, which emphasized revelation through dream visions, this author focuses on the painstaking process of searching the Scriptures for the less than obvious expression of God's will.[28] The claim of revelation is a theological judgment about the character and results of this human process.

As with 1 Enoch, it is impossible to state whether and to what extent the author of this text was a member of a defined, organized community. However, the narrative suggests that the author depicts a group of "exegetes" who come to certain conclusions about the right interpretation of the Torah and present them, in this text, as the true understanding of the Torah revealed at Sinai, exhorting

---

[28] I read the use of the verb "seek" or "search" to refer to a process of looking for something that is not obvious. The verb is used frequently with reference to books and texts.

Israel to obey them and find its salvation.[29] Strikingly different from
1 Enoch, the author emphasizes Israel's status as the covenantal people and proscribes interaction with the gentiles and certainly the
preaching of an eschatological *kerygma* that might lead to the salvation of the gentiles.

2.5. *Revelation as a Polemical Category*

As in 1 Enoch, the notion of revelation in Jubilees has polemical
overtones. In the most general sense, Jubilees' revelations about the
right interpretation and practice of the Torah are directed against a
nation that has violated the Torah. In part this may refer to outright
rejection of the Torah, not least some forms of hellenization.[30] In
other instances, however, revelations of the right interpretation of
the Torah imply the existence of differing interpretations. Pre-
eminently, this involves the observance of a different calendar. In
other cases, the authors present halakhot contrary to currently accepted practice.[31] The Sabbath laws are a case in point (50:6-13).
Thus, even if the text of Jubilees does not explicitly refer to opposing
teachers who "lead many astray with their lies," as does the Epistle
of Enoch, it indicates disputes about the Torah and undergirds its
own interpretation with the claim of revealed truth.

2.6. *Enoch and Enochic Revelations in the Book of Jubilees*

I have noted earlier that the Enochic corpus presents itself as primordial revelation that long preceded the Mosaic Torah and that,
by and large, it ignores the Mosaic Torah. It is striking, therefore,
that the pseudo-Mosaic Jubilees gives the Enochic revelations special mention and that the figure of Enoch has pride of place.
Indeed, the author of Jubilees casts Moses as a figure like Enoch.[32]
Enoch's case is special; he appears prior to Abraham and Moses
and thus his message is directed to all humanity. Moses is the pre-

---

[29] In his paper in this volume, "Pseudepigraphy and Group Formation in Second
Temple Judaism," John Collins is skeptical as to whether this text refers to a specif-
ic group. I use the term in lower case, presuming a plurality of students of the
Torah rather than the effort of a single person.

[30] Nickelsburg, "The Bible Rewritten and Expanded," 102-03.

[31] *Ibid.*, 99-100.

[32] Enoch learned his history, astronomy, and cosmology under the tutelage of angels, just as Moses learned the chronology and course of history and the eternal
Torah from the angel of the presence; Enoch wrote down everything as a testimony
(Jub. 4:18, 19, 24; 7:39; 10:17) just as Moses wrote his account as a testimony (1:1,
4, 9; 2:33; 3:14).

eminent prophet to Israel, the mediator of the covenant that constitutes Israel as God's chosen people and the mediator of the Torah
that is a constitutive part of that covenant. Nonetheless, the book
may also attest an ambivalence about the figure of Moses that is not
at odds with the viewpoint of the Enochic authors. The predictions
of Deuteronomy are uttered in a speech that *God directs to Moses,*
rather than as a part of *Moses' testament to Israel.* The content of the
Pentateuch is placed in the mouth of an angel who speaks to Moses.
Of course, this verifies that the Pentateuch, written by Moses, is
God's word; however, the explication of the revelatory process may
be a way of undergirding Moses' authority in circumstances that require this. Such a hypothesis provides some continuity between 1
Enoch's ambivalence about the authority of the Mosaic Torah and
the fact that Jubilees both embraces Enochic revelation and strongly affirms Mosaic authority.

3. The Nature and Function of Revelation in Some Qumranic Documents

In this section I shall discuss passages that are generally considered
to have been authored at Qumran or in a community closely related
or ancestral to it. My purpose is not to investigate the possible historical connections between the authors of these texts and the authors of 1 Enoch and Jubilees or, indeed, between the authors of the
sectarian texts. My concern is the forms, functions and social settings
of their notions of revelation.

3.1. *The Damascus Document*

3.1.1. *Column 1: An Account of the Formation of the Community of the End-Time*

The prologue to the Damascus Document recounts the origins of the
community in which it was generated. The setting is post-exilic and
is said to be 390 years after the destruction of Jerusalem, i.e., ca. 197
BCE. This is roughly contemporaneous with the time indicated for
the reforming activities described in the Animal Vision and, probably, the Apocalypse of Weeks.[33] The dominating factor in Israel's
post-exilic life is the nation's guilt and the ongoing presence of the
covenantal curses. This is paralleled in the Animal Vision, which describes the ongoing pollution of the cult and the nation's continued

---

[33] On the problems of the chronology of CD 1, see Collins, "Pseudepigraphy,"
nn. 11 and 12.

oppression by the gentiles. CD 1 and the Apocalypse of Weeks both ignore the sixth century return from exile and the rebuilding of the Temple, but emphasize the continuity in Israel's state of sin. In the Apocalypse of Weeks this is described as the rise of a thoroughly perverse generation (1 En. 93:9). The construal of this community as the remnant of Israel and as the sprouting of a plant (CD 1:4, 7) parallels the notion of the chosen and the language of the plant in the Apocalypse of Weeks (93:10), and its character as the community of the end-time is evident (CD 1:11-12).[34]

For the authors of CD 1:9, the Animal Vision (1 En. 89:94; 90:7) and the Apocalypse of Weeks, Israel's predicament is a function of its blindness. The corresponding remedy is revelation. In the Animal Vision this involves the opening of the eyes of the younger generation (1 En. 90:6). In the Apocalypse of Weeks (1 En. 93:10) it is the giving of sevenfold wisdom and knowledge. The author of CD 1 employs a string of expressions that construe the constituting events for this community as revelatory. God raises (קום) a Teacher of Righteousness to make them walk in the path of his heart, and he makes known (ידע) what he has done to the wicked who have strayed from the path (1:11-13). The process leading to revelation is described as seeking (דרש, 1:11), as it is in Jub. 23:26. The title "Teacher of Righteousness" parallels Enoch's title "Scribe of Righteousness." The metaphor of the two ways and the construal of obedience as "the path of righteousness" (1:16) have many counterparts in the Epistle of Enoch and appear in Jubilees 23:17, 18, 21, 26.

The opponents of the eschatological, enlightened community are those who seek slippery things (דרשו בחלקות), facile interpreters of the law (halakhot), who perpetrate lies. They are the counterparts of Enoch's deceitful teachers who lead many astray with their lies (98:15) and whose activity builds a structure of deceit on foundations of violence (93:11; cf. CD 1:20-21).[35]

3.1.2. CD 5:20-6:11: Revelation as the Interpretation of the Torah

This passage presents a scenario much like that of CD 1, albeit with a more detailed focus on the interpretation of the Torah. In the post-exilic period, certain individuals prophesied deceit and caused Israel to stray from God's commandments. In response to this God raised up (קום) knowledgeable and wise men who went to Damascus

---

[34] On the imagery of the planting in these texts, see P. Tiller, "The 'Eternal Planting' in the Dead Sea Scrolls," *Dead Sea Discoveries*, 4 (1997) 312-15.

[35] Similar language appears in 4QpNahum and 4QpPsa; see Nickelsburg, "Epistle of Enoch," 337.

to probe the well of the Torah under the leadership of the Searcher, i.e., Interpreter of the Torah (דורש התורה). All this happens with a view toward the end of time and the appearance of the one who teaches righteousness. The detailed focus on the interpretation of the Torah and the language of searching is most closely paralleled by the process in Jub. 23 and the language in which it is described

In summary: these two passages in the Damascus Document depict Israel in a state of apostasy, marked by the activity of false teachers of the Torah. In this situation, the eschatological community of the righteous arises, constituted by the revealed right interpretation of the law. The explicit references to a single individual figure differentiates these passages from their counterparts in 1 Enoch and Jubilees, although the plurality of persons, first mentioned in CD 1:8-10 and 5:2-7, corresponds to the plurality in the other texts.

3.2. *The Community Rule*

3.2.1. *1 QS 8:1-15*

Here we have another account of origins, with parallels to the previous texts as well as important nuances of its own. It is a time of uncleanness. The council of the community is formed with a view toward atoning for the land and exacting judgment on the wicked so that iniquity will be removed. The judicial functions of the council and the disappearance of wickedness is paralleled in the Apocalypse of Weeks (1 En. 93:10, 14).[36] The description of the council as an everlasting planting picks up a metaphor found in both CD 1 and 1 En. 93:10. The dominant metaphor of (the council of) the community as a building depicts its function as a kind of temple, implying the dysfunction of the Jerusalem sanctuary (cf. 1 En. 89:73; CD 4:15-5:15). Although it is rooted in an exegesis of Isaiah 28, with its counterposition of two structures, it finds a parallel in 1 En. 93:10 and its portrayal of a structure of deceit built on a foundation of violence. An important function of the community is the ongoing searching of the Torah (מדרש התורה, 8:15-16). This interpretation is not explicitly construed as revelation, although it is connected with previous revelations. The eschatological character of the community is indicated by its judicial function, which is connected with the extirpation of iniquity.

---

[36] For the notion of eschatological cleansing, albeit by a divine agent, cf. 1 En. 10:20-22, a passage with significant parallels to 1QS 4:17-22.

Although this passage contains no reference to a cadre of opposing, false interpreters of the Torah, the notion appears in 1QS 9:3-11. A literary association between these two passages is indicated by identical introductory words in 8:4 and 9:3 (בהיות אלה בירשאל) and by the common depiction of the community as a temple with atoning functions.[37] Those outside the community are "men of a lie," who stray from the right path (9:8-10). The eschatological orientation of the community is evident in 9:11.

3.2.2. *1QS 5:1-13: The Revealed Interpretation of the Torah*

This passage, which has a number of verbal parallels with 1QS 8 (cf. esp. 5:3-6 with 8:1-7), describes some of the regulations pertaining to persons who enter the covenant of the Community. A critical factor, perhaps *the* critical factor, in one's communal existence is the obligation "to return to the Torah of Moses in accordance with all that it commands with all his heart and all his soul, to everything that has been revealed (גלה) concerning it to the Sons of Zadok, the priests who observe the covenant and interpret (דרש) his will..." What distinguishes the members of the community and sustains their covenantal status is their proper observance of the Torah, rightly interpreted through divine revelation. The outsiders, by contrast, have neither sought (בקש) nor studied (דרש) the decrees of the covenant in order to learn (ידע) the hidden things (סתר) in which they stray (תעה). Here, revealed interpretation of the Torah is opposed not to false interpretation but to a lack of enlightenment with respect to its interpretation and observance.

3.3. *The Hodayot*

The Hodayot, especially the hymns of the teacher, are an important source for studying Qumranic notions of revelation. Here I can discuss only one of them.

3.3.1. *1QH 12(4):5-13(5):4: The Enlightened Teacher, his Disciples, and his Opponents*

This text does not speak *about* revelation and revealed interpreters of the Torah; it is the first person account of one *who claims to be* such a recipient and dispenser of revelation. The reason for this hymn of thanksgiving is the fact that the Lord has brightened his

---

[37] The parallel between the two passages does not appear in 4QS[d] 2 2.

face with his covenant, enlightened him like the perfect dawn (12:1-6) and has made known to him (ידע) the wondrous divine mysteries (12:27). The author, in turn, has enlightened the face of the many (12:27) and poured the drink of knowledge (12:11). The content of revelation is, first of all, the interpretation of the Torah. God has engraved his Torah upon the teacher's heart (12:10). Those "who walk in the path of your heart" have listened to him (12:24) and they will stand forever in God's presence and be established forever (12:27-28). The author may also allude to other kinds of revelation. The "vision of knowledge" (חזון דעת) may refer to eschatological revelation, while God's "wondrous mysteries" (רזי פלאכה) may refer to the same or imply cosmological secrets.

Much of the hymn is taken up with criticism of the author's opponents who ridicule and belittle him (12:8, 22). They change (מור) the Torah, giving vinegar rather than the drink of knowledge (12:10-11). In addition, they claim to have their own visions (12:20). Overall, the text is marked by a number of references to their lies and deception (12:7, 9-10, 16, 20), employing a vocabulary now familiar from the Epistle of Enoch, CD 1, and 4QpNah (cf. n. 22).

Especially noteworthy is this author's use of language from Isaiah 52-53 to describe his rejection by his opponents (12:8, 22-23). These passages, with their pairing of persecution and vindication, exaltation and judgment, are reminiscent of Wisdom of Solomon 2 and 5, where the suffering and eschatological exaltation of the righteous sage are depicted in the language of Isaiah 52-53.[38] Another application of Second Isaiah's servant material (Isa. 50:4) to the inspired teacher appears in 1QH 15(7):10; 16(8):36.

The eschatological character of the teacher's revelations may be indicated by the reference to "the vision of knowledge" and the use of an eschatological interpretation of Isaiah 52-53 which attributed judicial functions to the teacher.

3.4. The Habakkuk Pesher

The early columns of this text feature the opposition between the Man of Lies and his followers and the Teacher of Righteousness. The point of contention, on which the counterposition of truth and lies turns, relates both to the interpretation of the Torah (5:9-12) and

---

[38] G. W. E. Nickelsburg, *Resurrection, Immortality, and Eternal Life in Intertestamental Judaism* (HTS 26; Cambridge: Harvard University; London: Oxford University, 1972) 58-66. 1QH 12:8-12 parallels scene 1 in the story (Wis. Sol. 2). 1QH 12:21-23 parallels scene two (Wis. Sol. 5). Cf. also 1QH 12:23-25 with Wis. Sol. 5:5-7.

to the Teacher's inspired interpretation of prophetic eschatology
(2:5-10). The issue of revealed eschatology returns in the celebrated
passage in 7:4-9. What is striking here (in 2:5-10 and, indeed, in the
genre of the text itself) is the distinction between the revealed
prophetic word (God spoke [דבר] to Habakkuk) and the revealed eschatological interpretation granted to the Teacher (God made
known [ידע] to the Teacher). In contrast to 1 Enoch, who knows
Scripture but pretends that allusions to it came through direct revelation, here one assumes the existence of the ancient inspired texts,
then moving on to claim secondary revelation as the basis for its correct interpretation. What is not clear is the precise "mechanics" of
this revelation, i.e., the manner and form in which it was received.
The association of Torah and eschatology is explicit in 7:10-11 and
8:1-3. It is those "men of truth," who observe the Torah in accordance with the interpretation of the Teacher, who will endure in the
last age and pass muster in the coming judgment.

3.5. *Revelation and Apocalypse in the Qumranic Texts*

It remains to comment briefly on the genre apocalypse as it applies
to texts authored at Qumran or in its immediate orbit.[39] The topic is
complex, and I confine my comments (and, more often, questions) to
two issues. Both relate to matters familiar from apocalypses but
found in texts that are not generically apocalypses.

3.5.1. *Eschatology without Apocalypse*
One category we need to examine is "apocalyptic eschatology."
Should the term be used only for eschatology actually found in apocalypses or can it refer to dualistic, mythic eschatologies like those
found in apocalypses, even when these occur in texts that are not
apocalypses? Two texts from Qumran provide examples. The eschatological scenario in 1QS 4:19-26 has many parallels with 1 En.
10:20-22. In fact, neither of these texts is formally an apocalypse.
Should we refer to their eschatology as "apocalyptic," because it is
similar to the eschatology found in apocalyptic sections of 1 Enoch
and in other apocalypses? Three other questions come to mind. 1)
Should we reserve the term "apocalyptic" for texts that clearly posit
or presume revelation? 2) Should the term be applied more narrowly to texts whose revelatory base is an apocalypse? 3) Does the mythic, dualistic eschatology derive from a revelatory text or, more nar-

---

[39] On the issue of apocalypses at Qumran, see Collins, "Pseudepigraphy."

rowly, an apocalypse and does the author of this text find authority in such revelation?

We might address the same questions to three other examples which are found in fragmentary Qumran manuscripts: 4QPseudo-Daniel[a] (4Q243), 4QMessianic Apocalypse (4Q521), the so-called son of God text[40] and the text which Milik has identified as part of a Testament of Naphtali (4Q215), although it contains no verbal parallels to the Greek or medieval Hebrew testaments of Naphtali.[41]

3.5.2. Allusions to Heavenly Realia Described in Apocalyptic Texts

Two Qumran texts employ vocabulary found in the apocalypses and refer to heavenly entities described in the apocalypses. The first is 1QS 11:5-7:

> From the spring of his justice is my judgment,
>   and from the wonderful mystery is the light in my heart.
> My eyes have observed what always is,
>   wisdom that has been (hidden) from the sons of men,
> fountain of justice and well of strength,
>   and spring of glory (hidden) from the assembly of flesh
> (Trans. García Martínez).

These words could have been spoken by an apocalypticist about the apocalyptic experience. Does the text attest the author's apocalyptic experience or has the apocalyptic vocabulary been transformed to other ends, albeit with reference to heavenly realia? The same question about apocalyptic vocabulary can be applied to 1QH 12(4):5-6, 18.

A second text is 1QH 9(1):20-27.[42] Does it refer to the heavenly tablets described in 1 En. 81:1-4? Does the author presuppose and draw on such a text and/or is he using the language metaphorically? The cosmological reference in the preceding lines (10-19), which are also reminiscent of some wisdom texts, should also be considered in an answer to the question.

As we address ourselves to these and similar texts and to the questions I have suggested, it will be worth considering what difference it makes when material characteristic of apocalypses occurs in non-

---

[40] On these two texts, see García Martínez, 137-49; 162-79.

[41] On this text, see E. G. Chazon, "A Case of Mistaken Identity: Testament of Naphtali (4Q215) and Time of Righteousness (4Q215a)," in *The Provo International Conference on the Dead Sea Scrolls: New Texts, Reformulated Issues, and Technological Innovations* (ed. D. W. Parry and E. C. Ulrich; Leiden: E. J. Brill) [in press].

[42] G. W. E. Nickelsburg, "1 Enoch and Qumran Origins: The State of the Question and Some Prospects for Answers,"in *SBLSP* (1986) 347.

apocalypses, or vice versa. What difference does it make when one embodies references to hidden things, such as the eschatological future and cosmological realia, in texts of apocalyptic genre? To what extent does a discussion of these hidden things and the dualism presupposed by them take place prior to the rise of the apocalyptic genre? Why, and to what end, does the genre develop as an important staple in sectors of Second Temple Judaism? And why, given the existence of such apocalypse, is the material cited outside the genre?

I raise these questions to help us see more clearly the variegated character of notions of revelation and to sharpen our use of the term apocalyptic.

3.6. *Summary*

The Qumranic sectarian writings make many claims to revelation and posit revealed interpretations of the Torah and prophetic eschatology as constitutive of their origins and status as the eschatological community of the righteous. At the same time, they criticize their opponents for being unenlightened and promulgating false and deceptive revelations. The choice between these two options is the difference between life and death, salvation and damnation.

4. Conclusions and Synthesis

4.1. *The Content and Function of Revelation*

4.1.1. *Interpretation of the Torah*

A revealed interpretation of Torah is central to all these texts and functions as the catalyst for the founding of the respective communities. The precise nature of the Torah varies, however. The authors of 1 Enoch deprecate, or at least ignore, the centrality of the Mosaic Torah and speak much more in the idiom of the Israelite sapiential tradition. Explicit Torah in these texts is limited to instruction about the solar calendar. Other explicit instruction about right behavior focuses on ethical rather than halakhic issues and takes the form of prophetic Woes hurled against the wicked who oppress the righteous. Jubilees celebrates the Mosaic Torah, presenting it with explicit halakhic concerns and making little use of sapiential vocabulary. Nonetheless, it celebrates Enoch as the recipient of astronomical and calendrical revelation.

For the Qumranic authors, the Mosaic Torah is central, critical and constitutive of the status as the true Israel. The solar calendar is also crucial. More than in Jubilees, they employ the sapiential metaphor of the two ways to describe obedience and disobedience to the Torah.

4.1.2. *Eschatology*

Eschatological instruction is more prominent in 1 Enoch than is legal and ethical instruction. One finds, therefore, major parts of this text expressed in prophetic forms and idiom. The precipitating cause for the writing of this literature is the conviction that the judgment is imminent. That conviction is expressed in almost every major section of 1 Enoch. These eschatological revelations, although they speak in the biblical idiom, are presented not as interpretations of the prophets but as direct revelation. Of course, the pseudo-Enochic identity of the author precludes reference to the prophets. But the point is that these authors chose not to write commentaries on the prophets, but rather to present claims of direct revelation.

In Jubilees, eschatological revelations are attributed first to the ancient testimony of Enoch. Secondarily they are attributed to Moses, albeit in a way that clearly presupposes the text of Deuteronomy. For this author, the Pentateuch is a text to be interpreted, even if he does so by positing a Mosaic revelation parallel to the Pentateuch. Thus scriptural authority and pseudonymity go hand-in-hand.

In the Qumranic sectarian writings we are drawn into the life of an identifiable community with a high eschatological consciousness. Doubtless this was fed by the revelations found in the Enochic and Danielic texts in their possession, and they may have composed interpretations of these texts (cf. 4Q180-181). Nonetheless, their eschatology is explicitly tied to an interpretation of the prophetic texts, which is given expression in the pesharim. Specific references to the Teacher of Righteousness state that his eschatological consciousness was fed by an interpretation of the sacred prophetic texts. The evident waning of interest in the Enoch texts suggested by the dating of the manuscripts is perhaps the other side of the coin.[43] Perhaps both confirm the more general fact that the prophetic texts are gaining or have gained effective canonical status in Israel.

These facts notwithstanding, we should not isolate into watertight compartments immediate apocalyptic eschatological revelation and

---

[43] On the dating of the manuscripts, see Milik, *Books of Enoch*, 5-6.

revealed interpretation of prophetic eschatology. Two texts that we
have not discussed point in this direction and may provide a bridge
between the two approaches. The author of Daniel 9 claims to have
had an epiphany of the angel Gabriel, who bases his eschatological
prediction on an interpretation of Jeremiah. In a different form with
parallel function, the author of the Testament of Moses presents a
full-blown pseudepigraphic eschatological revelation that is, in effect,
a rewriting of the last chapters of Deuteronomy.[44] It claims to be a
secret final revelation granted to Moses on the eve of his departure
but its eschatology is presented with the structure and in the vocabulary of Deuteronomy 29-33. Here, in contrast to Daniel 9, pseudepigraphic revelation shapes the text and the interpretation of Scripture
is implicit rather than explicit.

4.1.3. *The Forms and Means of Revelation*

These previous considerations warn us not to make genre the dri-
ving factor in a discussion of revelation in Jewish texts of the Greco-
Roman period. Claims of direct apocalyptic revelation are compatible with explicit reference to prophetic interpretation or its *de facto*
presence. The same applies to the interpretation of the Torah.
Jubilees has it both ways, claiming to be a revelation given by an
angel and, at the same time, alluding to the process of "searching"
the commandments and the laws, a process of which we hear more
in the Damascus Document.

Once we grant the coincidence or co-existence of direct pseudepigraphic revelation and revealed interpretation of authoritative texts,
it becomes important to ask: Why the different forms? If people like
the Searcher of the Torah and the Teacher of Righteousness were
claiming revelation for their interpretations of the Torah and the
prophets, what were the necessity, specific function, and setting of
pseudepigraphic revelations about the Torah and the Prophets?

4.1.4. *Function and Historical and Social Setting*

The authors of both the apocalyptic writings and the Qumranic
texts claim revelation in order to authenticate their self-understanding as leaders of the eschatological community of the chosen, distinct
from the rest of unenlightened Israel and, in some cases, from other

---

[44] On the Testament of Moses as a rewritten form of the last chapters of Deuteronomy, see G. W. E. Nickelsburg, *Jewish Literature*, 80-81.

groups who also authenticated their self-understanding with claims of revelation. Thus claims to revelation undergird the authority of the leaders and strengthen community identity.

The precise historical realities behind these texts remain a mystery that we strain to discern through a glass darkly. Do the accounts of the Animal Vision, the Apocalypse of Weeks, CD 1 and 5 and 1QS 8 all point to the same event or have old traditions about the founding of an eschatological community been reused to describe the formation of a new community?[45] What are the historical points of continuity between the communities that generated the Enochic texts and the Qumranic sectarian documents?[46] Common Enochic authorship of texts that successively interpret one another indicates historical channels of transmission. The centrality of Enochic revelation in the Book of Jubilees again reflects historical continuity and the presence of the Enoch materials and Jubilees at Qumran requires a historical explanation. Happily, our situation is different from so much biblical scholarship. We are not working with texts gotten from various places which have striking similarities that suggest historical continuity. Here is one of the significant aspects of the Qumran discoveries. All of this material was found together, in one place. Now we need to ask: What was the historical road that brought the Enochic and Jubilees materials to Qumran? Recent refinements in the discussion of the history of the Qumran community and its relationship to the Essenes known from other sources add another part of the broader picture. As we address ourselves to these questions, we shall flesh out a more detailed picture of the history of Second Temple Judaism.

In addition to the history of specific groups in Judaism, our texts offer a better understanding of the institutions that ordered it. I think that behind 1 Enoch we can see people called scribes and "the wise." We need to relate these to the maskilim of Daniel who also wrote pseudepigraphic apocalypses and "led many to righteousness" through their instruction in the Torah or, at least, through their religious exhortations. And what of Qumran? How does the maskil of 1QS 3 relate to the Danielic maskilim? Is the Teacher of Righteousness similar to pseudo-Enoch, the Scribe of Righteousness? Which of these people were priests? How did they function in other roles related to the priesthood?[47]

---

[45] See Tiller, "'Eternal Planting'."

[46] For some helpful distinctions, see Collins, "Pseudepigraphy."

[47] On the possible priestly identity of the Enochic writers, see B. G. Wright, "Putting the Puzzle Together: Some Suggestions Concerning the Social Location of the Wisdom of Ben Sira," *SBLSP* (1996) 133-49.

4.2 *Implications for Broader Studies*

The conclusions of this paper have implications for the broader study of Judaism and our understanding of the rise of Christianity. Here it is possible only to present a few comments and to pose some questions.

4.2.1. *Judaism in the Greco-Roman Period*

It will be useful to probe the texts contemporary to 1 Enoch, Jubilees and the Qumran documents in order to examine their expressed attitudes about revelation, whether positive or negative.

The Wisdom of Ben Sira is an interesting case in point. His description of the activity of the scribe (ch. 39) indicates important parallels to some of our texts. For him the Torah and the Prophets are the Scriptures which he "searches" (39:1, 3, 5). However, his interpretation of the Torah, cast in sapiential form, looks very different from Jubilees. His attitude toward the prophets and prophecies is complex. Though their writings are effectively canonical, he speaks of his own interpretation as pouring forth wisdom like prophecy and sees himself as a mediator of the life-giving power of the Torah (24:32-33; 39:6). How does this relate to our texts?

4.2.2. *Continuity and Discontinuity with the Persian Period*

Seeking out the continuities and discontinuities between the texts of the Greco-Roman period and the biblical books of the Persian period is one of the most important agendas to have developed from the discovery and interpretation of the Scrolls and the related study of the Apocrypha and Pseudepigrapha. Yet the surface has scarcely been scratched. Such study has important ramifications for an understanding of the ongoing history of Israel and its religion. It also has a practical aspect. Clarification of these continuities and discontinuities will help us to lay to a deservedly uneasy rest the Christian specter of a legalistic Judaism.

What are the similarities and dissimilarities between the notions of revelation we have been studying and those found in the post-exilic prophets? Some of our authors act and talk like prophets. How does this tally with their "prophetic" predecessors? What are the connections between the scribes of the hellenistic period and Ezra the Scribe? Who were the people who collected, assembled and began to interpret the texts which become Scripture and what are the implications of the activity?

Careful study of these and related issues will probably reveal more continuity from the late Persian to the hellenistic period than common scholarly wisdom, expressed in the handbooks, has allowed.

4.2.3. *Early Christianity*

All of this impinges in a fundamental way on the study of early Christianity. Into what kind of categories did John the Baptist, Jesus of Nazareth, Paul and the authors of the gospel material fit? In what respects can we discover continuity with Judaism of the Greco-Roman period? In what ways does the spectrum of early Christian attitudes about the Torah relate to the matters we have been discussing? Can we find counterparts in our texts to the New Testament's propensity to quote and cite Scripture, on the one hand, and to argue and proclaim authoritatively without reference to Scripture, on the other hand? What do we make of the parallel between: a) the revealed Enochic wisdom that constitutes the eschatological community of the chosen and is to be proclaimed to all the sons of the whole earth; and b) the early Christian self-understanding and its proclamation of the gospel to all the nations?

These issues touch the heart of much that has been written about the discontinuity between Judaism of the Greco-Roman period and both its Israelite predecessors and its Christian successors.

THE TEMPLE SCROLL AND THE HALAKHIC PSEUDEPIGRAPHA OF THE SECOND TEMPLE PERIOD

LAWRENCE H. SCHIFFMAN

New York University

1. *The Temple Scroll*

Based on Y. Yadin's preliminary lectures on the Temple Scroll shortly after its recovery in 1967,[1] M. Goshen-Gottstein wrote that the scroll represented a new form of literature which he termed a "halakhic pseudepigraphon."[2] He assumed that the author did not intend his work to function as a real substitute for the Torah. In this respect, the scroll would simply have been a work based on the canonical Torah, transmitting the author's halakhic opinions. Yadin argued against this claim by saying that the author of the Temple Scroll perceived himself as a presenter of the true law and that there was no reason to assume that he was any more bold in his literary stance than the original editors of the Pentateuch.[3] Yadin cited M. Smith, who had recently written that the Pentateuch itself was, in many ways, pseudepigraphic in character and who saw the deuteronomic code as a prime example of this phenomenon.[4] Yadin therefore concluded that to the author and the members of the Dead Sea sect, whom he assumed had accepted the authority of this scroll, it

---

[1] Cf. Y. Yadin, "The Temple Scroll," in *New Directions in Biblical Archaeology* (ed. D. N. Freedman and J. C. Greenfield; Garden City, NY: Doubleday, 1971) 156-66, which is a written form of Yadin's lecture.

[2] *Ha-Aretz*, Oct. 25, 1967. Cf. his treatment of a similar issue in "The Psalms Scroll (11 QPsa), A Problem of Canon and Text," *Textus* 5 (1966) 22-33.

[3] Y. Yadin, *The Temple Scroll* (Jerusalem: Israel Exploration Society, 1983) 1.391-92 n. 8. These views were first presented in the Hebrew edition of *The Temple Scroll* (Jerusalem: Israel Exploration Society, 1977) 1.299-300, n. 8.

[4] See M. Smith, "Pseudepigraphy in the Israelite Literary Tradition," in *Pseudepigrapha I* (Entretiens sur l'antiquité classique 18; Vandœuvres-Genève: Fondation Hardt, 1972) 191-215, and discussion, 216-27. Cf. also R. Polzin, *Moses and the Deuteronomist, A Literary Study of the Deuteronomic History* (New York: Seabury Press, 1980) 25-72, on the alternation of the divine and Mosaic voices in Deuteronomy. For a totally different approach to the speeches of Moses, see M. Weinfeld, *Deuteronomy and the Deuteronomic School* (Oxford: Oxford University Press, 1972) 10-58.

was "a veritable Torah of the Lord."[5] To Yadin this meant that the Temple Scroll had canonical status.[6]

Needless to say, no decision on these two ways of looking at the scroll can be reached without examination of the text itself, especially the manner in which the author/redactor handled the various sources he had before him and the manner in which the authors (or author/redactors) of the various sources handled their sources. This issue was already examined by Yadin in his *editio princeps* and it is worth recapitulating his basic observations and the ensuing discussion.

In characterizing the nature of the scroll, which he seems to have believed had only one author, Yadin observed that the scroll demonstrates several forms of editorial activity. These are: "drafting the text in the first person with the object of establishing that it is God Himself who is the speaker; merging commands that concern the same subject; unifying duplicate commands, including those that contradict one another; modifying and adding to the commands in order to clarify their halakhic meaning; appending whole new sections."[7] The operative assumption in this characterization is that the author began with the canonical Torah in essentially the form in which we know it, with the exception of variations in his textual substratum[8] and that, based on this text, he performed the various editorial steps described above. For the purposes of our discussion, the most important editorial strategy is the rewriting of the biblical commands so that God speaks in the first person throughout the scroll.

Yadin took the view that these grammatical changes were intended to stress that God is the speaker. He cited, as we have mentioned above, the work of Smith, who had argued that this technique was used in parts of the Pentateuch in order to transform previously existing codes into the declared word of God. Essentially, our text replaces the Tetragrammaton with the first person in many passages and phrases the supplementary sections, composed by the author, in the first person. But Yadin also noted that in entire passages the pentateuchal construction has been maintained and the Tetragrammaton appears, with God spoken about in the third person.[9]

---

[5] Yadin, *Temple Scroll*, 1.392.

[6] Yadin is closely followed by D. W. Swanson, *The Temple Scroll and the Bible, The Methodology of 11QT* (STDJ 14; Leiden: E. J. Brill, 1995) 6-7.

[7] Yadin, *Temple Scroll*, 1.71.

[8] Cf. E. Tov, "The Temple Scroll and Biblical Criticism," *EI* 16 (1981-82) 100-11 [Hebrew].

[9] Yadin, *Temple Scroll*, 1.71.

Yadin further observed that the author intended to present the law as handed down directly by God without Moses' mediation. For this reason, the author altered Deuteronomy to stress that these are God's words, not Moses'. The author did not, however, have to alter other books which mention God in the third person since, in these passages, it is clear that these are the words of God. Yadin maintained that the author is consistent in his use of this technique.[10]

This issue was taken up in great detail by B. A. Levine[11] who, like Goshen-Gottstein, saw the scroll as a "pseudepigraphic composition." Levine followed the assumption that the reformulation of biblical material in the Temple Scroll was intended to attribute the laws in the document to God himself. He recapitulated Smith's main arguments, adding that while Deuteronomy stresses Moses' mediation in its introductions and conclusions, the author of our scroll chooses instead to follow the priestly tradition according to which all laws and commandments are attributed directly to God. Moses only "bears the message." Levine sees the scroll as methodically eliminating the intermediacy of Moses. At the same time, he observes that the scroll's author also eliminated claims that God had delivered the laws of the priestly code to Moses. In general, Levine argues, as did S. A. Kaufman,[12] that the scroll's author was simply continuing or extending the biblical process. Thus, Levine agrees with Yadin that the scroll presents a new Torah and not a commentary.

In his response to Levine's long review article, Yadin objects, among other things, to Levine's position regarding the role of Moses.[13] In this article, he appears to have "nuanced" his original claims. Here he notes those passages in which, despite the fact that Moses' name does not appear, it is clear that he is addressed. In discussing the gate of Levi, "the sons of your brother Aaron" (11QT 44:5) are mentioned. In 11QT 51:5-7 God refers to the forms of uncleanness, "which I declare to you [singular] on this mountain."[14]

---

[10] Yadin, *Temple Scroll*, 1.71-2. Some exceptions are discussed by G. Brin, "The Bible in the Temple Scroll," *Shnaton* 4 (1979-80) 210-12 [Hebrew]. Cf. also M. Weinfeld, "'Temple Scroll' or 'King's Law'?," *Shnaton* 3 (1978-79) 219 [Hebrew].

[11] B. A. Levine, "The Temple Scroll: Aspects of its Historical Provenance and Literary Character," *BASOR* 232 (1978) 17-21.

[12] S. A. Kaufman, "The Temple Scroll and Higher Criticism," *HUCA* 53 (1982) 29-43.

[13] Y. Yadin, "Is the Temple Scroll a Sectarian Document?," in *Humanizing America's Iconic Book. Society of Biblical Literature Centennial Addresses: 1980* (ed. G. M. Tucker and D. A. Knight; Chico, CA: Scholars Press, 1982) 153-69, esp. 156-57. Cf. Yadin, *Temple Scroll*, 1.406-7, in the "Addenda and Corrigenda" added to the 1983 English translation.

[14] A second manuscript, 11QT[b] reads "you" (plural) but has been corrected by an erasure into a singular (Yadin, *Temple Scroll*, 2.225).

Yadin concludes that Moses is indeed being addressed by God in the scroll. Hence, in Yadin's view, the scroll must be distinguished from the apocryphal books to which Levine compared it, such as Jubilees, Enoch and others.[15] Further, Yadin emphasized that "the transposition into first person was intended to turn the whole scroll into a Torah that God reveals to Moses, and not words uttered by Moses himself." To Yadin the scroll was "for the sect a sort of second, additional Torah delivered by God to Moses on Mount Sinai, just like the Masoretic one." This Torah, in his view, was revealed only to the members of the sect. It appears that he identified this scroll with the "hidden" law of the sect, the נסתר.[16] Only in this way can we understand the title of his popular book, *The Temple Scroll, The Hidden Law of the Dead Sea Sect.*[17] We should note that Yadin never really considered this text as a substitute for the canonical Torah, no doubt because so many issues were omitted completely, for example, the prohibition of murder. This was a selective work which was never intended to replace the original on which it was based.

The debate over the nature of the Temple Scroll was joined by B. Z. Wacholder. He also argued that this was a second Torah revealed at Sinai. His views were essentially the same as Yadin's on this matter and he saw the use of the first person direct address by God as evidence for his argument. But he saw the "I-thou" syntax as borrowed from the tabernacle texts of the Torah where the "thou" is clearly Moses. In Wacholder's view the "thou" throughout the Temple Scroll is Moses.[18] The notion that the Temple Scroll is addressed to Moses and that he is to be identified as the "thou" of the scroll would presume that Moses' name would have appeared in the lost beginning of the scroll or at its conclusion, as it does in Deuteronomy. But we will have to hold this matter in abeyance while we clarify some terms.

The truth is that there is some fundamental confusion in the views surveyed above. Certain basic facts have been agreed upon but no clear terms have defined. There are several issues which must be examined. The Temple Scroll may be simply a re-redacted Torah, i.e., the author/redactor reorganized passages, eliminated duplications

---

[15] Levine, "The Temple Scroll," 20.

[16] Yadin, *Temple Scroll*, 1.392, n. 9.

[17] New York: Random House, 1985. He describes the Temple Scroll as "what both author and sect believed to be the hidden law given by God to Moses and revealed and known only to the founder of the sect and his followers" (232).

[18] B. Z. Wacholder, *The Dawn of Qumran, The Sectarian Torah and the Teacher of Righteousness* (Cincinnati: Hebrew Union College Press, 1983) 1-9.

and in some ways continued editorial activity of the kind which is usually attributed to the biblical redactors. But clearly more has been done. There is no question that Moses' name does not appear in the preserved document. Nor is there any argument about the attempt of the author/redactor to present the scroll as a direct divine revelation. What is critical is the question of whether this revelation occurred through Moses' mediation, which is certainly the case with respect to the canonical Torah, or whether Moses has been eliminated. If he has not been removed, then we may easily understand the few references which appear in the text, where the second person turns out to be an oblique reference to Moses. It is possible, however, that the author *did* intend to eliminate Moses and accidentally overlooked some of the references to him in the scroll.

To make matters worse, this issue is bound up with other problems. If the scroll were the product of one author, then it would be possible to say that even the slightest oblique reference to Moses shows that he is meant to be everywhere present, in the second person pronouns. But we know that the scroll was put together from sources.[19] It is possible that the redactor tried to eliminate Moses from these sources and accidentally allowed the oblique references to slip through. In such a case, we could easily maintain that Moses' presence, not just his name, was supposed to be effaced from the entire document.

To clarify these possibilities we must develop a useful terminology. We shall discuss Moses pseudepigrapha below. For now we presume that a Moses pseudepigraphon takes a position similar to the canonical Deuteronomy, namely that Moses received the divine word and passed it on to Israel. A Moses pseudepigraphon does not claim Moses as the actual author, any more than does the Torah, but rather as the vessel through which God revealed Himself to Israel. A text eliminating Moses even from this intermediate role could be termed a divine pseudepigraphon (or, less politely, a God pseudepigraphon) since it places God in the position of revealing Himself directly, without even the mediation of Moses described in the canonical Pentateuch. This distinction is fundamental to our discussion since it determines whether the Temple Scroll is a Moses pseudepigraphon or a divine pseudepigraphon.

---

[19] A. M. Wilson and L. Wills, "Literary Sources of the *Temple Scroll*," *HTR* 75 (1982) 275-88.

2. *The Book of Jubilees*

To clarify the discussion we shall first examine Jubilees. This work has often been compared to the Temple Scroll and the two texts do indeed have a fair number of halakhic parallels. At the beginning of the text, the Prologue, which may or my not have been part of the original book, states that the book was given to Moses, "as the Lord spoke to Moses on Mount Sinai" when he received the "tables of the law and the commandments according to the voice [command] of God." Clearly the notion is presented that this book was received by Moses at Sinai. Subsequently, at the beginning of the actual book, the story becomes more complicated. In chapter 1 God commands Moses to come up to the mountain to receive the tablets of the law "which I have written." God teaches Moses the entire book of Jubilees, which is identical with the tablets of the law and the commandments, and commands Moses to write them in a book. When Moses learns about the future of Israel, he falls on his face and is informed of Israel's ultimate repentance. God orders Moses once more to write down the book of Jubilees which He will give on the mountain. After these events, God tells the angel of the presence to write the book for Moses.[20] The angel takes the tablets and commands Moses to write the book (Jub. 2:1). In fact, Moses is commanded several times to write the book which he received orally.

J. C. VanderKam has suggested that the confusion results from an error in which the *hifʿil* of כתב was incorrectly replaced by the *qal* in the relevant passages in the Greek forerunner of Ethiopic Jubilees. The correct text would have described the angel dictating the book to Moses rather than writing it for for him. VanderKam argues that the consistent picture in this book is that Moses received the Torah from God via an angel who dictated it to him.[21] VanderKam's suggestion has been proven correct by 4Q216 to Jub. 1:27 which has להכתיב, "to dictate."[22] Throughout the book, we can see occasionally that the you (or "thou" in Wacholder's terminology) is Moses. Moses is prominent in the narrative at the time of his own birth and career (chs. 47-48). This section makes it clear that Moses is still directly addressed, that God is still speaking to Moses and that he is revealing this book to him at Sinai.

---

[20] On this contradiction, see J. C. VanderKam, "The Putative Author of the Book of Jubilees," *JSS* 26 (1981) 209-15.

[21] VanderKam, "The Putative Author," 215-17.

[22] J. C. VanderKam in *Qumran Cave 4, VIII, Parabiblical Texts, Part I* (ed. H. W. Attridge *et al.*; DJD 13: Oxford: Clarendon Press, 1994) 11-12.

Now we confront the same problem: is this a Moses pseud-epigraphon or a divine pseudepigraphon? Who does the author of Jubilees claim to be the real author, God or Moses? The matter is even more complex because an angel functions as an additional in-termediary charged with dictating to Moses. In reality, God is por-trayed revealing a book to Moses and Moses is expected to reveal this book to the children of Israel. This text is actually a pseudo-God text; Moses is never portrayed as the author, only as the recipient and bearer of revelation. This approach accords with neither of the two approaches found in the Torah. It is neither the approach of the priestly code, where Moses is bypassed and God speaks directly to the children of Israel, nor is it the deuteronomic approach, where Moses makes a speech and appears as the "author." Rather, it com-bines both elements, relegating Moses to the role of a divine mouth-piece, through the agency of an angel, while maintaining him as an intermediary.

A comparison of Jubilees to the Temple Scroll leads to a number of conclusions. We may say that the Temple Scroll as it is preserved, without Moses' name, is a divine pseudepigraphon, even if Moses appears as a recipient of revelation, since he is never presented as the author. On the other hand, we may also consider the possibility that, like Jubilees, the Temple Scroll originally had an introduction which described Moses' receiving the law from God and delivering it to Israel. In any case, the elimination of his name and of his inter-mediary role from the body of the text itself would render the entire document the revelation of God to Israel though the agency of Moses. We still would have no aspect of Mosaic composition, only of divine composition.

Before examining a number of other so-called pseudo-Moses com-positions, we should briefly consider the theological ramifications of this discussion. Both Jubilees and the Temple Scroll make the claim that, with or without the mediation of Moses, the material they con-tain was revealed directly and that it is a divine Torah. In this re-spect they are positing a one-time revelation of God to Israel at Sinai in which this text was revealed. This approach must be strongly con-trasted with that of both the Qumran sectarians and the pharisaic-rabbinic tradition. Both the sect and the Rabbis assumed that God gave a revelation of the written Torah (the canonical document) and then gave some form of commentary as well. The Pharisees speak of the traditions of the fathers which the Rabbis later understood to be divinely given at Sinai. The Qumran sectarians, however, under-stood the law to be divided into the נגלה and the נסתר, that is, the revealed written law and the hidden or supplementary sectarian law.[23] The נסתר was not revealed at Sinai but is assumed to stem from the inspired biblical exegesis of the sectarians, a notion which is very different from that of the Temple Scroll. Yadin's claim that the נסתר can include the Temple Scroll[24] is therefore impossible, because the sectarian documents embodying the נסתר evoke a totally differently theological source of authority and different assumptions about the nature and duration of divine revelation to humanity.

3. The Pseudo-Moses Texts

The entire preceding discussion must be put into the framework of an examination of the so-called pseudo-Moses texts or Moses apocrypha.[25] This material has been recently reviewed by J. Strugnell and D. Dimant in the course of publishing various Cave 4 texts. Strugnell[26] has shown that 4Q376 and 1Q29, Liturgy of the Three Tongues of Fire, constitute the same work. He further claims that 4Q375 is a third manuscript of the same text, a view which we find somewhat questionable. He sees 1Q22, Words of Moses, as a text of similar genre.

In arguing for his identification of these texts and for the possibility that Words of Moses may belong to the same text, Strugnell makes an extremely important distinction between Moses' appearance in a document *ex parte sua* and *ex parte Domini*. In Words of Moses, Moses appears on his own behalf, not on behalf of God. He goes on to say that nothing in either 4Q375 or 1Q29 = 4Q376 "excludes such a pseudonymous author" and maintains that it is appropriate to suggest that they are Moses pseudepigrapha. But here he glosses over an important consideration. Other than 1Q22, none of these texts contains an actual address to Moses. If this is the case, then, like the Temple Scroll (as it is presently preserved), these would be not Moses pseudepigrapha, in the deuteronomic style, but divine

---

[23] See L. H. Schiffman, *The Halakhah at Qumran* (SJLA 16; Leiden: E. J. Brill, 1975) 22-32; revised in *idem.*, *Halakhah and Messianism in the Qumran Sect* (Jerusalem: Merkaz Shazar, 1993) 45-53 [Hebrew].

[24] Yadin, *Temple Scroll*, 1.392, n. 9.

[25] Cf. M. R. James, *The Lost Apocrypha of the Old Testament, Their Titles and Fragments* (London: Society for Promoting Christian Knowledge; New York: Macmillan, 1920) 42-51, which deals with Moses pseudepigrapha.

[26] J. Strugnell, "Moses Pseudepigrapha at Qumran: 4Q375, 4Q376, and Similar Works," in *Archaeology and History in the Dead Sea Scrolls: The New York University Conference in Memory of Yigael Yadin* (ed. L. H. Schiffman; Journal for the Study of the Pseudepigrapha Supplement Series 8; JSOT/ASOR Monographs 2; Sheffield Academic Press, 1990), 248-54, and J. Strugnell in *Qumran Cave 4, XIV, Parabiblical Texts, Part 2* (ed. M. Broshi *et al.*; DJD 19; Oxford: Clarendon Press, 1995) 129-36.

pseudepigrapha, in the priestly style, regardless of whatever other deuteronomic features they may or may not contain.

Strugnell asks whether there was indeed a school of pseudo-Moses that created documents of this genre in antiquity. He distinguished these documents from those such as Jubilees, where Moses serves as an amanuensis for an angel, and the Temple Scroll, where Moses functions as an amanuensis for God Himself. Strugnell characterizes the Mosaic pseudepigrapha as involving a "proclamation of law" by Moses (speaking in the first person) to Israel (in the second person) or occasionally to Aaron, but not to Moses. God is usually presented in the third person singular. In this way he has defined the Moses pseudepigrapha as following in the footsteps of Deuteronomy. Hence, he describes these texts as "Pseudo-Deuteronomies" or "Deutero-Deuteronomies." Strugnell notes the presence in the Torah of texts in which the "I" is God and refers to the Temple Scroll as a "divine pseudepigraphon." He suggests that there may be ideological links between these two types of pseudepigraphical writing. He further notes that the Moses pseudepigrapha as he has defined them are not connected to the Qumran community, a fact which we have noted regarding the Temple Scroll as well. He finally concludes that the evidence is not sufficient to sustain the conclusion that an actual pseudo-Moses school generated these texts. Strugnell speculates that the pseudo-Moses texts may have been produced by the same school of pre-Qumranian Jerusalem Zadokite priests that produced the Temple Scroll.

Finally, the Moses pseudepigrapha are taken up by D. Dimant in the context of her study of 4Q390.[27] In her discussion of "Pseudo-Moses," she writes that most of the fragments of 4Q390 contain "parts of a divine discourse" which is "written in the deuteronomic style typical of the divine addresses to Moses" and has a "close affinity with a similar divine address to Moses in the first chapter of *Jubilees*."[28] She points out the differences in the works studied by Strugnell and objects to the term "Pseudo-Moses" on the grounds that these texts have nothing in common with texts such as the Testament of Moses[29] and Jubilees. She feels they should be called

---

[27] D. Dimant, "New Light from Qumran on the Jewish Pseudepigrapha—4Q390," in *The Madrid Qumran Congress: Proceedings of the International Congress on the Dead Sea Scrolls, Madrid 18-21 March, 1991* (ed. J. Trebolle Barrera and L. Vegas Montaner; STDJ 11; Leiden: E. J. Brill, 1992) 2.405-47.

[28] Dimant, "New Light from Qumran," 409-10.

[29] See J. Priest, "Testament of Moses," in *The Old Testament Pseudepigrapha* (ed. J. H. Charlesworth; Garden City, NY: Doubleday, 1983) 1.919-34. Preserved in a Latin palimpsest from the sixth century, the document dates from somewhere between the second century BCE and the second century CE, with recent opinion

Moses apocrypha and that they are really pieces of rewritten Torah resembling the Temple Scroll.[30] On the other hand, she considers 2Q21, Apocryphon of Moses,[31] written in a third person narrative style, to be closer to her text. We should note that in this text God appears to speak in the first person, so that Moses' actions and words are described in the third person.

In general, Dimant seems to see the issue of narrative style as the key to identifying a Moses pseudepigraphon. We should note that the fragments she has published of 4Q390 never mention Moses although it is likely that he is being addressed by God in the text.[32] She emphasizes that this text describes the direct speech of God, addressed to Moses and modeled on the deuteronomic addresses to Moses. Indeed, the task of the addressee is to receive the divine commandments and to transmit them to Israel; in the same way, Moses is lawgiver and mediator of the divine message to Israel. In her view, one fragment, 4Q389 2 1-9, contains a direct speech of Moses himself. She compares this material to Jubilees 1, however, claiming that there we also have "pseudepigraphic divine speech addressed to Moses." This lends further support to the view that Moses is the addressee in 4Q390. Dimant states that the Temple Scroll was "certainly written as a divine address to Moses," a matter about which we have seen there is considerable controversy. She has no problem, therefore, in terming the Temple Scroll a Moses pseudepigraphon with halakhic rather than apocalyptic content.

4. *Conclusion*

The material we have surveyed here and the analysis of the views of various scholars enable us to set down some clear criteria for distinguishing a Moses pseudepigraphon from a divine pseudepigraphon. We may say at the outset that the contents of the text are not at stake. Deuteronomic content will not place a text in the class of Moses pseudepigrapha. We must distinguish three classes of material:

1   divine pseudepigrapha in which God speaks directly to Israel with no intermediary, as in the priestly code,
2   divine pseudepigrapha in which an intermediary appears, usually Moses cast as a mere amanuensis, as in the book of Jubilees,

---

tending toward a date during the Maccabean Revolt. The text is essentially a rewriting of Deuteronomy 31-34. Moses appears here as a mediator.

[30] Dimant, "New Light from Qumran," 410, n. 18.

[31] M. Baillet in *Les "Petites Grottes" de Qumrân* (ed. M. Baillet *et al.*; DJD 3; Oxford: Clarendon Press, 1962) 79-81.

[32] Dimant, "New Light from Qumran," 421, to ll. 3-4.

3 Moses pseudepigrapha, in which Moses appears as a full partner, so-to-speak, speaking for himself even while teaching the word of God, as in Deuteronomy and the Testament of Moses.

Concerning the Temple Scroll we reach the following conclusions: Certainly, the scroll is not a Moses pseudepigraphon as it does not allow Moses his own voice anywhere in the scroll. If he appears at all, it is in the second person, as the oblique addressee. It is possible that in the complete scroll, he appeared in the third person as the bearer of the divine message in the introduction (or prologue) and perhaps in a concluding section. If so, then the scroll would constitute a divine pseudepigraphon with Moses acting as an intermediary. While this is the case in Jubilees, where Moses' role is sprinkled throughout the text, in the Temple Scroll he does not appear in the body of the document except obliquely.

Either form of a divine pseudepigraphon with which we might identify the Temple Scroll implies the notion of direct divine revelation as it appears in the priestly code. Indeed, we may say that much of the literary activity of the author/redactor was directed at converting deuteronomic material to this priestly form, in order to present the entire text as direct revelation, possibly with Moses as a mouthpiece. The Temple Scroll, therefore, has little in common with 1Q22 Words of Moses in which Moses is directly addressed by God and then delivers a speech in which he instructs the people regarding the observance of the law. 1Q29 = 4Q376 Apocryphon of Moses[b?] never mentions Moses at all and so it resembles the Temple Scroll to some extent. Its fragmentary state does not allow us to determine if it is a divine pseudepigraphon, with or without the mediation of Moses, or a Moses pseudepigraphon. 4Q375 Apocryphon of Moses[a] is so deuteronomic in content that it is reasonable to assume that it was originally a Moses pseudepigraphon; the preserved material never mentions his name, however. Concerning 2Q21 Apocryphon of Moses (?) we may note that it resembles the Temple Scroll only insofar as God speaks in the first person but the appearance of Moses distinguishes it from the scroll. Finally, 4Q390 Pseudo-Moses, which also does not mention Moses at all, may be a text related to Moses, like Jubilees, but is best labeled a divine pseudepigraphon, with the possible mediation of Moses, and not a Moses pseudepigraphon.

In essence, then, the Temple Scroll stands alone in its literary character, at least in its present form. It is clearly a divine halakhic pseudepigraphon and only a true *deus ex machina* would ever allow us to know if it was delivered through the mediation of Moses or directly to the people of Israel.

THE AXIS OF HISTORY AT QUMRAN*

MICHAEL E. STONE

Hebrew University of Jerusalem

The present paper presents a series of observations arising from the consideration of which Pseudepigrapha occur at Qumran. The first point made is the existence of what we have called "the priestly-Noachic tradition." This traces the priestly teaching back from the Aaronic priests through Abraham to Noah. Next, Noah's role as a "bridge" over the flood is considered and his consequent transmission of antediluvian teachings. This leads us to broach the issue of the origin of evil and, consequently, the causes of the flood. The sectarians found this in the myths about Enoch, the Watchers, the giants and the consequent events.

This Enochic explanation of the origin of evil contrasts with that which relates it to Adam's sin. Adam apocrypha and legendary developments of the Adam stories are strikingly absent from Qumran, while there are many works associated with the axis from Enoch to Noah. The final part of the present paper discusses, therefore, the implications of the complementary distribution of these two ways of explaining evil. What did the world feel like when evil was attributed to angelic and demonic intervention rather than to human actions?

The Priestly-Noachic Tradition

"The following were the sons of Levi, by their names: Gerson, Kohath, and Merari.... The sons of Kohath by their clans: Amram, Izhar, Hebron and Uzziel" (Num. 3:17-19 RSV). Qahat, then, was the second son of Levi and the father of Amram, the father of Moses and Aaron (Exod. 6:18, Num. 3:19, etc.). Thus, Qahat forms a link in the priestly line that descended from Levi, through Amram, to Aaron.

The Aramaic Levi Document was apparently composed in the third century BCE. Seven copies of it have been found at Qumran, supplementing a fragmentary manuscript from the Cairo Geniza and some Greek extracts from Mount Athos. According to Aramaic Levi §§67-68, Qahat is exalted: he was born on the first day of the first month, at the rising of the sun. This is a particularly significant date according to the solar calendar (§68). Some, but not all, scholars have

* Research for this paper was supported by the Israel Science Foundation.

maintained that according to the solar calendar, the day started in the morning. Even if this is not the case, the daily order of sacrifices in the Temple began in the morning. Qahat is born on the morning of the first day of the year. This is a portentous beginning! Aramaic Levi §§66-67 relates the naming of Qahat in the following way: "[And I cal]led his name [Qahat and I sa]w that he would have an assembly of all the people and that he would have the high priesthood for Israel" ‏[וקרא]תי שמה]קהת [(67) וחזית]י די לה תהו]ה בנשת כל] עמא וד]י לה‎ ‏תהוה כהנותא רבתא] לכל יש[ראל‎. This is clearly a midrash on the name Qahat, which the author relates to the expression ‏ולו יקהת עמים‎ in the Blessing of Jacob in Gen. 49:10. The author of Aramaic Levi takes the strange word ‏יקהת‎ in Gen. 49:10 to be connected with the name Qahat. He explains the name Qahat by the meaning "assembly." This meaning is attested for the word ‏יקהת‎ in Gen. 49:10 by Aquila's translation σύστημα λαῶν and 4QPatr Bless] ‏בנשת אנשי‎, as well as by Midrash Bereshit Rabbah 99 (Theodor-Albeck, 1280 and note). Bereshit Rabbah explains ‏יקהת‎ as ‏מי שאומות עולם מתקהלים אליו‎ "he to whom nations of the world gather." The influence of Gen. 49:10 on Aramaic Levi §67 extends beyond the meaning of ‏יקהת‎. The explanation continues ‏עמא] כל‎ "all [the people" which also derives from the word "peoples" Gen. 49:10.

The Athos Greek text of Aramaic Levi §67 differs from the surviving Aramaic manuscripts in a number of readings. One is an additional phrase following the words ἡ ἀρχιεροσύνη ἡ μεγάλη "the great high priesthood" which corresponds to ‏כהנותא רבתא‎ "the high priesthood." This additional phrase is αὐτὸς καὶ τὸ σπέρμα αὐτοῦ ἔσονται ἀρχὴ βασιλέων ἱεράτευμα τῷ Ἰσραήλ "he and his seed will be an authority of kings, a priesthood for Israel." The expression ἀρχὴ βασιλέων probably means "authority of kings," though it could mean "beginning of kings." In either case, the phrase indicates that Qahat will have both royal and priestly attributes. It calls him "chief of kings" and ἱεράτευμα "priesthood," while the preceding phrase attributes to him ἡ ἀρχιεροσύνη ἡ μεγάλη "the great high priesthood." His line stands as the ἀρχή both of kings and priests. This is an extraordinary prediction, although its possible Hasmonean reference is precluded by the dating of the oldest Qumran manuscripts of the work.

The combination of royal and priestly language, however, is not unique to Aramaic Levi §67. In a similar vein, TLevi 11:6 gives a

---

[1] On this translation, see H. W. Hollander and M. de Jonge, *The Testaments of the Twelve Patriarchs: a Commentary* (Studia in Veteris Testamenti Pseudepigrapha 8; Leiden: E. J. Brill, 1985) 163. M. de Jonge discusses the relationship between Aramaic Levi and Greek Testament of Levi in "The Testament of Levi and 'Aramaic Levi'," *RevQ* 13 (1988) 376-85 and in his paper in the present volume.

name midrash for Qahat: "the first place of majesty and instruction" ὅ
ἔστιν ἀρχὴ μεγαλείου καὶ συμβιβασμός).[1] As in Aramaic Levi, both
royal and priestly aspects of Qahat are stressed by this name midrash,
for the "instruction" surely is the priestly duty of instruction that is
prominent in Deut. 33:8-11. This combination of the royal and the
sacerdotal was, of course, highlighted by the very application of Gen.
49:10 to Qahat in Aramaic Levi §67. After all, in Gen. 49:10, the
Blessing of Jacob, the ולו יקהת עמים was not pronounced over Levi at
all but over Judah, and the rest of Gen. 49:10 has clear royal associations. The whole section reads: לא יסור שבט מיהודה ומחקק מבין
רגליו, עד כי יבא שלה ולו יקהת עמים. RSV translates this difficult verse
as follows: "The scepter shall not depart from Judah, nor the ruler's
staff from between his feet, until tribute comes to him; and the obedience of the peoples is his." Aramaic Levi applies this verse, which was
originally directed to Judah and has unmistakable royal associations,
to Qahat who is clearly a link in the line of priestly descent.

The same combination of royal and priestly attributes occurs in
another fragment of Aramaic Levi from Cave 1 (1Q21). In that fragment we read: ב]ניך מלכות כהנותא רבא מן מלכות] "your [so]ns, kingdom of the priesthood is greater than the kingdom[." The context of
this phrase is lost, but it explicitly refers to a royal dimension, "the
kingdom," of the high priesthood and proclaims its superiority over
some other kingdom.[2] A similar expression occurs in 4QLevi[a] ar,
fragment 2, where we read, again in a fragmentary context, אף כהנין
ומלכין "also priests and kings" and then, in the next line, מלכותכן
"your kingdom."[3] The passage is Levi's exhortation directed to his
children, as the second person plural indicates. Again we observe the
same reference to the royal aspect of the priesthood, even though
the larger context has perished. Thus Aramaic Levi presents Qahat
as a central figure, a father of the high-priestly line, who will incor-
porate royal attributes in his priestly character. This is a very distinctive conception.

Four fragments of 4Q542 survive, and most scholars speak of
4Q542 as a "farewell address." In fact, strictly speaking, the surviving text only indicates that it is an exhortation. Since the speaker
mentions both "Amram my son" and "Levi my father," he is clearly
Qahat. Therefore 4Q542 has been styled "Testament of Qahat."[4]

---

[2] The use of מלכות "kingdom" leads one to think that this small fragment may
have preceded the material in Bodleian col. a. That passage compares a number of
contrasting "kingdoms." More cannot be added about the context than that.

[3] Given the fragmentary context, no reconstruction can be suggested.

[4] The first full edition of the manuscript is by E. Puech, "Le testament de Qahat
en araméen de la Grotte 4 (4QTQah)," *RevQ* 15 (1988) 23-54.

The first part of the text stresses the transmission of teaching from Abraham through Isaac, Jacob, Levi and Qahat to Amram, as well as an "inheritance" which the addressees received from their fathers and which they are to transmit to further generations.[5] In col. ii, this inheritance is specifically said to be "books," apparently books of priestly teaching. In the course of the second column, as well, the speech to "my sons" in general becomes directed specifically towards "Amram my son." So the fragments of Testament of Qahat, then, are concerned with the transmission of priestly teaching. Like similar "genealogies" of apocalyptic teaching, such as 4 Ezra 3:14, 12:35-39, 14. and 2 Enoch 22:11-23, 33:8-12, 47-48, they authenticate and authorize the tradition current at the author's time. Moreover, as in the case of certain pseudepigraphic apocalypses, the Qahat work may not be a *creatio ex nihilo*, but may reflect crystallization of traditions cultivated in a real social context. Of course, this cannot be demonstrated but the continuity of the tradition over generations can. The transmission of books of priestly teaching is central to the Testament of Qahat but the surviving fragments preserve no hints of the royal dimension of the priesthood. As we will demonstrate, the transmission of teaching is also a major theme of Aramaic Levi which knows both the priestly and the royal contexts and derives it from a Book of Noah.

The Noachic Genealogy

The Book of Jubilees similarly emphasizes the line of descent of teaching from antiquity. Jubilees chiefly stresses transmission from the antediluvian generations (7:38-39, 10:14; 21:10). In Jub. 21:10, moreover, Abraham concludes a catalogue of detailed sacrificial halachot that he has given Isaac by saying, "Because thus I have found written in the books of my forefathers and in the words of Enoch and in the words of Noah." Jubilees' introduction of Enoch into the teaching's genealogy is notable and the mention of Noah evokes

---

[5] It should be observed that 4QPseudo-Daniel[c] contains two fragmentary lists, one of high priests and the other of kings. The high priestly list (fragment 1) starts with Levi (or earlier, the line is broken) and continues down to Jonathan and Simeon the Hasmoneans. The royal list follows in the same fragment, but it is a torso. A small fragment of 4QPseudo-Daniel[a] is apparently part of the same list (fragment 28). These lists are discussed by J. J. Collins and P. W. Flint in DJD 22.157-58 and the texts are published in the same volume. See also J. J. Collins, "Pseudo-Daniel Revisited," *RevQ* 17 (1996) 111-35, especially 112. The priestly list reflects a concern for priestly genealogy analogous to, but different from, that discussed here. Moreover, the conjunction of the priestly and royal names, with the priestly preceding, is intriguing in light of the evidence adduced by us.

Aramaic Levi, a work discussed below. Even more significant than the introduction of Enoch is the priestly character of the transmitted teaching, thus strikingly resembling the Testament of Qahat and, as we shall see, Aramaic Levi.

Let us consider for a moment this line of descent and transmission which is set forth in 4QTestQahat and Jubilees 21. Except for the single manuscript from Cave 4, no other traces of the Testament of Qahat have been found at Qumran or elsewhere. Nonetheless, Testament of Qahat stresses a cardinal point, the descent of priestly teaching from Abraham and eventually, according to Aramaic Levi, from Noah. The same idea is to be found in works that circulated more widely. One of the main issues in Aramaic Levi is the investiture of Levi as priest and the transmission to him of the priestly teaching about the sacrificial cult. Levi, having been invested and anointed, is taught by Isaac (§§12-13):וכדי ידע די אנא כהין לאל עליון למראי שמיא שארי לפקדה ולאלפא יתי דין כהנותא "When he learned (realized?) that I was priest of the Most High God, of the Lord of Heaven, he began to instruct and to teach me the law of priesthood."

Levi's lessons are very substantial for they continue from §14 to §57. They deal in some detail with the preparation of the sacrifices, the wood of the altar and the elements that constitute each offering—the salt, the meal and so forth. At the end of Isaac's instruction about sacrificial cult we read, in text surviving only in Greek, οὕτως γάρ μοι ἐνετείλατο ὁ πατήρ μου Ἀβραάμ, ὅτι οὕτως εὗρεν ἐν τῇ γραφῇ τῆς βίβλου τοῦ Νῶε περὶ τοῦ αἵματος. "For thus my father Abraham instructed me, for thus he found in the writing of the Book of Noah[6] περὶ τοῦ αἵματος" (§57). The last phrase is ambiguous.[7] The title of the book might have been "The Book of Noah Concerning the Blood." It could have borne this name because God first gave the commandment about the blood to Noah, which will be discussed below. On the other hand, the ambiguous Greek might be translated "for thus he found concerning the blood in the writing of the Book of Noah." The words "concerning the blood" could, in this case, refer back to the subject of the instructions that had just been given.

---

[6] In a recently deciphered fragment of the Genesis Apocryphon the words כתב מלי נח are to be found. See R. C. Steiner, "The Heading of the Book of the Words of Noah on a Fragment of the Genesis Apocryphon: New Light on a 'Lost' Work," *DSD* 2.1 (1995) 66-71. For recent discussions of the Book of Noah, see F. García Martínez, *Qumran and Apocalyptic: Studies on the Aramaic Texts from Qumran* (Studies on the Texts of the Desert of Judah 9; Leiden: E. J. Brill, 1992) 1-44; M. E. Stone, "Noah, Books of," *Encyclopedia of the Dead Sea Scrolls* (forthcoming).

[7] The phrase survives only in Greek.

In either case, the teaching about sacrifices comes from ancient times and is connected with Noah both in Jubilees 21 and in Aramaic Levi §57. One is moved to ask why it is thus related to Noah. Considering that Levi was the eponymous ancestor of the priests, the attribution of the tradition of priestly learning and instruction to him should have sufficed to guarantee its authenticity. If Levi were not enough, then the connection to Abraham, the originator of belief in one God and "father of all believers," should have been adequate. Why was Noah introduced?

The writers of the three sequential Pseudepigrapha found in the Qumran caves and attributed to the ancestors of the Levites, viz., Aramaic Levi, Testament of Qahat and Visions of Amram,[8] obviously found it very important that the priestly tradition they enfolded be rooted in remote antiquity.[9] The specific connection of this tradition with Noah might be explained by the following. According to Gen. 8:20 Noah offers the first animal sacrifice. Gen. 9:4, in the following pericope, relates how he received the commandment about the blood.[10] Thus, Noah's connection to the sacrificial cult and to instructions concerning it was not by chance. The question remains, of course, whether a "Book of Noah (concerning the Blood)" actually existed, or whether Aramaic Levi invented this title to enhance the authority of the priestly tradition it was promoting.

The name "Book of Noah concerning the Blood" (if indeed this is the way it is to be parsed) fits in with a number of other pieces of evidence which relate to Noah and to a Book or Books of Noah:

a) One Hebrew scroll from Cave 1 at Qumran (1Q19) is known as "Book of Noah." Although this is a modern title, it was assigned because some fragments of 1Q19 do resemble parts of 1 Enoch that deal with Noah or that have been attributed by scholars to a Book of Noah.[11] 1 Enoch, however, was composed in Aramaic, while 1Q19 was written in Hebrew. Presumably, one language or the other must have been original to the Book of Noah, perhaps Aramaic. Indeed,

---

[8] The initial publication of some Amram fragments of this work is J. T. Milik, "4Q Visions de 'Amram et une citation d'Origène," *RB* 79 (1972) 77-97.

[9] We are not in a position at the moment to trace the exact relationship between these three works, except to say that Aramaic Levi is clearly the oldest. Whether the Amram and Qahat works were sectarian compositions or not remains unclear. Their Aramaic language weighs against it but is not completely decisive.

[10] With the exception of Abel's offering in Gen. 4:4, which has no continuation in the subsequent antediluvian generations.

[11] Fragments 2-3 deal with Noah's birth (parallel to 1 Enoch 106-107), while fragment 1 seems to have connections with the flood story and thus, perhaps, with 1 Enoch 8:4-9:4. The remaining fragments of 1Q19, however, do not seem to have any recognizable relationship to material connected with Noah and Enoch.

we cannot actually determine whether 1Q19 was a "Book of Noah" or another work embodying Noachic material. Certain fragments of 1Q19 exhibit a striking relationship with Noachic material but a number of other fragments of this scroll bear no evident relationship to anything known to us connected with Noah.

b) The Genesis Apocryphon devotes 15 columns to Noah. First, in cols. 2-5, it deals with Noah's birth from the viewpoint of his father Lamech. Next, col. 5, line 29, contains the expression "Book of the Words of Noah." There follows a first person narrative set in Noah's mouth and apparently attributed to the "Book of the Words of Noah" which continues to col. 17.[12] It might be an extract from or a summary of a Book of Noah, though this can only be determined after the full analysis of the rest of the fragments and perhaps not even then.[13]

c) Jub. 10:1-14 relates an angelic revelation to Noah about illness and demons, and concludes, "And Noah wrote down everything in a book, as we instructed him … [a]nd he gave everything he had written to Shem, his eldest son" (10:13-14). The demonological material is connected with Noah because of the idea that the giants, offspring of the Watchers and the daughters of men (Gen. 6:1 and 1 Enoch 6), were drowned in the flood and their spirits became demons. On literary grounds Jubilees 10:1-14 seems to be a discrete unit of text. Did it come from a Book of Noah?[14]

d) Scholars have attributed a number of other parts of 1 Enoch and Jubilees, with greater or lesser plausibility, to a Noachic source. We consider the following to be the strongest candidates: 1 Enoch 60, 65-69:25; 106-107.[15] An extensive development of Noachic traditions is to be observed in 2 Enoch 71-72 which rewrites the story of Noah's birth, transferring the special traditions to Melkizedek. This is, however, not in itself evidence for a literary work attributed to Noah.[16]

---

[12] Steiner, "The Heading of the *Book of the Words of Noah*," 66-71.

[13] The disproportion between the Noah material and the other parts of the Genesis Apocryphon may be less striking if M. Morgenstern's view of the length of the scroll is accepted. See: M. Morgenstern, "A New Clue to the Original Length of the Genesis Apocryphon," *JJS* 67.2 (1996) 345-47. Further Noachic fragments of the Genesis Apocryphon have been published by J. C. Greenfield and E. Qimron, "The Genesis Apocryphon Col. XII," *Abr-Nahrain Supplement* 3 (1992) 70-77; M. Morgenstern, E. Qimron and D. Sivan, "The Hitherto Unpublished Columns of the Genesis Apocryphon," *Abr-Nahrain* 33 (1995) 30-52.

[14] "The Words of Noah" are also mentioned in Jub. 21:10 which has been discussed above.

[15] Noachic teaching is transmitted in Jub. 7:20-39 and that is dependent in some fashion on 1 Enoch 6-11:1.

[16] An Aramaic text entitled 4QElect of God (4Q534) contains some physiognomic details, followed by information about the life of its hero. He will acquire wisdom with the knowledge of three books. Because of apparent references to the flood in

From these hints and references we can speculate with some plausibility that a Book or Books of Noah may have existed which dealt at least with three topics: (1) the birth of Noah ("Book of the Words of Noah"); (2) the sacrificial instructions ("Book of Noah Concerning the Blood"); and (3) medicine and demonology ("Book of Noah"). Whether these three topics were included in a single writing or in a number of different compositions cannot be determined.[17] What is significant for the present discussion is that Noah is singled out as the source of teachings about sacrifice and about medicine. It might be remarked that Jubilees 21:10 alone relates these traditions as far back as Enoch, rather than "just" to Noah. In other words, it has assimilated priestly teaching to other esoteric traditions known to it.[18] Thus, from our present perspective, Jubilees may have transferred the genealogy of other esoteric traditions to the priestly. Very little reason can be discerned to tie Enoch to the revelation of sacrificial halachot.

Later Jewish literature lays a similar stress on the transmission of special knowledge through the "Book of Noah." *Sefer 'Asaf ha-Rofe* "The Book of Asaph the Physician," a Jewish medieval medical work commences: "This is the book of remedies which ancient sages copied from the book of Shem b. Noah, which was transmitted to Noah on Mount Lubar, one of the mountains of Ararat, after the Flood." This material is drawn from the tenth chapter of Jubilees which we mentioned above and is, of course, also attributed to Noah in Jubilees. It has not yet been determined how this material reached the medieval author but its origin is indubitable.

Another such document is the somewhat older *Sefer ha-Razim* "Book of Mysteries," a Jewish magical book composed during the first millennium.[19] Its superscription traces the transmission of esoteric knowledge which originates with Adam and is transmitted by

---

col. ii, it has often been thought to be a horoscope of Noah. The matter cannot be regarded as settled. One of the most recent contributions to this debate is García Martínez, *Qumran and Apocalyptic*, 1-44. He surveys the evidence for the existence of a Book of Noah and the interpretation of 4QElect of God.

[17] Indeed, it is quite possible that some or all of these topics were not part of a discrete Book of Noah but were included in a broader or differently focused retelling(s) of the Genesis stories.

[18] E. G. Chazon remarks, "Perhaps the way 4Q265 (and the similar material in Jubilees) incorporates purity material into the Eden story (see below) could be linked to the attribution of priestly tradition to Adam." She has been kind enough to read this paper and has made this and a number of other pertinent observations.

[19] For an English translation see M. Morgan, *Sepher Ha-Razim: The Book of Mysteries* (Pseudepigrapha Series 11; SBL Texts and Translations 25; Chico, CA: Scholars, 1983).

Noah. Noah's connection with the antediluvian esoteric knowledge fits with his role as a "bridge" over the rupture of the flood.[20]

Noah is the object of very substantial concern and he plays a special role as the originator of sacrificial instruction. Noah is a second Adam and the founder of postdiluvian humanity. Conjunctions and disjunctions with the antediluvian period are stressed – the continuity of the tradition, the new order of the world and the shortened lives, as well as the origins of the demons from the giants. The sudden clustering of works around Noah indicates that he was seen as a pivotal figure in the history of humanity, as both an end and a beginning.

In short, we find three works at Qumran connected with three priestly descendants, the first and oldest of which with Levi. Aramaic Levi attributes its priestly teaching to Noah, though it is not certain that a Book of Noah existed which contained this teaching. In any case, the Noah traditions are ancient. This teaching relates above all to the sacrificial cult, the special prerogative of the priests and is rooted in Noah as the initiator of sacrificial cult. Therefore, in effect, this procedure incorporates Noah into the priestly genealogy. Consequently, the function of the Amram, Qahat and Levi works is to undergird the priestly teaching. The introduction of Noah draws attention to his pivotal role as a bridge over the Flood. He is a second Adam for the new, postdiluvian world order.[21]

The Priestly-Noah Tradition in the Qumran Library

The character of the pseudepigraphic books found at Qumran does not differ greatly from that of the Pseudepigrapha transmitted by the various Christian Churches. As distinct from the sectarian books proper, which are new both in genre and in content, the Qumran finds of Pseudepigrapha are important precisely because they link up

---

[20] Other such "bridges" existed, such as the antediluvian stelae discovered after the flood; we find this legend in a range of forms and sources, from Jubilees through Josephus and on into Jewish and Christian apocrypha. See M. E. Stone, *Armenian Apocrypha Relating to Adam and Eve* (Studia in Veteris Testamenti Pseudepigrapha 12; Leiden: E. J. Brill, 1996) 151 and 198. The stelae tradition is also to be found in J. Malalas, *Chronographia* (ed. L. Dindorf; Bonn, 1831) 6, lines 7-18 (*Anonymi Chronologia*).

[21] This understanding of Noah is prominent in 4 Ezra 3. Adam and Noah themes are drawn together in the Paraphrase of Genesis and Exodus and Dibre Hamme'orot, col. 1: see E. G. Chazon, "The Creation and Fall of Adam in the Dead Sea Scrolls," in *The Book of Genesis in Jewish and Oriental Christian Interpretation: Reworked versions of papers read at a symposium held in May 1995 in Jerusalem* (eds. J. Frischman and L. Van Rompay; Leuven: Peeters Press, 1997) 13-24.

with the material transmitted through other channels and enrich known literary types. In a sense, this reasoning is circular. Qumran Pseudepigrapha contribute "more of the same," precisely because they are defined by their being "much the same" as the Pseudepigrapha transmitted in other channels.[22] Their significance lies in the very substantial addition they make to our knowledge about Judaism in that ancient period.

There are other genres, some allied with those found in the Pseudepigrapha and others rather different from them, which also enrich our knowledge of Jewish Pseudepigrapha in the period of the Second Temple. These exhortations and parabiblical books, testimony books, pesharim, hymns, prayers and commentaries all cast light on the Pseudepigrapha. By setting the new pseudepigrahic writings in this double context, that of known Pseudepigrapha and that of other contemporary writings, many new insights are gained. As books, however, the Pseudepigrapha from Qumran are Pseudepigrapha (this is *ex definitione* the case). They are, moreover, exceedingly important.

In studying the Qumran library one is struck by differences in the distribution and frequency of occurrence of various books. Because many documents from the Dead Sea Scrolls have not yet been published, many others are extremely fragmentary, and some have not survived at all, it is difficult to make absolutely certain statements about what existed and what didn't. Some indications may be gained, however. Neither Baruch nor Ezra, both of whom formed lodestones for many pseudepigraphical writings, seems to have played a major role in the manuscripts discovered in the Judean Desert. Judith is not there, nor Maccabees (of course!); of the twelve sons of Jacob, we have material definitely associated only with Levi and Naphtali, and those texts are not identical by any means with the Testaments of the Twelve Patriarchs.[23]

There seem to have been a number of pseudo-Mosaic writings at Qumran but there is no evidence of the Assumption or Testament of

---

[22] We are, of course, conscious of the problems inherent in the term "Pseudepigrapha" and the debates surrounding its denotation. See M. E. Stone, "Categorization and Classification of the Apocrypha and Pseudepigrapha," *Abr-Nahrain* 24 (1986) 167-177; M. E. Stone and R. A. Kraft, reviews of J. H. Charlesworth, *Old Testament Pseudepigrapha* in *RSR* 14.2 (1988) 111ff.

[23] The importance of this fact for the ongoing debate over the Jewish or Christian character of the Testaments of the Twelve Patriarchs is considerable. J. T. Milik has claimed to have found fragments of Judah and Joseph texts as well, but this has been challenged. See H. W. Hollander and M. de Jonge, *Testaments of the Twelve Patriarchs*, 17, 29.

Moses.[24] There are also, it seems, no apocrypha of Job (a Targum exists) or Psalms of Solomon. We would not expect to find many fragments of Jewish works composed in Greek, and this is indeed the case.[25] Although some Solomon traditions, some Daniel ones, and some others are found, the range of previously known Pseudepigrapha preserved at Qumran is rather limited, particularly when viewed from the perspective of the Pseudepigrapha in general.[26]

We have discussed the Pseudepigrapha from Qumran which relate the priestly teaching to Noah, observing Noah's role as "bridge" between the ante- and postdiluvian worlds. Consequently, it is intriguing to ask about Qumran pseudepigrapha bearing on the antediluvian and diluvian periods. Which works occur in many copies and which in few? How does this pattern of distribution relate to the sectarian understanding of history?

The combination of sources we presented above, in which we traced the priestly traditions from Noah down to Aaron, would have been impossible without the Qumran finds. The new manuscripts have made available to us many completely unknown works, or works known previously by title alone. As far as the Pseudepigrapha are concerned, Qumran enriches our knowledge of the texts and provides a great quantity of new data. Once this data is integrated with what we already know, it will enable us to present a more textured and fuller picture of the Judaism of the Second Temple period as expressed in the Pseudepigrapha.

Yet I find myself struck by the fact that the Pseudepigrapha and the pseudepigraphic traditions mentioned above—and these are among the most prominent at Qumran—do not include a series of books found among the received Pseudepigrapha. Except for the texts studied by J. M. Baumgarten (4Q265) and E. G. Chazon (see below), few

---

[24] See the long note by John Strugnell in DJD 19.131-36; see also *idem.* "Moses-Pseudepigrapha at Qumran: 4Q375, 4Q376 and Similar Works," in *Archeology and History in the Dead Sea Scrolls: The New York University Conference in Memory of Yigael Yadin* (ed. L. H. Schiffman; JSP Supplement 8; JSOT/ASOR Monographs 2; Sheffield; JSOT Press, 1990) 221-56. Some observations on Strugnell's view were made by M. Morgenstern, "Language and Literature in the Second Temple Period," *JJS* 47.3 (1997) 141-42. On the Testament of Moses, see most recently J. Tromp, *The Assumption of Moses: A Critical Edition with Commentary* (Studia in Veteris Testamenti Pseudepigrapha 10; Leiden: E. J. Brill, 1993).

[25] In Cave 7 a number of Greek manuscripts have been discovered including what are evidently Greek fragments of Enoch and of Epistle of Jeremiah.

[26] A more detailed discussion of the range of Pseudepigrapha at Qumran and their relationship to the pseudepigrapha in general is to be found in the writer's paper: "The Dead Sea Scrolls and the Pseudepigrapha," *DSD* 3.3 (1996) 270-96. There the Pseudo-Ezekiel works, a major corpus at Qumran, are discussed and the relevant bibliography is given.

texts deal with Adam. Even 4Q265 is halachic and the Adam material in it is close to Jubilees. "Exposition on the Patriarchs" (4Q464) contains some traditions about creation, but none about Adam.[27] Chazon has drawn attention to traditions about the creation and fall of Adam in three apparently non-sectarian works, Dibre Hamme'orot, Paraphrase of Genesis and Exodus, and Sapiental Work A.[28] Although these works share some exegetical tradition, they have no legendary expansions and variations of the biblical narrative such as may be observed in the primary Adam books. Their most distinctive tradition is the drawing together of the Adam and Flood narratives by the use of terminology.[29] Viewed from the perspective of the primary Adam books, however, the material analyzed by Chazon is remarkable for its lack of legendary expansion and reworking.[30] Legendary Adam texts seem to be rare or non-existent.[31] As we shall see below, this is no small matter, but indeed very significant.

In contrast to this situation, the frequency of occurrence of those works which were preserved among the Dead Sea Scrolls is very striking. The incident of the Watchers and the daughters of men (Gen. 6:1 ff.), and the Enochic traditions associated with it, seem to have been very important to the sect. The number of copies of 1 Enoch (6), of Jubilees (15) and of the Book of the Giants (8) is re-

---

[27] M. E. Stone and E. Eshel, "An Exposition on the Patriarchs (4Q464) and Two Other Documents (4Q464ᵃ and 4Q464ᵇ)" *Le Muséon* 105 (1992) frg. 3, col. 1:7-9 and comments there. See also DJD 19.215-30.

[28] Chazon, "The Creation and Fall of Adam."

[29] Chazon justly comments, "In both Dibre Hamme'orot and Paraphrase of Genesis and Exodus this [i.e., the drawing together of the Adam and Flood narratives] highlights the sin-punishment cycle and human responsibility for sin. So, this tradition did exists at Qumran alongside the prevalent Enoch-Watchers-Noah axis." This view, like Dibre Hamme'orot itself, is probably non-sectarian and does not play a substantial role in the sectarian writings proper.

[30] In her paper Esther Chazon compares the three texts she selects with two other accounts of the creation and fall of Adam current at Qumran, viz. Ben Sira 17:1-10 and Jubilees 2-4; see "Creation and Fall of Adam," 19-21.

[31] The exact character of the fragment 4Q500, originally published by Baillet (DJD 7.78) and identified by Baumgarten as referring to Eden as God's garden, is not really clear. According to his interpretation, this text links the Garden of Eden with the Temple. See J. M. Baumgarten, "4Q500 and the Ancient Conception of the Lord's Vineyard," *JJS* 40 (1989) 1-6. 4Q422 is a Paraphrase of Genesis and Exodus, published by Elgvin and Tov in DJD 13.417-41. Its first fragment (*ibid.*, 421) contains text from Genesis 2, but seems to have no apocryphal narrative or legendary elements. Vermes' survey of Genesis 1-3 in Hebrew and Aramaic literature of the age does not add any information to the above, as far as legendary materials are concerned; see G. Vermes, "Genesis 1-3 in Post-Biblical Hebrew and Aramaic Literature before the Mishnah," *JJS* 43 (1992) 221-25. Nothing substantial is contributed to the search for legendary Adam texts by J. R. Levison, *Portraits of Adam in Early Judaism. From Sirach to 2 Baruch* (JSP Supplement 1; Sheffield: JSOT Press, 1988), although he casts considerable light on the figure of Adam.

markable. The Noachic texts, too, belong to this circle of writings. As we observed, even if Morgenstern is correct, the amount of Noah material in the Genesis Apocryphon is disproportionate to the subjects of the other parts of that work. Further Noah writings have also been found at Qumran. The numerous copies of these Pseudepigrapha and the absence of developed Adam traditions are a signal witness to the sect's concentration on the period from Enoch to Noah. This must necessarily have given their understanding of biblical history a particular configuration. The Watchers begat the giants. The giants drowned in the Flood and their spirits survived. After the Flood, these spirits formed the demonic order and they were reduced by God's grace to one tenth of their original number. These traditions combine to create a specific understanding of the state of the world. The evil that precipitated the Flood stems from angelic sin and not from human disobedience. In the postdiluvian world, this evil persists, though in an attenuated form (cf. Jubilees 10). It is perpetrated and perpetuated by the demons.

This view of the world emerges from the reading of these Pseudepigrapha together and combining elements in them. We must observe, moreover, that most of these writings antedate the foundation of the Qumran sect.[32] They probably stemmed from groups or tendencies in third century Judaism analogous with those from which the Qumran sect itself derived. Their presence at Qumran, some in an astounding number of copies, and the fact that they were quoted in the sectarian writings proper, shows how important they were to the sect.[33] Any assessment of the Qumran sect's ideas must take into account that the sectarians viewed this period of the past as pivotal. They accepted and must have been profoundly influenced by the interpretation of it to be found in these Pseudepigrapha. The Pseudepigrapha dedicated to the Enoch to Noah axis provided an explanation of how the world reached its present state.[34]

---

[32] The status of the Qahat and Amram works remains unclear. Chazon also noted that the three documents she studied are non-sectarian.

[33] This point was tellingly made about the Jubilees manuscripts by J. C. VanderKam, "The Jubilees Fragments from Qumran Cave 4," in *The Madrid Qumran Congress: Proceedings of the International Congress on the Dead Sea Scrolls, Madrid, 18-21 March 1991* (ed. J. Trebolle Barrera and L. Vegas Montaner; Studies on the Texts of the Desert of Judah 11; Madrid: Complutense; Leiden: E. J. Brill, 1992) 2. 635-48. On citations see J. C. Greenfield, "The Words of Levi Son of Jacob in Damascus Document 4.15-19," *RevQ* 13 (1988) 319-22. Note also J. C. VanderKam, "4Q228: Text with a Citation of Jubilees," in DJD 13.177-85. The character of 4Q228 remains unclear.

[34] Legendary Adam material is to be found in Jubilees, of course, which follows the text of Genesis. This merely makes its absence from the other Qumran documents the more striking.

In such a context, the prevalence of Enoch, Giants and Noah texts in the Qumran library and the absence of legendary Adam material takes on a redoubled significance. The Adam and Eve stories, as used, for example, in the Books of Adam and Eve, are designed to explain death, illness and the loss of the paradisiacal state. These are the result of the curses laid upon the protoplasts. These aspects of the human state are accounted for at Qumran by the Enoch-Noah pseudepigrapha.

Let us consider this point further. There is little literature at Qumran dealing with Adam and Eve and, in particular, with the issues of their sin and its consequences that were to become so central. Paul, even if we do not follow Augustine's reading of him, knew and developed views in which Adam's sin had dire consequences for the history of humanity—death, illness and all the curses of Gen. 3:16-19 at the very least. Yet this aspect of the Adam traditions is not at all prominent in the Qumran texts. Jub. 3:23-29 deals with the curses of the protoplasts in terms close to those of Genesis, not even seeing death as a result of their sin, cf. also Ben Sira 17:1-10.[35]

Indeed, words like 4 Ezra's about the "evil seed" (4 Ezra 4:30-32, cf. 3:20-22) are quite rare in ancient Jewish literature outside Paul and they may represent a tradition which Paul developed but to which few witnesses survive.[36] Both Paul and 4 Ezra relate the present state of the world to Adam and to the consequences of his sin.[37] We cannot deal here with the question of whether the sin is considered Adam's, Adam and Eve's or whether there is a tendency to exculpate Adam. That raises a different set of issues. It is nonetheless true that these ideas do not play a role at Qumran in the slightest measure commensurate with that played by the Pseudepigrapha located on the axis running from Enoch to Noah.[38]

We may speculate about what happens when the parlous state of the world is attributed to angelic disobedience for which humans

---

[35] Chazon, "Creation and Fall," 20.

[36] M. E. Stone, *Commentary on 4 Ezra* (Hermeneia; Minneapolis: Augsberg-Fortress, 1990) 95; E. Brandenburger, *Adam und Christus: Exegetisch-Religionsgeschichtliche Untersuchung zu Röm 5:21-21* (WMANT, 7; Neukirchen: Neukirchener Verlag, 1962). 2 Baruch expatiates quite largely on Adam's sin and its consequences: see 4:3, 56:6, *et al.* This is discussed by Levison, *Portraits of Adam*, 129-44. 2 Baruch's view of Adam's sin is diametrically opposed to 4 Ezra's, see *ibid*, 143.

[37] This is so, even in other texts in which the propensity to sin is not considered to be innate.

[38] The paucity of Adam texts from Qumran, moreover, does not mean that the Dead Sea Sect was not interested in how the world got to be the way it is. That issue lies, of course, at the basis of the dual determinism which formed part of the conceptual undergirding of the sect's *Weltanschauung*.

cannot be held responsible. This can be contrasted with a view that attributes it to the disobedience of the father of humanity. These are two different readings of Genesis and they must have produced very different attitudes in those who accepted them.

The intensive use at Qumran of these (largely) pre-Qumran documents shows that the sect stressed the Enoch-Noah axis. We cannot yet reply fully to the question of how this relates to the dual determinism of the sect which explains the state of the world by the nature of its genesis. A few remarks, however, may be in order. The sect preserved, cultivated and cherished the Enochic texts, Jubilees, Book of the Giants, Aramaic Levi, Qahat and Amram. This shows that it favored one particular explanation of the situation of the world. It is not an explanation that necessarily contradicts the approach, say, of the Treatise on the Two Spirits in 1QS cols. 3-4, but it refers to the origins of evil and degeneration of the world in another set of terms, drawn from the re-mythologized world of the Pseudepigrapha. In this perspective, the axis from Enoch to the Flood and Noah, from the fall of the Watchers to the re-seeding of the earth by Noah, is the crucial axis for the creation of the present world state. The actions preceding, indeed precipitating, the Flood and the subsequent re-creation are mythical and play the role that Adam and Eve's actions did in other contexts.

A second and apparently allied focus of sectarian interest seems to have been the levitical priesthood. This is evidenced not only by Aramaic Levi Document but also by the new apocrypha of Amram and of Qahat and by 4Q451.[39] The attitudes of the sect towards the priesthood, as reflected in their own legal codes, are well known. Yet, we have shown above that the strong interest in and exaltation of the levitical line antedated the foundation of the sect. I have addressed myself elsewhere to differing attitudes to the priestly role in documents reflecting third century Judaism.[40] Both in the Aramaic Levi Document and in Jubilees this levitical concern is related back to Noah: Abraham and Isaac learned the laws of sacrifice from the Book of Noah and passed them on to Levi. The claims of Aramaic

---

[39] J. T. Milik, "Écrits préésséniens de Qumrân: de Hénoch à Amram," in *Qumrân: Sa piété, sa théologie et son milieu* (ed. M. Delcor; Bibliotheca Ephemeridum Theologicarum Lovaniensium 46; Louvain: Leuven University, 1978) 91-106, attempts to reconstruct a pre-Qumran literary corpus, but his views are rather too speculative.

[40] M. E. Stone, "Ideal Figures and Social Context: Priest and Sage in the Early Second Temple Age," in *Ancient Israelite Religion. Essays in honor of Frank Moore Cross* (ed. P.D. Miller, P. D. Hanson and S. D. McBride; Philadelpia: Fortress, 1988) 575-86.

Levi Document about the levitical priesthood are even more far-reaching than those of the Qumran sectarian documents proper. At this point, once more, the Pseudepigrapha cultivated at Qumran provide an underpinning for dominant aspects of sectarian ideas. They illuminate the type of Jewish movements from which the Qumran sectarians might have derived. They provide us not only with information about Qumran origins, but also about the obscure history of Judaism in the third century.

Let us accept, for the moment, the schematic presentation of the remythologized view of history proposed above. If it reflects some sort of reality, then evil, suffering, fruitlessness of the earth, illness and consequentially death are the results of the fall of the angels and all that stemmed from it. This is made abundantly clear in Jubilees 10, as far as illness and other afflictions are concerned, and in more general terms in the Book of the Watchers (1 Enoch 6-11:1, 69:4-13). It is not human actions, Adam and Eve's disobedience, that generated the state of the world; it was the angels' actions and their consequences. This starkly contrasts with the usual understanding of the Adam and Eve story.[41] According to it, whether the evil heart is inherited or not, the state of the world is caused by Adam and Eve's transgression.

One might then raise a number of subsequent speculations. One is that the deliberate tying of the sacrificial cult in particular back to Noah does not necessarily make it antediluvian. The commandments in Genesis 8 and 9 about sacrifice indicate that sacrifice is part of the world-order established after the flood.[42] If this is so, then the tradition we have traced differs from that of *Sefer ha-Razim*, which is ultimately attributed to Adam. It also differs equally from traditions such as those in 2 Enoch 69-72 or the later Cave of Treasures in which the high priesthood is traced back ultimately to Adam. Both the Flood and Noah's role in establishing the new world order were very important. Perhaps his wife's name, 'Em Zara' "mother of seed,"[43] indicates something of the role of new creator and father of humankind which Noah and his wife played. Like Deucalion and Phyrra they re-seeded the earth.

---

[41] See above note 29.

[42] The story of Abel's sacrifice, Gen. 4:4, just says, "And the Lord had regard for Abel and his offering." Abel's action in v. 3 is described as הביא "brought." On the other hand, according to Gen. 8:20, Noah builds an alter and offers whole burnt offerings ויעל עלות.

[43] See discussion in Stone, *Adam and Eve*, 91 and 165. The name appears, as has recently been made public, in newly deciphered text from the Genesis Apocryphon.

Of course, these observations far from exhaust the role and importance of the Enochic material at Qumran. I must leave it to others to describe in detail how the Enochic material functioned there. However, it must be remarked that through the Enochic material (which includes Giants) we can explain the fall of the angels, the origins of the demons and their plagues, as well as the Flood and the destruction of the earth. The present world order is the postdiluvian state. Into that state, among other things, Noah introduced sacrifice. Noah was thus father of humans, recipient of information to protect humans against the demons and originator of the sacrificial cult.

The displacement of the true cult from Jerusalem was most likely a catalytic factor for the wing of Judaism to which the sect belonged. That wing of Judaism, however, was older than the sect proper and preceded the events leading up to the expulsion of the Oniad priests (ca. 175 BCE) and the decrees of Antiochus IV (167 BCE). The alienation from the Jerusalem Temple sprang from other, yet unrevealed, sources in the mist-enshrouded third century. But it was this alienation that can explain both the stress on the Noachic fount of sacrificial law and practice and the importance of the genealogy of the priestly teaching.

Much remains to be done and study must precede further talk. The integration of the texts newly discovered at Qumran with those which have been known for centuries will continue to produce rich fruit as we meditate upon it.

THE ANGEL STORY IN THE BOOK OF JUBILEES

James C. VanderKam

University of Notre Dame

I. Introduction

The angelic interpretation of Gen. 6:1-4 and surrounding passages is relatively widespread in Jewish and Christian literature of the Greco-Roman period. It is especially frequently attested in the literature that can be associated in some way with Qumran, whether in compositions that were inherited by the community living there or in texts that may have been written by members of it. The first and most detailed exposition of the angelic interpretation is found in the Enochic Book of the Watchers (BW = 1 Enoch 1-36). It later reappears in works such as Jubilees, the Genesis Apocryphon, the Pesher on the Periods, etc.

In the history of scholarship on 1 Enoch and Jubilees, little has been written about the specifics of the angel stories in them and how they are related to one another, if in fact they are related. The classical commentaries on the ancient pseudepigrapha tend not to be commentaries at all but series of notes and collections of parallels. The only detailed, systematic analysis of the BW and later embodiments of the angel story has been made by D. Dimant.[1] As she has shown in great detail, even so early a work as the BW preserves more than one version of the story. In fact, she distinguishes three different ones in chs. 6-16. They are:

1. a story about angels who became impure with the daughters of men, became the fathers of giants (= נְפִלִים), and sinned; it is a midrashic interpretation of Gen. 6:1-4 lacking any connection with the flood.

2. a story about angels who taught magic and secrets to humanity and led them into sin (they also became the fathers of demons, who are נְפִלִים?); it is also apparently a midrashic interpretation of Gen. 6:1-4 which is connected with the flood as a punishment for humanity's sin.

---

[1] "'The Fallen Angels' in the Dead Sea Scrolls and in the Apocryphal and Pseudepigraphic Books Related to Them" (unpublished Ph.D. dissertation, Jerusalem: Hebrew University, 1974).

3 the story about Azael; it is a story about the works that Azael taught to humanity which led them into sin, and it interprets Gen. 6:11-12. It supplies an explanation for the corruption before the flood and a reason for the punishment constituted by the flood.[2] Dimant further believes that versions 1 and 2 were combined first, as both interpret the same biblical base, and that the Azael story was subsequently merged with the combination under the influence of the shared feature of angelic teachings. After isolating and discussing these versions of the angel story, she pursued her investigation into later literature and found that the versions and motifs in the BW lived on in Jewish and Christian literature, although at times in rather different settings.

One of the works that Dimant analyzed was the Book of Jubilees.[3] She showed that Jubilees presents the first version of the angel story, that is, the one in which the angels became defiled with women and fathered giants. As she writes: "...in chaps. 5 and 7 the author of Jubilees used only the story about the angels who became impure as it is related in 1 Enoch 6-11, without including other elements that are found in the BW, such as the figures of Shemihazah and Azael. The way in which he presents the account gives evidence that the author of the book was aware of all details in the story about the angels who became impure."[4] She maintains that Jubilees' surprising statement that the angels originally descended on a positive mission from God and were seduced only after they reached the earth is probably not a part of the way in which this story was first formulated. In her view, it could be in opposition to the picture in the BW in which the descent of the angels is part of their sin; it may also be the "first sign of a tendency that will grow stronger—to weaken the motif of the angels who sinned."[5] As she understands the story in Jubilees, the flood was a punishment not only of the giants but also of humanity and the animals. She finds that Jubilees is later than the BW but is not dependent on it: "...rather, it makes use of a related aggadic tradition. It is possible that the author of Jubilees knew in separate form the traditions that are joined in the aggadic source in 1 Enoch 6-11."[6]

---

[2] *Ibid.*, 65.

[3] *Ibid.*, 92-103. One of the few to treat the version of the story in Jubilees, if only briefly, was M. Delcor, "Le mythe de la chute des anges et de l'origine des géants comme explication du mal dans le monde dans l'apocalyptique juive. Histoire des traditions," *RHR* 190 (1976) 22-24.

[4] E.g., *ibid.*, 99. The translations from Dimant's dissertation are mine.

[5] *Ibid.*, 100.

[6] *Ibid.*, 102-03.

The purpose of this paper is to subject Jubilees' presentation of the Watcher story to a somewhat different examination. The chief goal of the study is to clarify the new elements in Jubilees' way of formulating the story in ch. 5 and the first part of ch. 6, although information from elsewhere in the book (especially ch. 7) will be adduced where relevant. This study will permit some conclusions about the relationship between Jubilees' version and those in the BW. It will be shown that the author of Jubilees did in fact know the story from the BW but shaped the different elements in it to his own purposes.

II. The Angel Story in the Book of Jubilees

A. *The Place of the Story in Jubilees*

Whatever relationship may obtain between the BW and Jubilees, there can be no doubt that they are very different types of works.[7] The BW focuses on sin and ultimate punishment. The editor devotes a large percentage of his text to these themes and their ramifications. As he sets forth the story about the angels, he at times bases himself solidly on the biblical text, but he does not place the angel story in the same context that Genesis does. We read nothing in 1 Enoch 1-5 of Genesis 1-4 or of the genealogy in Genesis 5, nor is much space allotted to the flood narrative that follows Gen. 6:1-4. One gets the impression from the BW and the other Enochic compositions that the Eden story in Genesis 3 played only a modest role in their authors' understanding of the origin and character of sin. The writers in this tradition clearly knew about the early chapters of Genesis; that is obvious from passages such as 1 Enoch 24-25, 32:6, and 1 Enoch 85 in the Animal Apocalypse, to name only three. The approach favored in the Enochic tradition as it has survived saw Gen. 6:1-4 as providing an explanation for the supernatural growth of evil which became so monstrous that it justified the extreme measure of God's sending the flood, a deluge that was the first judgment and presaged the final one. A story about a piece of forbidden fruit and another about a fratricidal act may have seemed insufficient to explain how frightfully conditions had deteriorated on the earth. Only a supernatural boost for wickedness could account for the pre-flood situation and for God's comprehensive and definitive punishment of the practitioners of iniquity.

---

[7] Dimant stresses this point, especially for all of 1 Enoch and Jubilees, at the beginning of her chapter on Jubilees (*ibid.*, 92-93).

Jubilees is, of course, tied much more systematically and closely to the biblical text than is the BW. It begins its narrative with Genesis 1 and continues through the remainder of Genesis and the first half of Exodus. Hence it places its rendition of Gen. 6:1-4 directly after the Genesis 5 genealogy and before the flood story. It resembles the BW in so far as it does not take up all parts of Gen. 6:1-4 at once. In fact only 5:1 (parallel to Gen. 6:1-2, 4) is drawn from the biblical pericope, and it is not until several verses later that Gen. 6:3 is handled. Moreover, Jubilees does not accord such a dominant role to the angel story as the BW and other Enochic compositions do. Not only does it assign a smaller percentage of its text to the story; it also does not present it as the pre-eminent cause of human evil. The writer treats the Eden narrative in some detail (the 31 verses of ch. 3); hence, the angel story has not displaced it. Moreover, the myth of the angels plays no part in Jubilees 1 where God predicts the historical course of Israel's apostasy, repentance, and renewal. To be sure, the chapter is concerned with the nation of Israel and its fate, not with antediluvian conditions. But one would not be too surprised if the results of angelic sin were mentioned at some point, if only in passing, in a chapter of this kind. The same is the case for the apocalypse in Jubilees 23, which also fails to mention the sin of the angels. The story is a major theme for a few chapters in Jubilees (5:1-10; 7:20-25; see also 4:15, 22; 8:3), but after ch. 10:1-14 it is largely forgotten, reappearing only once in the Abraham section (20:5) and in the Exodus tale at the end of the book (ch. 48; 49:2). The angel story is not nearly so dominant a theme in Jubilees as it is 1 Enoch.

The use of the story shows something about the procedure favored by the author. His habitually adheres closely to the text of Genesis-Exodus, and where he diverges from it he does not deviate in so massive a way as do the authors of the individual sections in the BW. Moreover, as will be shown shortly, the text of Genesis is the springboard for the addition of any material from elsewhere in the Bible.

B. *The First References to the Angel Story*

1. *Jub. 4:15*

The author of Jubilees makes no allusion to the angel story until he is well into his reworking of the Genesis 5 genealogy. Of Jared, the sixth from Adam and the father of Enoch, he writes: "He [Malalael] named him Jared because during his lifetime the angels of the Lord who were called Watchers descended to earth to teach mankind and to do what is just and upright upon the earth" (4:15).[8] As noted above, Dimant considers the theme of the positive errand, for which the Watchers came, to be a secondary motif in the version of the angel story presented in Jubilees. Whatever its status may be in a hypothetical original form of the story, there is at least no external evidence for an addition or gloss here in the text of Jubilees. Moreover, the statement serves an important purpose: it protects the reputation of heaven by distancing it from evil. That is, evil does not come from heaven to earth, as it does in 1 Enoch, but originates on the earth. The angels did not make their sinful, lustful resolve in heaven as they do in 1 Enoch 6 and, as Dimant has commented, their descent was thus not part of their sin.[9]

The explanation for the appearance of the Watcher motif in the Jared paragraph is obvious to anyone who has read 1 Enoch 6:6: his Hebrew name suggests descent, and it is one in a series of etymological associations for the names in Genesis 5 that were developed in the Enochic tradition. It appears from the text that Jared's father must have been prescient because he named his son before the watchers actually descended. The positive purpose for which they descended (note that they descend, they do not fall) may be related to the notion, found in the BW (1 Enoch 8), that the angels taught. There, however, the motif is a negative one; here it is purely positive. Ironically, the angels descended to teach humanity the very virtues that they themselves soon lost when they came into contact with women.

It may not be entirely accidental that Jared is surrounded by other names which echo themes from the angel story. Jared's mother is named Dinah, a term that suggests judgment, while later we learn that his son Enoch's wife Edni was the daughter of one Daniel. The fact that the angels came to earth to teach righteousness should also be suggestive of the name and title of another character in the drama: Enoch's name seems to have suggested education (note that he learned instruction and taught humanity according to Jub. 4:17),[10] and he was identified as the scribe of righteousness (1 Enoch 12:4) who recorded the deeds that would be punished at the final judgment (Jub. 4:19, 23-24).

---

[8] Translations of Jubilees and citations of the Ethiopic text are from J. C. VanderKam, *The Book of Jubilees* (2 vols.; CSCO 510-11, Scriptores Aethiopici 87-88; Leuven: Peeters, 1989).

[9] *Ibid.*, 99-100. On the reason for this motif in Jubilees, see J. C. VanderKam, "Enoch Traditions in Jubilees and Other Second-Century Sources," *SBLSP* 1 (1978) 242-45.

[10] See Delcor, "Le mythe de la chute," 23-24.

2. *Jub. 4:22*

Jubilees' second allusion to the angel episode before the story itself is, naturally, in the Enoch paragraph which immediately follows the one about Jared. The allusion comes after the verse which notes his marriage to Edni and the birth of Methuselah. In the section that corresponds with the first reference in Genesis to Enoch's walking with האלהים, the text says: "He was, moreover, with God's angels for six jubilees of years. They showed him everything on earth and in the heavens—the dominion of the sun—and he wrote down everything. He testified to the Watchers who had sinned with the daughters of men because these had begun to mix with earthly women so that they became defiled. Enoch testified against all of them" (4:21-22). From these few words we can glean that the writer of Jubilees knew much of the Enochic literature,[11] and here we see that the version of the Watcher story used by our author included mixing angelic and human realms and the defilement that resulted. Enoch's testifying against or to the watchers is familiar from 1 Enoch 12-16. Jub. 4:21-22 is now known to have a Hebrew parallel in 4Q227 frg. 2. The scribe who made a supralinear addition in line 1 has even emended the text to fit the same framework as Jubilees by reading למדנוהו rather than למדוהו. Line 2 mentions the six weeks of years also found in Jub. 4:21; the 294 years involved is now known to be the largest unit in the Qumran calendrical cycles. These the angels taught to Enoch. The final sentence of 4:22 appears as ויעד על כולם in 4Q227 2 3.[12]

C. *The Angel Story in Jubilees 5-7*

By the time the readers of Jubilees reach the section where the story of the watchers is told, they have a good idea about the main themes. The story itself begins in Jubilees 5, directly after the reference to the births of Noah's three sons, the final element in Genesis 5. In the paragraphs below, after a brief description of the relations between Jubilees' story and the text of Genesis, some of the key items in Jubilees' version will be treated in more detail.

---

[11] See VanderKam, "Enoch Traditions in Jubilees," 235, where it is shown that Jub. 4:21 betrays the author's knowledge of 1 Enoch 17-36 and 72, while 4:22 reflects his familiarity with 1 Enoch 6-16.

[12] 4Q227 has been published by VanderKam and Milik in *Qumran Cave 4, VIII. Parabiblical Texts Part 1* (DJD 13; Oxford: Clarendon, 1994) 171-75.

1. *Jubilees and Genesis*

Apart from allusions in chs. 4, 8, 10, and 20, the primary angel story is found in Jubilees 5-7; these chapters are closely related to Genesis 6-9. Jubilees shortens the flood story considerably, especially by omitting the latter part of Genesis 6 (vv. 13-21), almost all of Genesis 7 (it lacks equivalents to Gen. 7:1-10, 13-15, 21-23) and large sections of Genesis 8 (missing are 8:1-3, 6-13, 15-17). Some missing parts appear elsewhere (e.g., in the calendrical section at the end of Jubilees 6), but Jubilees eliminates virtually all instructions to Noah about the ark and thus also does away with the duplication in Genesis at this point. If one looks at the sections of Jubilees which have no strict parallel in Genesis, they are: Jub. 5:6-7 (punishment of the angels and their children); 5:9-21 (their children are killed, the angels bound, a new nature is promised, and judgment and the day of atonement are treated; vv. 20-21 quickly summarize the orders to Noah about the ark); 5:29 (calendrical notes about events during the flood); 6:2 (Noah's atoning sacrifice); 6:1-15 (oath about not consuming blood); and 6:17-38 (a calendrical section).

2. *Jub. 5:1 and Gen. 6:1-2, 4*

Jubilees, like 1 Enoch 6:1-2 (cf. 7:1-2), begins the story by citing from the Genesis paragraph.

Genesis 6	Jubilees 5
ויהי כי החל האדם לרב על פני האדמה	wa-kona'ama waṭanu daqiqa 'egʷāla
ובנות ילדו להם	'emma-ḥeyāw yebzexu diba gaṣṣa kʷellā medr wa-'awāled tawaldā lomu
ויראו בני האלהים את בנות האדם כי טבת	wa-re'yewwon malā'ekta 'egzi'abḥēr
הנה ויקחו להם נשים מכל אשר בחרו	ba-'aḥatti za-'iyobēlewu zentu'esma sannāyt la-re'iy 'emāntu wa-naš'ewwon loton lomu 'anesteyā 'em-kʷellon 'ella xarayu
וילדו להם המה הגברים אשר מעולם אנשי השם	wa-waladā lomu weluda wa-'emuntu ra'āyt

At this point Jubilees stops quoting from Gen. 6:1-2, 4 and moves into its own expansion of the tradition.

The differences between Gen. 6:1-2, 4 and Jub. 5:1 are relatively minor and usually obvious. Jubilees presupposes בני האדם at the beginning of Gen. 6:1, rather than the simple האדם in the biblical text. It also presupposes כל before האדמה. In Gen. 6:2, Jubilees renders

the MT phrase בני האלהים with "the angels of God", in agreement
with the Old Greek, the Old Latin, the Ethiopic Genesis, and
Josephus, Ant. 1.73. The note about the date in Jubilees fits a larger
pattern in the book in which events are tied to a timeline that begins
with creation. The jubilee period in question is the twenty-fifth one,
as 4:33 had indicated. Oddly, the writer may not have specified the
year (see below). Jub. 5:22 indicates that the flood did not come until
the twenty-seventh jubilee. The number of the jubilee for the descent of the angels may be significant: the twenty-fifth one would be
the last jubilee in the first half of the history, since the book covers
50 jubilee periods (50:4).

The meaning may be that the first half of the narrated history concluded with the ominous event of the angelic desire for women which
led to an illicit mixing of beings from different orders and eventually
to the evil that had to be punished in the flood. Perhaps this is one
reason why the writer is so insistent that the Israelites not intermarry
with the peoples of Canaan after they enter the land in the fiftieth jubilee. In the section that speaks of the angels' seeing the women, MT
mentions the daughters of men but Jubilees employs a pronoun instead. Somewhat redundantly, Jubilees adds that the women were
beautiful "to see". Note that the author does not resort to the doubling
of adjectives describing the women as 1 Enoch 6:1 does, nor does he
elaborate the matter in the style of Targum Pseudo-Jonathan which
adds after "beautiful," "they painted their eyes and put on rouge, and
walked about with naked flesh".[13] Jubilees has a suffixal expression
with the verb "they took". The major difference, however, is in the
final sentence in Jubilees: "They gave birth to children for them and
they were giants." These words correspond with וילדו להם המה הגברים
(Gen. 6:4). Thus הגברים are understood as giants in Jubilees, and at
least in this passage there is no indication that the other two phrases
at the end of Gen. 6:4 were understood to be different classes of giants.

3. *Jub. 5:2-11*

Jubilees departs from the Genesis framework after briefly retelling
the basics of the story. Thus the writer bypasses Gen. 6:3 at this
point and postpones his treatment of it until 5:8. At 5:2 he adduces a

---

[13] Translation of M. Maher, *Targum Pseudo-Jonathan: Genesis* (The Aramaic Bible
1B; Collegeville: The Liturgical Press, 1992) 38 (other quotations from this targum
are also those of Maher). Targum Neofiti adds rather unhelpfully "female" before
"daughters". For a study of the targumic treatments of Gen. 6:1-4, see P. S.
Alexander, "The Targumim and Early Exegesis of 'Sons of God' in Genesis 6," *JJS*
23 (1972) 60-71.

number of verses from Genesis 6 that indicate the all-pervasive character of sin on the earth as a result of the watchers' transgression. The passages that underlie the wording in Jubilees are Gen. 6:12b, 6:5b, 6:12, 6:7a, in that order. These statements lead to Jubilees' reproduction of Gen. 6:8 (= Jub. 5:5) in which the reader learns that God was pleased with Noah alone (*alone* [*baḥtitu* = לבדו] is an addition found in no version of Genesis). Jub. 5:2 claims about the beings living on the earth: "All of them corrupted their way [*fenotomu* = דרכם] and their prescribed course [*šerʿatomu*; Goldmann וחקותיהם[14]]. They began to devour one another and wickedness increased on the earth." Evil led to the divine verdict that all people and living beings would be obliterated from the earth which God had created (5:4). The *prescribed course* that the wicked corrupted was the law or statute appropriate for their place in creation, the constitution that God had prescribed for each class of beings.

Jub. 5:6-11, an extra-Genesis section, details the punishments meted out to the various sinners. In 5:6 the author still refers to the angels as "his [that is, God's] angels". They had incurred his wrath by mixing with women and following the prescribed course of humanity rather than their own; hence God removed them from their positions of authority. Since they had departed from the way set for them and no longer carried out their responsibilities, they had to be removed from their appointed stations. The punishment for the immortal watchers was to be bound alone in the depths of the earth— a motif familiar from 1 Enoch 10:12.

The next sinners to be handled are "their children". In something of a flashback, the writer says that while their angelic fathers watched, the children killed one another with the sword until there were no survivors. It was only after viewing this gruesome spectacle that the fathers were bound in the earth. The interesting item here is that this is the context in which the author of Jubilees chose to reproduce Gen. 6:3: "He said: 'My spirit will not remain on people (*sab*ʾ) forever for they are flesh. Their lifespan is to be 120 years." In this context, with the verse surrounded by references to the children of the angels, the term translated *people* (*sab*ʾ) obviously refers to the giants who were identified as the children of the angels in 5:1, a point that Dimant has noted.[15] The writer delayed reproducing Gen.

---

[14] M. Goldmann, "The Book of Jubilees," in *The Apocryphal Books* (ed. A. Kahana; rpt.; Jerusalem: Makor, 1970) vol. 1 (Hebrew). 11QJub 3 reads at Jub. 5:2: הׁשחיתו דרכם וחקתם.

[15] "The Angels," 96.

6:3 until this stage in the text because he wanted to provide some context for the divine limit on lifespans. The text of Genesis hardly seemed to provide an adequate reason for the sentence.

Anyone familiar with text-critical problems will immediately notice that Jubilees, like a number of other ancient witnesses (Peshitta, Old Greek, some Old Latin, Ethiopic Genesis, Targum Onkelos), reads "remain" (*yenabber*) rather than "judge," as in the MT. Whether this is actually a textual variant and whether all of these versions have the same one can be debated,[16] but the Ethiopic texts suggest strongly that Jubilees' Hebrew original read ידור, as in 4Q252, not ידון, or that at the very least the author understood ידון to mean ידור.[17] The general context indicates an interesting point. In the Qumran pesharim it is at times clear that where the biblical lemma contains a reading differing from the one in the MT the pesher indicates that the commentator knew both the variant and the reading familiar from the MT.[18] Even if we consider ידור to be a legitimate variant reading, it can hardly be doubted the writer of Jubilees also knew about the reading ידון because in the immediate sequel he begins talking about the *judgment* at considerable length. Jub. 5:6-11 concentrates on the judgment for the angels and giants, and the judgment theme returns in 5:13-16 where the fact that each is judged impartially according to a fixed set of standards appropriate to each kind is emphasized. All of this could have been suggested by the flood context, but it is likely that the variant ידון played a part in triggering the idea of judgment that receives extended attention in the context.

Jub. 5:8 = Gen. 6:3 specifies that 120 years is a limit on life spans. Whatever group may be intended as the object of this limit in Genesis, it is unmistakable in Jubilees that the giants are the recipients of the decree, as we have seen. The setting in Jubilees makes it evident that the author has not read the purpose of the 120 years in the same way as the person who wrote 4Q252 did. In the latter, the 120 years are a period between Noah's 480th year and the flood which came in his 600th year.

---

[16] See M.J. Bernstein, "לא ידור רוחי באדם לעולם 4Q252 i 2: Biblical Text or Biblical Interpretation?" *RevQ* 16 (1993-94) 421-27.

[17] On the possible meanings of ידון, see C. Westermann, *Genesis 1-11: A Commentary* (Minneapolis: Augsburg, 1974) 375.

[18] W. Brownlee seems to have been the first to have noted this point. See his *The Text of Habakkuk in the Ancient Commentary from Qumran* (JBLMS 11; Philadelphia: SBL, 1959) 118-23.

[In the y]ear four hundred and eighty of Noah's life, Noah reached the end of them. And God [2] [sa]id: 'My spirit will not reside in man for ever'. Their days shall be fixed at one hundred and twenty [3] [y]ears until the end of the waters of the flood."[19]

In Jubilees the 120 years are a limit set on how long the giants will be allowed to live. The span of time involved would fit in well with the Jubilees chronology if, with Berger, we translate *ba-ʾaḥatti za-ʾiy-obēleyu* in Jub. 5:1 (it dates the year when the marriages between angels and women took place) as meaning the first year (some manuscripts add the word for *year*) of the jubilee. If so, the lives of the giants could have extended to as many as 120 years but they would still have died comfortably before the flood. The first year of the jubilee in question is the year of the world 1177, and the flood came in the year 1308. Thus, even if they were born in the same year as the marriages, the giants would all have perished by 1297, some 11 years before the flood. This sentence entails that the giants, like their angelic fathers, cannot have been the ones who were punished by the flood according to this context in Jubilees.

4. *Jub. 5:12*

One possibly puzzling verse in this section is Jub. 5:12: "he made a new and righteous nature [*feṭrata* which Goldmann renders literally as בריאה] for all his creatures so that they would not sin with their whole nature until eternity. Everyone will be righteous—each according to his kind—for all time." The passage is the immediate sequel to the section about how creatures corrupted their way and were obliterated from their positions. The new and righteous natures should in some way be related to these themes. The notion of a certain way or prescribed course is repeated frequently in the context and is obviously highly significant for the author. For example, Jub. 5:2 accuses all animate beings of corrupting their way and prescribed course; 5:3 makes the same charge against the same creatures. According to 5:10, the condemnation of the great day of judgment will fall "on all who have corrupted their ways and their actions before the Lord." Jub. 5:13 deals with "all who transgress from their way in which it was ordained for them to go". Divine judgment is passed on "each one in accord with his way" (5:15) because the deity showed no favor to "all who corrupted their ways and their plan(s) before the flood" (5:19). Later one learns that Noah

---

[19] F. García Martínez, *The Dead Sea Scrolls Translated* (Leiden: E. J. Brill, 1994) 213. Other translations from the scrolls are also from this work.

was the lone exception to this blanket charge: "his mind was righteous in all his ways, as it had been commanded concerning him. He
did not transgress from anything that had been ordained for him"
(5:19). But in the immediate context, when Jub. 5:12 speaks about a
"new and righteous nature" and says that "[e]veryone will be righteous—each according to his kind", the intent should be that creatures (not just people) were again to be given the ability to operate
within their created orders, in contrast to the systematic corruption
of those orders by all living beings before the flood.

　　Charles argued that the person who translated Hebrew Jubilees into
Greek had failed to notice that, in this passage (vv. 10b-12), the verbs
were converted forms of the perfect, not simple perfects. Hence, in his
view the entire passage should be rendered in the future tense: he will
make a new and righteous nature, etc.[20] The final judgment and new
creation are, therefore, what the writer has in mind. However, K.
Berger is correct in maintaining that the verse need not be taken es-
chatologically in the strict sense of the term. It refers to the renewal
after the flood that is remarked upon in other sources as well.[21]

　　In this connection 1 Enoch 10-11 resembles Jubilees to some extent. It speaks about the punishment of the angels and the destruction of "all the souls of lust and the sons of the Watchers, for they
have wronged men. Destroy all wrong from the face of the earth,
and every evil work will cease. And let the plant of righteousness and
truth appear, and the deed will become a blessing; righteousness and
truth will they plant in joy for ever" (10:15-16).[22] 4QEn^c 1 v 5-6
shows that the sequel read: "[And now all] the righteous shall escape
and they shall be [alive until they beget] thousands; and all the days
[of your youth and] of your old age shall be completed in peace."[23]
It is difficult to sort out which statements in the context refer to the
eschaton and which to the immediate postdiluvian age, but at least

---

[20] *The Book of Jubilees or the Little Genesis* (London: Adam and Charles Black, 1902)
44-45, n. to vv. 10b-12.
　　[21] K. Berger, *Das Buch der Jubiläen* (JSHRZ 2.3; Gütersloh: Gütersloher Ver-
lagshaus [Gerd Mohn], 1981) 351, n. b to v. 12. See also G. Davenport, *The
Eschatology of the Book of Jubilees* (SPB 20; Leiden: E. J. Brill, 1971) 47-49; he includes
Jub. 5:1-19 under the category of "non-eschatological passages that contain significant eschatological elements".
　　[22] The translation comes from M. A. Knibb, *The Ethiopic Book of Enoch: A new edition in the light of the Aramaic Dead Sea Fragments* (Oxford: Clarendon Press, 1978) vol.
2.
　　[23] Translation of J. T. Milik, *The Books of Enoch: Aramaic Fragments of Qumrân Cave 4*
(Oxford: Clarendon Press, 1976) 190 (text, 189). For the first part of v. 17 the
Ethiopic has: "And now all the righteous will be humble". R. H. Charles, *The Book
of Enoch or 1 Enoch* (Oxford: Clarendon Press, 1912) 25, claimed that the "writer has
here gone over wholly to a description of the Messianic times."

the passage shows a great change after the flood. The targumic tradition expressed in Pseudo-Jonathan (and Neofiti) may be pointing in this direction with its lengthy rendering of Gen. 6:3[24]: "The Lord said in his Memra, 'None of the evil generations that are to arise (in the future) will be judged according to the order of judgment applied to the generation of the Flood, (that is) to be destroyed and wiped out from the world." One arrangement applied to that generation but a new one would be in effect after the flood. Gen. 9:11-17, which mentions the covenant with Noah and the fact that a flood would never again be sent, may have played a part in the development of this theme. Although the postdiluvian renewal was to be no more successful than the first effort to give creatures a righteous nature, a least a new beginning was made. As God had resolved to obliterate every living thing on the earth that he had created because all had corrupted their way (Jub. 5:4), so he determined to give them a new nature, a new creation after the flood.[25]

5. *Jub. 5:17-18; 6:1-2*

Jub. 5:17-18 introduce the subject of the day of atonement without mentioning it by name. The narrator (the angel of the presence) turns from the story to address Moses concerning the people of Israel: "Regarding the Israelites it has been written and ordained: 'If they turn to him in the right way, he will forgive all their wickedness and will pardon all their sins'. It has been written and ordained that he will have mercy on all who turn from all their errors once each year." The wording indicates a citation, presumably from a heavenly tablet, but the earthly source for it is not obvious. Charles suggested that it was "[p]robably based on Jer. xxxvi.3",[26] and he also mentioned Jer. 18:8 and Jon. 3:8 as possible sources. The Jeremiah passages speak of God's repenting from carrying out what he planned if Israel would turn from its wickedness; Jon. 3:8 describes the Ninevites' penitence. None of these is overly close to the wording in Jubilees. While some of Jubilees' wording echoes Lev. 16:16[27] and

---

[24] See J. Bowker, *The Targums and Rabbinic Literature: An Introduction to Jewish Interpretations of Scripture* (Cambridge: University of Cambridge Press, 1969) 154-56.

[25] See C. Werman, "The Attitude Towards Gentiles in the Book of Jubilees and Qumran Literature Compared with Early Tannaitic Halakha and Contemporary Pseudepigrapha" (unpublished Ph.D. dissertation, Jerusalem: Hebrew University, 1995) 60-61 (Hebrew).

[26] *The Book of Jubilees*, 45.

[27] In Lev. 16:16 where the MT reads החטאם the Ethiopic Leviticus has the cognate *xati'atomu*; a related plural form appears in Lev. 16:34. Jub. 5:17 uses the same term. The Ethiopic word corresponds with עונות in Lev. 16:21, 22.

21[28], Lev. 16:34 may be the chief source for the quotation: "This shall be an everlasting statute for you, to make atonement for the people of Israel once in the year for all their sins [מכל חטאתם אחת בשנה]." Even though the day of atonement is not named in the text, the affinity of the wording with Lev. 16:34 indicates that this is the subject. Hence the topic of the day of atonement surfaces in Jubilees long before the historical event which supposedly gave rise to it, the grieving of Jacob at the "death" of Joseph (34:18-19).

Jub. 5:17-18 is only the first reference to atonement in the book's presentation of the flood story. Jub. 6:1-2, which should correspond with Gen. 8:19-20 (Noah's postdiluvian sacrifice), reads, "On the first of the third month he left the ark and built an altar on this mountain. He appeared on the earth, and took a kid, and atoned with its blood for all the sins of the earth because everything that was on it had been obliterated except those who were in the ark with Noah." Actually Jub. 6:3-4 reproduce the Genesis version of Noah's sacrifice. Jubilees, offering of atonement is an addition to the text of Genesis.[29] The clause "he appeared on the earth", while it is the better reading in the Ethiopic manuscript tradition, is probably not original. Earlier editors had already noted that two Ethiopic verbs, which resemble each other in appearance, probably underlie the mistake: "He appeared" is 'astar'aya, while "he atoned" would be 'astasraya.[30] Hence, the original reading was "he atoned for the earth". The likelihood that "he atoned" is the preferable reading increased considerably when the Genesis Apocryphon was deciphered. This work, which is closely related to Jubilees, reads as follows[31]: "Col. X 12 [...] the ark settled [on] one of the mountains of Hurarat [...] 13 [...] I atoned for all the whole earth[32] [...] 15 [...] I burned incense on the altar [...]."

The facts that Jubilees alludes to the day of atonement in 5:17-18 and to Noah's atoning sacrifice in 6:1-2 and that both passages are absent from the base in Genesis suggest that the topic was significant for the author. What could have been the textual or other types of stimuli which made him or his tradition read atonement into the narrative? It turns out to be an unusual theme in ancient treatments

---

[28] In Lev. 16:21 where the MT has פשעיהם the Ethiopic version has 'abbasāhomu, the other word for "sin" in Jub. 5:17.

[29] A Syriac citation from this section simply blends the reference to the goat into the sacrifice of the next verses (see VanderKam, *The Book of Jubilees*, 1.264; 2.333).

[30] For the details, see VanderKam, *The Book of Jubilees*, 2.36.

[31] The context is broken but enough remains to see that it is the same as Jub. 6:1-4//Gen. 8:19-20.

[32] The text reads: לכול ארעא כולהא כפרת.

of the Genesis flood story. The discussion at this point in Genesis Rabbah says nothing about atonement; rather, the issue debated there is whether Noah's sacrifice was a burnt offering or a peace offering (Gen. Rab. 34:9). Other texts seem more concerned with noting that Noah rebuilt the altar on which Cain and Abel had presented their offerings (Pirke de R. Eliezer 23; some targums).[33]

Both Jubilees and the Genesis Apocryphon say that Noah atoned for (all) the earth. Thus the earth had been defiled in such a way that atonement was required for it. It seems from the context in Jubilees that the author has in mind every wrong that had been committed on the earth and had polluted it.

In his note to Jub. 6:2, Charles says about the phrase "made atonement for the earth," "[t]hough Jewish Haggada knows nothing of this particular act of atonement, it is easy to justify such a conception from Lev. xviii.26-28; Num. xxxv.33, 34. The earth itself as being defiled needed expiation. Unnatural vices and murder pollute it."[34] Berger adds: "Die Entsühnung des Landes war wohl wegen des vergossenen Blutes notwendig: V 9; VII 25; vgl. Num 35.33f; VII 33. Noah kann als einziger mit seinem Opfer universale Sühne schaffen..."[35]

Lev. 18:26-28, the first biblical passage to which Charles alluded, is set in a context of laws prohibiting actions such as those committed by Egyptians and Canaanites. These practices defiled the land and caused the previous inhabitants to be vomited from it (vv. 24-25). That is, the people became defiled through such practices and thus defiled the land, which had to be punished for its iniquity (v. 25). It is worth noting that illicit degrees of sexual relations are the subject of the paragraphs immediately before vv. 26-28, including the law prohibiting relations with a woman in her menstrual uncleanness (v. 19). This was one of the angels' offenses, according to the Greek version of 1 Enoch 15:4 (ἐν τῷ αἵματι τῶν γυναικῶν ἐμιάνθητε). The pertinent verses in Leviticus say:

> **26** But you shall keep my statutes and my ordinances and commit none of these abominations, either the citizen or the alien who resides among you **27** (for the inhabitants of the land, who were before you, committed all of these abominations, and the land became defiled); **28** otherwise the land will vomit you out for defiling it, as it vomited out the nation that was before you.

---

[33] For references see Bowker, *The Targums*, 170-71.
[34] *The Book of Jubilees*, 49.
[35] *Das Buch der Jubiläen*, 355, n. b to 6:2.

Jubilees does draw attention to the illicit nature of the angelic marriages and thus of the sexual relations involved. While Jub. 5:1 ("So they married of them whomever they chose") simply repeats Gen. 6:2 *verbatim*, the topic returns in ch. 7. Noah, as he is prescribing laws for his descendants, "testified to his sons that they should do what is right, cover the shame of their bodies, bless the one who had created them, honor father and mother, love one another, and keep themselves from fornication, uncleanness, and from all injustice. For it was on account of these three things that the flood was on the earth, since (it was) due to fornication that the Watchers had illicit intercourse—apart from the mandate of their authority—with women. When they married of them whomever they chose they committed the first (acts) of uncleanness" (7:20-21). Lev. 18:26-28, which is directly preceded by laws about illicit sexual relations, could have reminded Jubilees' author about the connection between such offenses and defilement of the land on which they were committed. It is also worth noting that the subject of the fourth-year planting appears in the next chapter (Lev. 19:23-25), just as it follows Noah's warnings to his children in Jub. 7:34-37.

The second passage, Num. 35:33-34, which both Charles and Berger noted, occurs in a chapter that speaks about cities for the Levites and cities of refuge along with the related topics of murder and blood revenge. The verses immediately before the relevant section deal with murder and the requirement that a murderer be put to death, with no ransom (כֹּפֶר is used in vv. 31, 32) being acceptable.

> [33] You shall not pollute the land in which you live; for blood pollutes the land, and no expiation [יְכֻפַּר] can be made for the land, for the blood that is shed in it, except by the blood of the one who shed it. [34] You shall not defile the land in which you live, in which I also dwell; for I the Lord dwell among the Israelites.

Here we find atonement connected with pollution of the land by blood. The blood that was shed on the earth is, of course, a major point in Jubilees' version of the angel story, as it is in the BW. Animate beings ate one another (5:2); the giants engaged in mutual slaughter before their fathers' eyes (5:9); and 6:7-8 repeat the law in Genesis about consuming and shedding blood (cf. also vv. 10, 12, 13). But this point, too, is developed to a greater extent in ch. 7:

> They fathered (as their) sons the Nephilim. They were all dissimilar (from one another) and would devour one another: the giant killed the Naphil; the Naphil killed the Elyo; the Elyo mankind; and people their fellows. [23] When everyone sold himself to commit injustice and to shed innocent [or: much] blood, the earth was filled with injustice.

²⁴ After them all the animals, birds, and whatever moves about and whatever walks on the earth.³⁶ Much blood was shed on the earth. All the thoughts and wishes of mankind were (devoted to) thinking up what was useless and wicked all the time. ²⁵ Then the Lord obliterated all from the surface of the earth because of their actions and because of the blood which they had shed on the earth. (7:22-25)

Noah subsequently expressed his fear that when he was gone his children would shed blood on the earth and thus also suffer obliteration (v. 27). He mandated great care in the treatment of blood and noted the need to cover it. In 7:33 the writer shows that he does indeed have Num. 35:33 in mind: "For the earth will not be purified of the blood which has been shed on it; but by the blood of the one who shed it the earth will be purified in all its generations."

While these passages lie behind the introduction of atonement into Jubilees' story, an adjustment had to be made in the special case of Noah and the flood because the blood of the murderers was not available to atone for the defiled earth. Noah alone was in a position to offer such a sacrifice.

The sins committed on the earth received atonement through the sacrifice of a goat. The goat should, although a different word is used in Jubilees than in the Ethiopic Leviticus, remind us of Leviticus 16 and its ceremonies for the day of atonement which involved two goats, one for the Lord and one for Azazel. Azazel is intriguing in this connection because of the similarity between his name and the name of a leading angel in the Watcher story—Asael. It is now clear from the Aramaic fragments of Enoch that the original form of the angel name in that book was עסאל or עשאל, neither of which closely resembles the עזאזל of Lev. 16:8, 10, etc. But at some point in the tradition the two were brought into closer connection so that by the time one reaches the Ethiopic version of 1 Enoch the two names are difficult to distinguish.

4Q180 1 7-8 and 4QEnGiantsª 7 i 6 (see also 11QTª 26:13 which reproduces Lev. 16:21 but imports the name עזזאל into it) now show, by the spellings they give to the name, that the identification between the Azazel of Lev. 16:8, 10, 26 and the Asael of the BW was current in the late Second Temple period. In 4Q180 1 the name occurs twice and obviously within the context of a version of the angel story: line 7 reads פשר על עזזאל והמלאכים אש]ר, and line 8 has וי]לדו

---

³⁶ For what appears to be an incomplete sentence here, see VanderKam, *The Book of Jubilees*, 2.47, n. to v. 24.

לֶהֶם נברים ועל עזאזל.[37] Then, in 4QEnGiants[a] 7 i 5-6, part of a section that mentions the sons of the watchers (line 5) and the watchers
themselves (line 6), Azazel appears: אדין עני לוא לנא [אל]ה לעזא[ז]ל
ועבד ל[ה. Milik translates as: "Then, he (sc. God?) punished, not [6]us,
but 'Azâzel, and has made him". Milik comments about the passage:
"'Azâzel appears here in his expiatory role (Lev. 16:8, 10, 26), for he
seems to be punished for the sins of the giants. He was evidently not
a simple he-goat, but a giant who combined goat-like characteristics
and those of man."[38] The fact that not only a Qumran text in the
Enoch tradition (the Book of Giants) but also one which clearly expresses the determinist view of the community (4Q180) identify the
puzzling creature of Leviticus 16 with the archfiend of the angel
story raises interesting possibilities for explaining the introduction of
the notion of atonement into Jubilees' recension of the tale.[39]

It seems likely that the writer of Jubilees knew a version of the angel
story in which Azazel played a part, but he modified it and turned it to
his own purpose of establishing a legal and cultic precedent. He did not
name Azazel, just as he did not name Shemihazah or any other angel.
But he took the associations with Azazel and turned them into a lesson
about the day of atonement and the need to atone for the earth after
impure acts and shedding of blood. The nearest the BW comes to connecting Asael and Leviticus 16 is in specifying the place where he is
bound as *Dudael* which, as Charles argued, may be the same as the
בית חדודי of Tg. Ps. J. Lev. 16:21-22 and בית חדודו/י in m. Yoma 6.8.[40]
Another possible allusion comes in 1 Enoch 10:8: "And the whole
earth has been ruined by the teaching of the works of Azazel, and
against him write down all sin [*xāṭi'ata*]."[41] The line may reflect Lev.

---

[37] J. M. Allegro, *Qumran Cave 4 I (4Q158-4Q186)* (DJD 5; Oxford: Clarendon Press, 1968) 78. See also D. Dimant, "The 'Pesher on the Periods' (4Q180) and 4Q181," *Israel Oriental Studies* 9 (1979) 78-81.

[38] *The Books of Enoch*, 313.

[39] For Azazel in connection with 1 Enoch 6-11, see Delcor, "Le mythe de la chute," 35-37.

[40] *The Book of Enoch*, 22-23. For a more comprehensive study of possible points of contact between the Asael material in 1 Enoch 6-11 and Leviticus 16 (with ancient interpretations of the matter), see P. Hanson, "Rebellion in Heaven, Azazel, and Euhemeristic Heroes in 1 Enoch 6-11," *JBL* 96 (1977) 220-26. Hanson adds the suggestions that "make an opening in the desert" in 1 Enoch 10:4 arose from the verb פטר (= both "to send" and "to break open") that Tg. Ps. J. Lev. 16:22 uses to translate שלח; the "rough and jagged" rocks in Asael's place of imprisonment is a translation of עזאזל (222-24).

[41] The Greek versions here have τὰς ἁμαρτίας πάσας (Panopolitanus) and πάσας τὰς ἁμαρτίας. See Hanson, "Rebellion in Heaven," 224. Hanson writes about this and other parallels: "These details lead us to conclude that the Azazel episode arose as an expository elaboration which sought to deepen the meaning of the Šemiḥazah

16:21-22 (note especially לכל חטאתם in v. 21). Nevertheless, the language of atonement is not employed in these parts of 1 Enoch; rather, before the flood the earth complains about the lawless beings on it (7:6), and the need for renewal of the corrupted earth is mentioned (1 Enoch 10:7, 20, 22).

Even if 1 Enoch has such traces of Leviticus 16, Jubilees has greatly transformed the tradition. In Jubilees, atonement is necessary, as one could learn from the Mosaic law, and it has a positive function. Rather than laying all sin to the charge of one leader of the angels, Jubilees makes Noah an agent of atonement and calls on Israel to confess its sins annually in order to obtain pardon from God who is the just judge. In using the angel story to establish halakhic points and not to focus on eschatology, the author follows the same procedure he will use in ch. 7 where the sins that led to the flood will become the subject of laws about shedding and covering blood.

III. The Angel Story in Jubilees and 1 Enoch 6-16

Can one make a case that Jubilees is dependent for the angel story on 1 Enoch 6-16? No definitive argument can be fashioned, but it does seem the most economical explanation for the data, despite the large-scale differences between what the two books say about the subject.

First, the paragraphs about Jared and Enoch (Jub. 4:15-26) and the other Enochic sections in Jubilees (5:1-10; 7:20-39; 10:1-17) provide evidence that 1 Enoch 1-36 lay before the author. They supply many details from one version of the angel story, including points such as the angels' descent in Jared's time, their sinful marriages with women, the gigantic children, the violence and blood, the punishments and Enoch's testimony against the Watchers. The Jared pun is from 1 Enoch 6, the story itself is in 1 Enoch 6-11, and the testimony against the watchers is in 1 Enoch 12-16.[42]

Second, while Jubilees lacks many of the details of the stories in 1 Enoch 6-16 (such as the names Shemihazah and Asael, the specific teachings of Asael, the many angel names), it does in fact have the

---

story by relating it to the *yom kippur* text in Lev. 16. The basic structure of the episode was supplied by the mythic pattern of the Šemiḥazah story, for the exposition modeled the elaboration on the account of the punishment of Šemiḥazah. But the details unique to the Azazel episode can be recognized as stemming from the expository techniques of interpreters writing from the perspective of apocalyptic eschatology as they now relate their narrative to yet another biblical text, Lev. 16" (224).

[42] For the specific evidence, see VanderKam, "Enoch in Jubilees," 1.231-41.

basic elements of the story about the angels who sinned with women and became the fathers of giants, as Dimant has shown. One could say that 1 Enoch 9:8-9 summarizes the story as it appears in Jubilees: "And they went in to the daughters of men together, and lay with those women, and became unclean, and revealed to them these sins. And the women bore giants, and thereby the whole earth has been filled with blood and iniquity." The theme of angelic instruction is not present in Jubilees 4-5, but it does appear in part (that is, Asael's military curriculum is not mentioned) in 8:1-4 where Kainan discovers rock inscriptions containing the Watchers' astronomical teachings (see v. 3). Furthermore, Jubilees and 1 Enoch 6-16 share the nature of the punishments meted out to the angels and the giants. It may be that the theme of the evil spirits is also related: Jubilees may present them as emanations from the angels rather than from the bodies of the giants (although "fathers" in 10:5 could be ancestors) as one could infer from some expressions in 1 Enoch 15 (cf. v. 8). It is even possible that Jubilees reflects knowledge of the Azazel tradition in its teachings about atonement, and its emphasis on violation of created orders is reminiscent of the charge made against the angels in 1 Enoch 12-16.

Third, while he knows much that appears in these chapters in 1 Enoch, the writer certainly does not reproduce everything and at times he opposes or strongly modifies an element in his source. So, his teaching that the angels descended for a righteous purpose and were later corrupted contradicts the reason given in 1 Enoch 6 and elsewhere in these chapters. Also, Jubilees downplays the eschatological implications of the story as they appear in 1 Enoch 6-16. The story becomes an example for moral exhortation and a basis for legal inferences in Jubilees, while in 1 Enoch 6-16 it serves to model the final judgment and conditions before it.

It is reasonable to conclude, therefore that the writer of Jubilees was familiar with the BW, borrowed heavily from it, but transformed the material to meet the goals for which he was writing his book.

QUMRAN AND THE BOOK OF NOAH*

CANA WERMAN

Ben Gurion University

A Book of Noah has been mentioned in various sources in antiquity but its identity is still in question. Although I am aware that claims of non-existence are the most difficult to prove—for, after all, discovery of a single copy alone is enough to put such claims to rest—I would like to present evidence that casts doubt on the existence of the book. The Noah book is mentioned both in Qumran literature and in the Pseudepigrapha, apparently strong evidence for its existence. These sources, however, do not agree about the contents of the book.[1]

What, according to these ancient sources, does the Book of Noah embody?

a In the Genesis Apocryphon the following appears at the bottom of col. 5: "A copy of the Book of the Words of Noah." We learn from the recently published columns brought to light by Morgenstern, Qimron, Sivan and the late Prof. Jonas Greenfield[2] that the life story of Noah is given in the Apocryphon. Noah recounts his following the path of righteousness (col. 6), a vision concerning the sin of the Watchers (cols. 6-7), the events of the Flood and the departure from the ark (col. 8-10), his tour of the land (col. 11), the sacrifices he offers and details of the covenant that God made with him (cols. 11-12). Further, Noah tells of the vineyard he planted (col. 12), a vision of the fate of humankind (cols. 13-15); and the world was divided among his sons (cols. 16-17).

b According to the Introduction to the Book of Asaph (a medieval composition based on an ancient source), the Book of Noah deals with remedies and healing.

---

* *This work was supported in part by The Memorial Foundation for Jewish Culture.*

[1] The last scholar who dealt with this problem was F. García Martínez, *Qumran and the Apocalyptic. Studies on the Aramaic Text from Qumran* (STDJ 11; Leiden: E. J. Brill, 1992) 1-44.

[2] M. Morgenstern, E. Qimron and D. Sivan, "The Hitherto Unpublished Columns of the Genesis Apocryphon," *Abr-Nahrain* 33 (1995) 30-54; J. C. Greenfield and E. Qimron, "The Genesis Apocryphon Col. XII," *Abr-Nahrain suppl.* 3 (1992) 70-77.

c According to Jubilees (ch. 10), the Book of Noah consists primarily of phrases meant to lead evil spirits astray. Chapter 21 relates that Abraham discovered "in the book of my ancestors, the words of Enoch and the words of Noah," the laws concerning נותר (portions of sacrifices left over beyond the legal time which must be burned).

d The Aramaic Levi Document states that the Book of Noah deals with laws pertaining to the slaughter of animals and the handling of blood.[3]

Even the most superficial examination of these sources shows that the material attributed to the Book of Noah is different in each case. The Genesis Apocryphon includes a biography of Noah from youth to old age. Yet, despite its richness of detail, the scroll never refers to healing, as one would expect from the Introduction to the Book of Asaph; nor is there any mention of prayers to banish evil spirits, as in Jubilees; finally, laws related to blood, found in Aramaic Levi, are totally absent except for the prohibition of eating blood.

In addition, the author of Jubilees was acquainted with the Genesis Apocryphon and even made use of it. Nonetheless, he attributes material to the Book of Noah that is completely different from the Noah material cited in the Genesis Apocryphon. Instead, the author of Jubilees used material from Aramaic Levi and from the Introduction to the Book of Asaph, but with changes. Jubilees does include laws concerning the slaughter of animals and the handling of blood that are found in Aramaic Levi but, unlike Aramaic Levi, it does not cite the Book of Noah as the source for these laws, although some of these strictures are recited by Noah himself to his sons in Jubilees. Jubilees emphasizes that the Book of Noah includes words and prayers needed to banish evil spirits, while the Introduction to the Book of Asaph holds that the Book of Noah listed remedies for the diseases caused by the evil spirits.

Did the author of Jubilees really know these documents? Himmelfarb has suggested that Jubilees used the precursor of the Introduction to Asaph.[4] I will demonstrate that Jubilees also made use of the Apocryphon and Aramaic Levi.

---

[3] The Athos Manuscript *e*, *57. I use the translation published by J. C. Green-field and M. E. Stone, "The Aramaic and Greek Fragments of a Levi Document," in *The Testaments of the Twelve Patriarchs. A Commentary* (ed. H. W. Hollander and M. de Jonge; SVTP 5; Leiden: E. J. Brill, 1985) 457-69. I use VanderKam's translation of Jubilees: J. C. VanderKam, *The Book of Jubilees*, CSCO 511, Leuven, 1989.

[4] M. Himmelfarb, "Some Echoes of Jubilees in Medieval Hebrew Literature," in *Tracing the Threads: Studies in the Vitality of Jewish Pseudepigrapha* (ed. J. C. Reeves; Atlanta: Scholars Press, 1994) 127-36. In the Introduction to Asaph, the evil spirits

There are three major points of agreement between Jubilees and
the Apocryphon in dealing with the life of Noach. Both mention
נטע רבעי (Jub. 7:1-4; 34-37; Gen. Apoc. 12), the fourth year's fruits
of a young tree; the sacrifices that Noah offers after leaving the Ark
(Jub. 6; Gen. Apoc. 10), and the division of the world among Noah's
sons (Jub. 11-12; Gen. Apoc. 16-17). It is hard to believe that this
congruence is coincidental. The question is only, "Which document
is earlier?"

TABLE 1

Genesis Apocryphon	*Jubilees 7*
and I began—with all my sons—to work the land and I planted a large vineyard at Mt. Lubar	Noah planted a vine at the mountain (whose name was Lubar, one of the mountains of Ararat) on which the ark had come to rest
and by the fourth year it produced wine for me;	It produced fruit in the fourth year. He guarded its fruit and picked it that year during the seventh month. He made wine from it, put it in a container, and kept it until the fifth year— until the first day at the beginning of the first month.
And when the first festival came, on the first day of the first festival of the [seventh?] month...I opened	
this vessel and I began to drink from it on the first day of the fifth year.	He joyfully celebrated the day of this festival. He made a burnt offering for the Lord—one young bull, one ram, seven sheep each a year old, and one kid—to make atonement through it for himself and for his sons. First he prepared the kid. He put some of its blood on the meat (that was on) the altar which he had made. He offered all the fat on the altar where he made the burnt offering along with the bull, the ram, and the sheep.... Afterwards he sprinkled wine in the fire that had been on the altar before hand ... and offered a pleasant fragrance that was pleasing before the Lord his God.
On this day I called my sons and grand-sons and all our wives and their daughters and we gathered together and we went [to the place of the altar?]	He was very happy,
...and I blessed the Lord of Heaven, the Most High God, the Great Holy One who delivered us from destruction	
...they drank and...	and he and his sons happily drank some of this wine.
I poured on ... and the wine	

In col. 12 of the Apocryphon we find the story of Noah planting the vineyard. In the fourth year after planting, the vineyard produces wine which Noah stores until the fifth year. Then he and his family drink the wine and pour it on the altar as a libation. Jubilees relates this story at the beginning of ch. 7 (see Table 1 above).

In Jubilees the story varies at several points. There the wine is first poured on the altar; only then does Noah drink. Also, only his sons drink with him, not the other members of the family. According to the Apocryphon, however, Noah first drinks the wine, then he calls his family to come to the altar and drink the wine, and then wine is poured on the altar. Why these differences? As already shown by Prof. Kister and others, Jub. 7:35-37 not only gives this story but also offers a halakha about fourth year fruits that contradicts the story.[5] According to this halakha, the fruit of the fourth year is brought to the Temple, the *bikkurim* are brought to the altar, while the rest of the fruit is given to the priests. In the Apocryphon the fruit of the fourth year is stored until the fifth year and then the owners are permitted to eat it. It appears likely that the author of Jubilees altered the narrative in order to blur the contradiction between the story and the halakha that he was interested in promulgating. Jubilees sees Noah and his sons as priests, like the other main characters in Jubilees, Abraham, Isaac, Jacob and Levi. Thus, they are allowed the fruit, after the wine of the *bikkurim* is poured on the altar. The year's storage found in the

---

produce diseases in the children of Noah, while in Jubilees the emphasis is on the evil spirits leading the children of Noah astray. In the Introduction, a list of remedies is revealed to Noah while, in Jubilees, Noah is granted the secret of leading the evil spirits themselves astray, in addition to the remedies (130). According to Himmelfarb, Jubilees does not deal with remedies in order to downplay elements that could suggest magic practices on the part of the heroes.

Note that in the Introduction the evil spirits attack the children of Noah and bring disease to them. This is the beginning of a logically developed section that continues with Noah praying for his children. The evil spirits are then, for the most part, imprisoned but a minority remain free to threaten the children of Noah and can continue to produce disease. Noah then receives insight into the remedies needed to combat the illnesses.

In Jubilees the development is more obscure; there we find an emphasis on the moral aspects of the interactions, and the diseases are hardly mentioned at all. In fact there is no need for remedies as such; what is required is the means to deal with the evil spirits. Noah conquers not the diseases but the evil spirits themselves: "And the evil spirits were precluded from pursuing Noah's children" (10:13). Nonetheless, the remedies are mentioned: "We told Noah all the medicines for their diseases with their deceptions" (10:12). The retention of the remedies as a minor theme is apparently a consequence of the author's familiarity with and use of the source of the Introduction.

[5] M. Kister, "Some Aspects of Qumran Halacha," in *The Madrid Qumran Congress* (ed. J. Trebolle Barrera and L. Vegas Montaner; STDJ 11; Leiden: E. J. Brill, 1992) 2.571-88.

Apocryphon is a problem for Jubilees, but the author makes use of it to proclaim the celebration of the first day of the month of Nissan, a holiday of the priestly group not found in rabbinic halakha.[6]

Since the story itself does not serve the halakhic interests of the author of Jubilees, it is unlikely that he invented it; more likely, he knew it from another source. Where else if not from the Apocryphon? If the story was of no interest to him, why use it? Apparently the story as given in the Apocryphon was widely known at the time and could not be ignored.

Examination of the description of Noah's deeds after leaving the ark in these two sources reinforces the conclusion that the author of Jubilees knew the Genesis Apocryphon (see Table 2). The Genesis Apocryphon emphasizes atonement in describing this scene ("and I atoned for the whole Earth" 10 i 13) and, in particular, atonement through the use of blood.[7] Two groups of burnt offerings are recorded, each characterized by a different use of blood. In the first group of burnt offerings, that of the ritually pure animals, the blood is poured on the base of the altar.[8] The turtledove is included in the second group rather than in the first, because it is not a major source of blood (see Lev. 1:5; 16). Jubilees, on the other hand, offers a single category of burnt offerings in a detailed listing of the sacrifices which Noah offered, with both beasts and birds listed together and with no mention of blood at all.[9]

---

[6] Y. Yadin, *The Temple Scroll* (Jerusalem: Israel Exploration Society, Institute of Archaeology of the Hebrew University of Jerusalem, Shrine of the Book, 1983) 2.89-91.

[7] The idea of atonement for the earth by the blood of sin-offerings is unique to the Genesis Apocryphon and is not to be found in the Bible or elsewhere in Qumran literature. In the Bible, the role of sin offerings is to purify the Temple from the impurity produced by the sins of man and his ritual impurities. See J. Milgrom, "The Function of the Hattat Sacrifice," *Tarbiz* 40 (1970) 1-8 (Hebrew).

In fact, in the Bible, there are two things that defile the earth: murder and fornication. In the case of the former, only the blood of the killer can atone, purifying the earth (Num. 35:33; if, however, the murderer is not identified, the blood of a calf may be used [Deut. 21:1-9]). In the case of fornication, God exiles the sinners (Lev. 19); no sacrifice or blood can atone.

[8] According to Lev. 1:5, the blood of a burnt-offering is to be sprinkled on the altar itself, and not to be poured on its base. It is likely that the deviation from the Bible in the Apocryphon is the result of the propinquity of the burnt-offering to the sin-offering in this passage. The blood of the sin-offering (Lev. 4:25) should be poured on the base of the altar, after it was placed on the altar's horns.

[9] In his single list, the author of Jubilees preserves the Apocryphon's original two lists of sacrifices, separated by the interjection of salt, a non-animal sacrifice. See Table 2. Notice that the words, "with its blood" are not found in mss. 20 and 25 (VanderKam considers ms. 25 the most authoritative); this would indicate that blood is not mentioned by Jubilees in this context, rather surprising in view of the book's great concern with blood throughout. It is difficult to avoid the conclusion that the author made deliberate efforts not to mention blood here.

TABLE 2

Genesis Apocryphon	*Jubilees 6*
...and I atoned for the whole Earth ...[he-goat] first	He appeared on the earth, took a kid, and atoned [with its blood] for all the sins of the earth because everything that was on it had been obliterated except those who were in the ark with Noah.
...and after it came...I burned the fat on the fire; secondly...I poured out *their* blood on the base of the altar; then I burned all *their* flesh on the altar	He placed the fat on the altar.
	Then he took a bull, a ram, a sheep, goats, salt, a turtledove, and a dove and offered (them as) a burnt offering on the altar.
and thirdly, the turtledoves...upon the altar as an offering... I put on it fine flour mixed in oil together with frankincense as a meal-offering	He poured on them an offering mixed with oil, sprinkled wine, and put frankincense on everything.
I put salt on all of them.	

In the Apocryphon, this section begins with the declaration by Noah that his sacrifices are an atonement for the whole earth. Jubilees uses a different introductory phrase (see Table 2 above), "He appeared on the earth." The author immediately makes the point that atonement is only meant for the inhabitants of the ark.

Why this change in emphasis? According to Jubilees, the sin of the generation of the Flood is the sin of the consumption and the shedding of blood.[10] Thus, the giants, humankind and animals all sinned (see Table 3 below). In Jubilees 5, the punishment for the misuse of blood is death, blood for blood, as in Num. 35:33, "So you shall not pollute the land wherein you are: for blood it defileth the land: and the land cannot be cleansed of the blood that is shed therein, but by the blood of him that shed it." Jubilees 5 specifies the punishment for all that generation: the giants killed one another by the sword

---

[10] C. Werman, "The Story of the Flood in the Book of Jubilees," *Tarbiz* 64 (1995) 183-202 (Hebrew).

(5:6-9), the Watchers are bound and wait in Sheol for their death at the End of Days (5:10-11), men and animals, other than those in the ark, are wiped out in the Flood (5:20). The earth, defiled by blood, is cleansed by the blood of the giants, of humankind and of animals. In Jubilees there is no longer any need for atonement for the earth after the flood.

TABLE 3

Jubilees 5	*Jubilees 7*
Injustice increased on the earth	When everyone sold himself to commit injustice **and to shed innocent blood**. The earth was filled with injustice (23)
all animate beings corrupted their way, from people to cattle, animals, birds and everything that moves about on the ground	After them all the animals, birds, and whatever moves about and whatever walks on the earth
All of them corrupted their way and their prescribed course	**Much blood was shed on the earth** (24)
He said that He would obliterate people and all animate beings that were on the face of the earth that he had created.	Then the Lord obliterated all from the face of the Earth because of their actions **and because of the blood that they had shed into the earth**.

Jubilees' use of the difficult word "appeared," describing Noah's exit from the Ark, "...he appeared on the earth," can be understood as a replacement for the atonement idea given by the Apocryphon: "...I atoned for the Earth." The change in verb reflects the author's need to de-emphasize the notion, introduced by the Apocryphon, that the earth is still defiled after the Flood.

The author of Jubilees was apparently also familiar with the Aramaic Levi Document. In Aramaic Levi, we find Isaac instructing Levi on sacrifice and slaughtering. In Jubilees 21, it is Abraham who instructs Isaac, with similar rules (see Table 4).

It is clear that the two lists are similar. The similarity is even greater if we note that Jubilees deals not only with peace offerings, as generally assumed until now, but burnt offerings as well. Inclusion of the law of burnt offerings in the list of subjects in ch. 21 is justified.

TABLE 4

Aramaic Levi Document	*Jubilees 21*
	Prohibition against eating blood. Burnt offering and peace offering:
Warning to lave the body before sacrificing. Warning to wash hands and feet.[11] (Slaughtering) Washing hands and feet.[12] Kinds of wood needed for the altar. Sprinkling of blood.	Sprinkling of blood.
Washing hands and feet after sprinkling blood.	
Burning parts of the burnt offering.	Burning parts of the burnt offering. Burning the fat of the peace offering. Meal offering and libation. Prohibition against eating נותר.
Salt.	Salt.
Meal offering, libation, and frankincense.	
Measures of wood, salt, flour, oil, wine and incense for each sacrifice.	Kinds of wood needed for the altar. Warning to lave the body before sacrificing. Warning to wash hands and feet.
Warning to wash hands and feet after sacrifice.	Warning to wash hands and feet after sacrifice.
Warning about blood during sacrifices.	Warning about blood during sacrifices
Warning about blood during profane slaughter.	(Warning about blood during profane slaughter [found in ch. 7]). Prohibition against eating blood.

---

[11] The biblical basis for the double requirement of washing, once of the body and again of the hands and feet, is found in Exod. 30:20-21: "When they go into the tabernacle of the congregation, they shall wash with water that they die not; or when they come near to the altar, to minister, to burn offerings made by fire unto the Lord: so they shall wash their hands and feet that they die not...."

[12] The question arises, why, after the first laving, is there a requirement for a second, of the same limbs? This requirement to wash the hands and feet a second time apparently reflects the need produced by the slaughtering of the burnt-offering before the priest approaches the altar. Indeed, Second Temple literature indicates that it was the priests who carried out the slaughtering, and not the one bringing the sacrifice.

In line 3 of frg. 4Q220 of Jubilees,[13] we find the difficult זבח שלמים
עלה, referring not only to peace offerings but to burnt offerings as
well. Lines 4 and 5 of the fragment clearly speak about burnt offerings that are completely burnt on the altar. At the end of line 5 we
find an allusion to peace offerings where the fat is the item which is
burnt on the altar.

Which list came first? It is likely that Aramaic Levi is earlier. This
is most obvious in the polemic nature of Jubilees' attitude towards
matters of blood, not found at all in Aramaic Levi. In Jubilees the instructions for covering blood and the warning against the appearance of drops of blood on the limbs of the slaughterer as well as on
his clothing are part of the prohibition against eating blood.[14] Thus,
the demand to cover the blood and the warning against the appearance of blood are part of the conditional covenant between God and
Noah; the covenant is valid only to the extent that these prohibitions
are honored.[15] In Aramaic Levi there is no connection between the

---

[13] *Qumran Cave 4.VIII* (DJD XIII; ed. H. W. Attridge, T. L. Elgvin, J. T. Milik, S.
Olyan, J. Strugnell, E. Tov, J. C. VanderKam and S. White; Oxford: Clarendon,
1994):

> 3 [If you sa]crifice a burnt-offering (and) a peace-offer[ing] you are to [sa]crifice it
> in a pleasing way, and you are to sprinkle their blood on the alt[ar.]
> 4 [All] the meat of the burnt-offering you are to off[e]r on the al[tar] with the
> flour of its offering mixed with [o]i[l,]
> 5 [with its libation. You] are to offer the whole on the altar as a fire-offering, a
> pleasing fragrance before God. [The fat]
> 6 [of the pe]a[ce sacrifice] you are to offer on the fire which is on the altar, and
> the fat [which is on...]

[14] Note that the section of Jub. 21 which deals with the burnt-offering and the
peace-offering begins and ends with the prohibition against consuming blood. See
Werman, "The Events of the Generation."

[15] Compare the biblical order to the order in Jubilees. In Gen. 8-9:

–God smells the sweet savor of the sacrifice.
–God decides in his heart not to visit another flood on the earth.
–God blesses Noah and his sons and commands them to be fruitful and multiply,
  places their dread upon all creatures, permits them to eat meat, prohibits
  their consumption of blood and stipulates the prohibition against spilling the
  blood of man.
–God makes a covenant with the inhabitants of the earth that he will not visit
  another flood on the earth.
–The rainbow is given as a token.

In Jub. 6:
–God smells the sweet savor of the sacrifice.
–God makes a covenant with Noah.
–God details the conditions of the covenant, to be fruitful and multiply, grants
  rule over all other creatures, gives permission to eat meat, prohibits the eating
  of blood, prohibits the spilling of the blood of man.
–Noah and his sons accept the conditions of the covenant.
–A rainbow is given as a token of the covenant.

instructions for washing and the care needed in dealing with blood and the prohibition against eating blood. In fact, this prohibition is not found at all in Aramaic Levi.

If the Aramaic Levi Document were dependent on Jubilees, some remnant of the repeated and central polemical position against eating blood and its relationship to the other laws would be expected. None is present.

Jub. 7:10 offers further evidence that Jubilees is dependent on Aramaic Levi: "... because this is the way I found it written in the book of my ancestors, in the words of Enoch and in the words of Noah." Here we see that Jubilees mentions two figures who are related to Aramaic Levi. Halakhot dealing with incense are, according to Jubilees 4, derived from Enoch. In Aramaic Levi there are halakhot related to incense; because of this reference to incense, Jubilees, almost mechanically, adds Enoch in ch. 21.[16]

Aramaic Levi ascribes halakhot dealing with blood to the Book of Noah. It is no surprise, therefore, that the stanza dealing with blood in Jubilees 21 also contains a reference to the Book of Noah. Jubilees, however, does not attribute the halakhot related to the handling of blood to the Book of Noah; the author insists that such halakhot were transmitted orally. Because of the need of the author of Jubilees to retain the oral nature of Noah's laws concerning blood, only the halakha relating to the prohibition against the eating of

---

Jubilees differs from the Bible also in choosing the object of the covenant. On the one hand, God promises to desist from cursing the earth and from obliterating all living beings on it (Gen. 8:21) and, in another version, not to bring the waters of a flood to destroy the earth and obliterate all flesh (Gen. 9:11). In Jub. 6, on the other, God restricts his promise to forgo destruction to the earth alone. God will not bring another flood to destroy the earth but he does not commit himself to desist from killing all living beings (6:4, 16). See Werman, "The Story of the Flood."

[16] I still am not sure of the source of the requirement for adding frankincense to the meal offering that accompanied the burnt-offerings found in Aramaic Levi, Genesis Apocryphon as well as Jubilees (6:3; 7:3; 32:4-6, and see: C. Albeck, "Das Buch Jubiläen und die Halacha," *Jahresbericht Hochschule für die Wissenchaft des Judentums* (1930) 22. In the Bible, frankincense is only given with an independent meal offering; its memorial, a handful of its flour and the added oil and all the frankincense, is burnt on the altar while the remainder is eaten by the priests (Lev. 2:1-3). It is probable that the halakhic outlook reflected here derives from the requirement to join frankincense to the flour and oil which are burnt in the meal offering. By extension, the requirement for frankincense was broadened to include the meal offering that was given with the burnt-offering, both to be burned on the altar. It is likely that this requirement is connected to that of pouring all the wine on the fire, as in the Temple Scroll and Jubilees (Albeck, "Das Buch Jubiläen," 22; Yadin, *The Temple Scroll*, 118-19) and not on the edges of the altar, as we find in the halakha of the Sages, and to use special wood, as in Aramaic Levi and Jubilees. Wine on the fire together with frankincense produce the sweet aroma, a requirement of every sacrifice.

נוֹחַ, a relatively minor point, is acknowledged to be part of the Book of Noah.

In summary, the Genesis Apocryphon includes the story of the life of Noah. The author of the Book of Jubilees knew this scroll and used it; despite this, he did not hesitate to attribute to the Book of Noah material totally different from that found in the scroll. Instead, he preferred the testimonies of other works, the Aramaic Levi Document and the antecedent of the Introduction to the Book of Asaph available to him. Even with these materials we feel the deft use of the editor's pen.

For these reasons, it is not likely that an actual Book of Noah was available to the author of Jubilees. When we examine Jubilees' attitude to the Book of Enoch, we see that the author of Jubilees faithfully reports its contents.[17] However, inventive author that he is, he adds halakhic material related to incense and to fruits of the fourth year to his recounting of the Enoch material. If the author of Jubilees had a manuscript of the Book of Noah before him, we might expect him to do the same, that is to give the contents faithfully and then to add his own material. His failure to do so argues against his having such a book to refer to and casts doubt on the existence of such a book. Jubilees knows of a Book of Noah only by hearsay, from three secondary sources that contradict one another as to the nature of this putative book.

---

[17] Jub. 4:17 summarizes the Astronomical Book of 1 Enoch: Jub. 4:18 summarizes the Apocalypse of Weeks found in the Epistle of Enoch. Jub. 4:19 summarizes the Book of Dreams. Jub. 4:21 summarizes the second part of the Book of the Watchers. Jub. 4:23 summarizes chs. 106-107 at the end of the Epistle. See J. C. VanderKam, "Enoch Traditions in Jubilees and other Second-Century Sources," *SBLSP* (1978) 233-35; *idem, Enoch and the Growth of an Apocalyptic Tradition* (CBQMS 16; Washington DC: Catholic Biblical Association of America, 1984) 179-88; P. Grelot, "Henoch et ses écritures," *RB* 82 (1975) 481-88; J. T. Milik, *The Book of Enoch, Aramaic Fragments of Qumran Cave 4* (Oxford: Clarendon, 1976) 25, 45, 61-62; García Martínez, *Qumran and the Apocalyptic,* 76.

QUMRAN PSEUDEPIGRAPHA IN EARLY CHRISTIANITY

Is 1 Clem. 50:4 a Citation of 4QPseudo-Ezekiel (4Q385)?

BENJAMIN G. WRIGHT

Lehigh University

For many and varied reasons, ancient Christians found much non-biblical Jewish literature worth using and preserving. For instance, before their discovery as part of the scrolls of Qumran, important Jewish works like 1 Enoch and Jubilees were known only in the versions transmitted in Christian communities. Christians put this literature to use as proof texts for various ideas and, as a result, early Christian writers frequently cite passages from Jewish works.

The manner of citation used by Christian writers often provides clues to the origin of a particular quotation. To give just one example, the several citations by church fathers given in the name of the biblical prophet Ezekiel combined with ancient testimony concerning more than one book by this prophet (Epiphanius, Pan. 64.70 and Josephus, Ant. 10:79) witness to the existence of an ancient Apocryphon of Ezekiel.[1] In many more instances, however, scholars still do not know the origins of the citations, which frequently appear out of context and with vague citation formulae. The discovery and publication of so many Jewish pseudepigrapha among the Qumran scrolls provide an expanded range of texts that can be used in attempts to identify some of these early Christian citations. The most prominent example from Qumran thus far is 4QPseudo-Ezekiel.

With the recent, accelerated work on the manuscripts from Qumran Cave 4 came the publication of several fragments deriving from a Hebrew Ezekiel pseudepigraphon, originally designated 4QSecond Ezekiel, but now called 4QPseudo-Ezekiel.[2] Its original editors, John

---

[1] On the *Apocryphon of Ezekiel* see M. R. James, "The Apocryphal Ezekiel," *JTS* 15 (1914) 236-43; J. R. Mueller, *The Five Fragments of the Apocryphon of Ezekiel: A Critical Study* (JSOPSS 5; Sheffield: Sheffield Academic Press, 1994); and J. R. Mueller and S. E. Robinson, "Apocryphon of Ezekiel," in *The Old Testament Pseudepigrapha* (ed. J. H. Charlesworth; Garden City, NY: Doubleday, 1983) 1.487-95.

[2] The literature on 4QPseudo-Ezekiel is constantly growing, but the most important publications of the Hebrew text are: J. Strugnell and D. Dimant, "4Q Second Ezekiel," *RevQ* 13 (1988) 45-59; *idem*, "The Merkebah Vision in *Second Ezekiel* (4Q385 4)," *RevQ* 14 (1990) 331-48; M. Kister and E. Qimron, "Observa-

Strugnell and Devorah Dimant, included in this work all the numbers from 4Q385-4Q390, but Dimant, who now has sole responsibility for their publication, currently limits its scope among these numbers to four copies: 4Q385 fragments 1-5, 12, 24 (PsEz[a]); all of 4Q386 (PsEz[b]); possibly several fragments of 4Q387 (PsEz[c]); 4Q388 at least fragment 8 (PsEz[d]). The present status of 4Q387 is somewhat uncertain. In her paper delivered at the Madrid Qumran Conference, she originally reported 4Q387 and 4Q388 as separate copies of 4QPseudo-Ezekiel, and thus the four copies of the work in her lot.[3] In her contribution to the *festschrift* for David Flusser, however, she lists 4Q387 as a copy of a Pseudo-Moses pseudepigraphon.[4] A fifth copy of this Ezekiel pseudepigraphon is contained among the 4Q391 fragments (PsEz[e]) published by Mark Smith in DJD 19.[5]

This Cave 4 pseudepigraphon is framed as a dialogue between the biblical prophet and God. Several of the extant fragments reprise portions of the biblical Ezekiel, especially the Merkabah Vision (Ezekiel 1, 10) and the Vision of the Dry Bones (Ezekiel 37). Other passages, although probably originating under the influence of biblical texts, nevertheless do not follow them closely. Still others show little or no relationship to the biblical Ezekiel at all.

In the light of the initial publications of Strugnell and Dimant, Menahem Kister and Richard Bauckham, in separate articles, have argued that three patristic texts, two of which are cited with vague introductions and one whose introduction attributes it to Enoch, may have originated in 4QPseudo-Ezekiel. Kister argues first that Barn. 12:1, which reads, "Similarly again he describes the cross in another prophet, who says, 'And when shall all these things be accomplished? The Lord says, "When a tree shall bend and stand erect and when blood shall flow from the tree",'" parallels closely, and perhaps has as its source the text of the Ezekiel pseudepigraphon found in 4Q385 2, "And I said, 'O, YHWH, when will these things happen?' And YHWH said to me, '...And a tree shall

tions on 4Q Second Ezekiel," *RevQ* 15 (1992) 595-602; M. Smith, "Pseudo-Ezekiel," in *Qumran Cave 4 XIV: Parabiblical Texts Part 2* (ed. M. Broshi et al.; DJD 19; Oxford: Clarendon Press, 1995) 153-93.

[3] D. Dimant, "New Light from Qumran on the Jewish Pseudepigrapha—4Q390," in *Proceedings of the International Congress on the Dead Sea Scrolls, Madrid 18-21 March 1991* (ed. J. Trebolle Barrera and L. Vegas Montaner; Studies on the Texts of the Desert of Judah 11; Madrid: Universidad Complutense; Leiden: E. J. Brill, 1992) 2.409.

[4] D. Dimant, "The Apocalyptic Interpretation of Ezekiel at Qumran," in *Messiah and Christos: Studies in the Jewish Origins of Christianity* (ed. I. Gruenwald, S. Shaked and G. G. Stroumsa; Tübingen: J. C. B. Mohr, 1992) 49, n. 74.

[5] For the 4Q391 fragments, see Smith, "Pseudo-Ezekiel."

bend and stand erect...'."[6] He also notes a similarity between 4Q385 3 and Barn. 4:3. In this case Barnabas attributes a passage to Enoch that ends "For to this end the Lord has cut short the days that his Beloved should make haste and come to his inheritance." In the Qumran fragment Ezekiel asks God to "Let the days hasten on fast until all men will say, 'Indeed the days are hastening on in order that the children of Israel may inherit'." About this text, however, Kister only muses that Barnabas may be a free rendering of a text like 4Q385, and indeed this parallel has less to commend it than the first.

The citation from "scripture" given in Apoc. Pet. 4:7-9 is the only such citation in the book.[7] It clearly refers to Ezekiel's vision of the Valley of the Dry Bones, but the citation contains several important variations from the biblical version which correspond to the vision as it is reported in 4Q385 2. Bauckham relies on four major pieces of evidence to argue that the passage, rather than a quote from Ezekiel 37, is actually from 4QPseudo-Ezekiel: (1) the beginning of 4Q385 2 5 is in the same sequence as the Apocalypse of Peter, (2) in both of these instances the effect is "to produce a formula characteristic of Ezekiel," (3) both 4QPseudo-Ezekiel and the Apocalypse of Peter present the phrase "bone to its bone" as what Yahweh commands Ezekiel to say, a major difference from the biblical text, (4) the phrase "joint to its joint" in 4Q385 2 5-6 parallels the reference to joints in Apocalypse of Peter, but has no basis in the Masoretic text.[8] Bauckham concludes that "the *Apocalypse of Peter*...reflects the major characteristic feature of this passage [4Q385 2] of *4Q Second Ezekiel* in its rewriting of Ezekiel 37. That the *Apocalypse of Peter* is actually quoting *4Q Second Ezekiel* seems therefore very likely."[9]

Bauckham ends his discussion with a significant point about this citation of 4QPseudo-Ezekiel. He remarks, "That *4Q Second Ezekiel* was cited as scripture by the author of the *Apocalypse of Peter* is of interest in demonstrating that this work was not confined to the Qumran community and increases the probability that it did not originate there."[10] Of course, such a conclusion indirectly raises the issue of whether the extant patristic citations usually identified as

---

[6] Kister notes several difficulties with identifying 4Q385 2 as the source of the quote; M. Kister, "Barnabas 12:1; 4:3 and 4Q Second Ezekiel," *RB* 97 (1990) 66.

[7] Richard Bauckham, "A Quotation from 4Q Second Ezekiel in the *Apocalypse of Peter*," *RevQ* 15 (1992) 437.

[8] Bauckham, "Quotation," 442-43.

[9] Bauckham, "Quotation," 443.

[10] Bauckham, "Quotation," 443. Strugnell and Dimant reach the same conclusion in "4Q Second Ezekiel" based on the vocabulary and ideas of the work.

part of the Greek Apocryphon of Ezekiel come from the same work as that found in Qumran. Bauckham is less certain about that prospect, but, even though the Greek citations and the Qumran work contain no common passages, the form and content of several of the patristic citations would fit well with the Qumran work as we know it.[11]

The fact that some early Christian writers were familiar with the Qumran Pseudo-Ezekiel makes it a prime candidate for comparison with patristic citations that make allusion to passages from Ezekiel or that sound like the biblical Ezekiel, even though they may not be explicitly associated with the prophet. In his seminal article on the Apocryphon of Ezekiel known to early Christian writers, M. R. James listed several unidentified citations that Alfred Resch thought might come from that work.[12] Now, after the discovery of the Qumran manuscripts, one of Resch's suggested apocryphal Ezekiel texts, 1 Clem. 50:4, may be proposed to be a citation of the same Jewish Pseudo-Ezekiel work found in multiple copies among the scrolls.

Clement of Rome knew non-biblical Ezekiel traditions. 1 Clem. 8:3 almost certainly originated in an Apocryphon of Ezekiel.[13] In 50:4 Clement cites a prophetic passage as scripture by the introductory formula, "It is written" (γέγραπται γάρ). The citation itself consists of three clauses. The first, "Enter into your inner chambers for a little while, until my anger and wrath pass away," is a shorter, variant form of Isa. 26:20.[14] The citation lacks several elements of the Isaiah passage, namely Isaiah's initial imperative "Go my people" and the middle portion of the biblical verse which exhorts the people to close the door of the chamber and to hide. Two nouns for God's anger occur in Clement's text while Isaiah has only one. The second

---

[11] Bauckham, "Quotation,"444. Dimant, "Apocalyptic Interpretation," 49, n. 73, has claimed that "no direct connection" exists between the two works, presumably meaning that there is no textual overlapping. This much is true. The discussion should probably center on the compatibility of the patristic citations with the Qumran work and the date and place of the works, as far as that can be determined.

[12] James, "Apocryphal Ezekiel," 243. See A. Resch, *Agrapha: Ausserkanonische Schriftfragmente* (TU 30/3-4; Leipzig: J. C. Hinrichs, 1906).

[13] For the arguments in favor of 1 Clem. 8:3 originating in the Apocryphon of Ezekiel, see B. G. Wright, "A Fragment of Apocryphal Ezekiel Contained in First Clement," paper presented at the Annual Meeting of the Society of Biblical Literature, Atlanta, Georgia, 22-25 November 1986, and Mueller, *Five Fragments*, 101-20.

[14] For the complete Greek and Hebrew texts, see the Appendix to this paper.

clause of 50:4, "And I will remember a good day," has no obvious biblical parallel. Finally, the third clause, "And I will raise you up out of your graves," is taken from Ezek. 37:12. In this section the verb "raise" and the noun for "tombs/graves" differ from the manuscript tradition of the Greek translation of Ezekiel. The divergences from the texts of Isaiah and Ezekiel in the first and third parts of Clement's citation together with the absence of any biblical source for the second clause indicate that Clement is not likely creating a composite citation here, but is citing some text that he has found in this form in some source.[15]

1 Clem. 50:4 is not the only place where Ezekiel and Isaiah 26 come together in Jewish and Christian literature. Several texts that concern Ezekiel himself or material from his book invoke Isa. 26:19-20. In Pan. 64.70 Epiphanius begins with a citation of the Greek of Isa. 26:19, "For the dead will rise and those in their tombs will be raised up," and then segues into a parable about two men, one lame and the other blind, who despoil a king's garden, which Epiphanius says came "from Ezekiel's own apocryphon."[16] A later rabbinic midrash, Song Rab. 7:8, relates that Hananiah, Mishael and Azariah went to Ezekiel to ask if they should bow down to Nebuchadnezzar's idols. Ezekiel responds that his teacher Isaiah told him, "Hide yourself a little while until my anger passes away," a citation of Isa. 26:20. Finally, 4Q385 4, a fragment containing Ezekiel's vision of the merkabah, most likely alludes to Isa. 26:20. Strugnell and Dimant transcribe line 3 חבא כמעט ק]ט. The verb חבא appears nowhere in Ezekiel, but Isa. 26.20 begins חבי כמעט רגע.

This same conjunction of biblical texts may be present in 4Q385 12, another of the 4QPseudo-Ezekiel fragments; and this conjunction is very reminiscent of the prophetic citation in 1 Clem. 50:4. Although the text of 4Q385 12 is fragmentary, the almost certain reconstruction of line 3 as ב]ן [אדם reveals that the fragment is about Ezekiel. The first full sentence in line 1 that begins "And all the people rose up" probably indicates that the events of the fragment concern Ezekiel 37, the Vision of the Dry Bones.[17] Specifically, the sentence is probably the culmination of a longer paraphrase of the

---

[15] On Clement's citation practices, see D. A. Hagner, *The Use of the Old and New Testaments in Clement of Rome* (SNT 34; Leiden: E. J. Brill, 1973).

[16] The Greek translation of Isa. 26:19 quoted by Epiphanius differs significantly from the Masoretic text which says, "Your dead shall live, their corpses shall rise."

[17] R. Eisenman and M. O. Wise mistakenly give this fragment as "Pseudo-Jeremiah"; *The Dead Sea Scrolls Uncovered* (New York: Penguin, 1992) 58.

events of Ezek. 37:9-10. It is only here in the biblical Ezekiel that a
group rises up. After the dry bones come together in 37:7-8, God
commands Ezekiel to prophecy to the breath. The four winds come
and bring breath into the people. The people then "stood up on
their feet (ויעמדו על רגליהם)." In fact these verses may provide a
plausible reconstruction of the end of 4Q385 12 1. I would suggest,
based on Ezek. 37:10, that the line should read, ויקומו כל העם
וי[עמדו על] רגליהם. The condition of line 2 prevents any certainty
as to what is happening, but the first person singular pronoun suggests that Ezekiel is the speaker. The vocabulary of line 2 does not
reflect any passage from the biblical book, and apparently God's
statement to Ezekiel in Ezek. 37:11 was not included in 4QPseudo-
Ezekiel, but was replaced with something else.[18] Since line 3 begins
with a *vacat*, whatever is happening in line 2 probably constitutes the
end of a section.

The continuing storyline of Ezek. 37:12-14, however, provides a
good framework for the new section beginning with 4Q385 12 3.
God speaks to Ezekiel, "And YHWH said to me, 'Son of [Man]...'."[19]
The next 2 lines, 4-5, are the ones of immediate interest. The words
that can be read with confidence are, ישכבו עד אשׁ[ר, "and they will
lie/rest until...." Preceding them are the letters הם, which I take as a
feminine plural nominal ending with a third person plural masculine
possessive pronoun. The extant portion of line 5 begins with the
combination of letters יכם, a second person plural possessive ending,
and the line ends with the phrase "and from the land (ומן הארץ)."

Any reconstructions here must be tentative, but the context of this
fragment in Ezekiel 37 and the combination of Isa. 26:20 and Ezek.
37:12, which I believe appears in lines 4-5, may provide some assistance. Beginning with line 4, if the storyline follows Ezekiel 37, the
people stand up and then God tells Ezekiel to say to them, "Thus
says the Lord God, I am going to open your graves (קברותיכם) and
bring you up out of your graves (מקברותיכם), my people" (37:12).

---

[18] One possible reason for the replacement may be that Ezek. 37:11 is clearly
about community restoration. Since 4QPseudo-Ezekiel understands Ezekiel 37 to
be about resurrection, this verse was not really appropriate in this interpretive context.

[19] In the MT there is a *setumah* at the end of 37:12. Verse 13 reiterates the
thought of 37:12 that God will "open your graves." 4Q385 12 only has the idea of
opening graves (if my reconstruction makes sense) once, eliminating the doubling of
the thought found in the biblical text. The *vacat* of line 3 may perhaps represent an
early tradition of the *setumah/petuhah*. If so, this would be especially important since
this work is not Bible, but a biblical rewriting.

Keeping Ezekiel 37 as the frame, the הם- in line 4 might be reconstructed קברותם, "their tombs." There is a small stroke of a letter
visible on the microfiche photo (PAM 44.195) before the ה that is, at
least, not inconsistent with a ו that is necessary for the plural ending
on the noun.

The words following the הם- of line 4 do not come from Ezekiel
37. They may, however, recall the thought expressed in Isa. 26:20
and represent an interpretation of the Dry Bones Vision as concerning resurrection of the righteous. Since there is no conjunction pre-
fixed to ישכבו the preceding word probably began the sentence and
might thus be reconstructed something like "in their graves"
(בקברותם). The כי-sequence in line 5 may be reconstructed in con-
sonance with what has preceded as קברותיכם "your tombs/graves,"
a frequently occurring term in Ezek. 37:11-14.

Thus, the whole section from lines 4-6 would be an interpretive
paraphrase of the events narrated in Ezek. 37:10-14 with an allusion
to Isa. 26:20 interposed. The passage then would read, with some
supplied material, "And Yahweh said to me, 'Son of [Man, say/
speak(?)] to them(?) ...[in] their [graves] they will lie/rest until [my
anger passes[20] and I will raise you up from] your [graves] and from
the earth....'" This last phrase also may continue the storyline of
Ezekiel 37 in which, after the section about being raised from their
graves, God promises the people to restore them to their land. What
the intervening material, represented here by ellipsis dots, may have
been would depend on how wide the columns were, which at present is an unknown.

Reconstructing the fragment in this way may begin to provide a
coherent reading, but several interpretive difficulties require consideration. First, if lines 3-5 speak about God's intention to raise the
faithful from their graves, as I have suggested, then how does one account for its position *after* the statement that the people have already
risen up? The easiest explanation is the one that I have given above,
that 4QPseudo-Ezekiel simply follows the order of events in Ezekiel
37.

It also, however, represents a literary feature used elsewhere in
4QPseudo-Ezekiel, in 4Q385 2, part of the Dry Bones Vision itself,
which presumably preceded 4Q385 12 in the work. Beginning in
4Q385 2 2 Ezekiel speaks about those in Israel who have been faithful, after which he asks in line 3, "And these things [presumably
what YHWH has already told him] when will they happen and how

---

[20] This tentative restoration is taken from Isa. 26:20.

will they be paid back for their piety?" God commands Ezekiel to prophesy to the bones, which come together. After God tells Ezekiel to prophesy again, flesh appears on the reconstituted bones. God then tells Ezekiel to prophesy a third time, and the people come alive. Finally "a great crowd of people stood and they blessed YHWH Sabaoth who made them live." Only after the people stand and bless God does Ezekiel again ask, "O YHWH, when will these things happen?" God gives another reply which seems to include the strange prophecy about a tree bending and becoming erect. Thus, Ezekiel's questions might be taken in the first instance to address the restored community of the text and, in the second, the community that is reading the work.

I understand 4Q385 12 to be working rhetorically in a similar manner to 4Q385 2. After the people rise up, God speaks to Ezekiel about what will happen in the future still to come. This most likely represents the future of the group who composed or used the text. The Dry Bones Vision is understood in the Qumran text not to be concerned with community restoration but a prophecy about the resurrection of the righteous who have been faithful to the law.[21] And just as the dry bones were raised to life in Ezekiel, so God will raise those who are now, according to the authors/readers of the text, in their graves. Thus the text functions on two levels. On one level, it describes a resurrection which God accomplished before the eyes of Ezekiel and, on the other, it prophesies a resurrection that will yet occur for the community who used this work. 4Q385 2 has a past and future aspect and so does 4Q385 12, in the way in which I have attempted to interpret it.

A second interpretive issue which requires explanation is the change from third to second person between lines 4 and 5. This switch may also represent a way of including the reading/interpretive community in the events themselves. In this case, like the one above, God raised the Israelites up in the past, *and* he will raise the present community, here addressed in the second person. Other Qumran texts also exhibit changes in person for apparently similar reasons. One example is 4Q462.[22] This text presents its own inter-

---

[21] On resurrection at Qumran see the magisterial work of E. Puech, *La croyance de Esséniens en la vie future: Immortalité, résurrection, vie éternelle?* (Paris: Librairie Lecoffre, 1993). On 4QPseudo-Ezekiel in particular, see 2.605-16.
[22] M. S. Smith, "4Q462 (Narrative) Fragment 1: A Preliminary Edition," *RevQ* 15 (1991-92) 55-77 and M. Smith, "4QNarrative C," in *Qumran Cave 4 XIV: Parabiblical Texts Part 2*, DJD 19.195-209.

pretive problems, but it seems to be a "pre-sectarian" or "non-sectarian" text that uses historical allusions to highlight "the return of the Jewish people from the diaspora."[23] Line 9 says, "they captured his people [a reference to the Babylonian captivity?]; the light was with them and upon *us* [emphasis mine]...." Here the text seems to shift from the third person "them" of the historical allusion to the "us" of the present community.

Are the texts in 1 Clem. 50:4 and 4Q385 12 the same and do they derive from the same Pseudo-Ezekiel? Again several problems require solutions. First, one clear problem is that there is no manuscript evidence that the middle clause in 1 Clement, "and I will remember a good day," was present in the Qumran work. Second, even though a reconstruction of the fragment based on Isa. 26:20 and Ezekiel 37 is plausible and works well there, it certainly may not be the only possibility. There are obvious differences between the patristic quotation and the Qumran fragment. 1 Clement's citation enjoins the faithful to "enter into their inner chambers," a phrase more in line with Isa. 26:20 instead of, if my reconstruction makes sense, "rest [in their graves]." Clement's phrase "for a little while" is apparently missing from the Qumran fragment.

These differences complicate the question of whether 1 Clement's prophetic text originated in Pseudo-Ezekiel. One possible view of the problem is that the Qumran Pseudo-Ezekiel and the Christian 1 Clement are simply using a common exegetical tradition that juxtaposes Isa. 26:19-20, which speaks of raising the dead, and Ezekiel 37, which is clearly interpreted as being concerned with resurrection. This would seem to be a natural conjunction. These two texts, as I noted above, are, after all, conjoined elsewhere.

If 1 Clement is citing the text from an Ezekiel pseudepigraphon, however, it is clearly not the same version as the one from Qumran. Both 4Q385 12 and 1 Clem. 50:4 probably derive from a Jewish pseudepigraphon that was not composed by the Qumran community. Internally, on the basis of 4QPseudo-Ezekiel's vocabulary, Strugnell and Dimant suggest that it was not composed by the Qumranites.[24] Its use by the Epistle of Barnabas and the Apocalypse of Peter also argues for its non-sectarian origin.[25] If these Christian

---

[23] The characterizations, "pre-" and "non-sectarian" are Smith's ("Preliminary Edition," 77).

[24] For Strugnell and Dimant's suggestion, see Strugnell and Dimant, "4QSecond Ezekiel," 58, and subsequently Dimant, "Apocalyptic Interpretation," 50.

[25] Bauckham, "Quotation," 442-43, makes this suggestion. See above.

works along with 1 Clement knew Pseudo-Ezekiel, then this Jewish pseudepigraphon at some point must have been translated into Greek and subsequently was transmitted in that language by early Christians.

I do not regard these remaining problems as insurmountable, however, and my view is that 1 Clem. 50:4 most likely derives from the same apocryphal Ezekiel work that was found in Cave 4 at Qumran. This conclusion seems more reasonable if 4QPseudo-Ezekiel originated outside of the Qumran community.

To conclude, then, 4Q385 12 interprets Ezekiel 37 as evidence that God will resurrect his people. This interpretation is consistent with other 4QPseudo-Ezekiel texts. The fragment may well represent the use of Isa. 26:20 in conjunction with Ezek. 37:12 to further this understanding of the biblical text, and this combination of texts enables some plausible reconstructions of the fragment. While it is difficult to know whether 1 Clem. 50:4 is citing the same work as 4QPseudo-Ezekiel, the similarities are close enough that on the basis of scholarly intuition I suspect that they derive from the same Jewish pseudepigraphon. At the very least, the use of Pseudo-Ezekiel in other Christian literature shows that it may have been available to the author of 1 Clement. Certainly 4Q385 12 and 1 Clem. 50:4 illustrate the methodological difficulties attendant in these kinds of situations and, if Clement's quotation is any indication, as previously unknown pseudepigrapha from Qumran are published, scholars may discover more of the sources for some of the many unattributed citations in the Christian church fathers.

APPENDIX

1 Clem. 50:4 (SC 167.182):
γέγραπται γάρ· εἰσέλθετε εἰς τὰ ταμεῖα μικρὸν ὅσον ὅσον, ἕως οὗ παρέλθῃ ἡ ὀργὴ καὶ ὁ θυμός μου, καὶ μνησθήσομαι ἡμέρας ἀγαθῆς, καὶ ἀναστήσω ὑμᾶς ἐκ τῶν θηκῶν ὑμῶν.

4Q385 12:

ן יהוה ויקומו כל העם וין]עמדו[עלןרגליהם	1
]ל את יהוה צבאות ואף אני מן.[ן.חי עמהסן	2
vac[at ויאמר יהוה אלי בן]אדם ...[.ן.] להסן	3
בקברוןתהם ישכבו עד אשןר יעבור זעם ואני	4
פתח את קברותן]יכם ומן הארץ ן	5
]אשר[26	6a
]ל מצן[	6

Ezek. 37:12
MT:

הנה אני פתח את קברותיכם והעליתי
אתכם מקברותיכם עמי והבאתי אתכם
אל אדמת ישראל

LXX:
Ἰδοὺ ἐγὼ ἀνοίγω ὑμῶν τὰ μνήματα καὶ ἀνάξω ὑμας ἐκ τῶν μνημάτων ὑμῶν καὶ εἰσάξω ὑμᾶς εἰς τὴν γῆν τοῦ Ισραηλ.

Isa. 26:20
MT:

לך עמי בא בחדריך
וסגר דלתיך בעדך
חבי כמעט רגע
עד יעבור זעם

LXX (vv. 19-20):
ἀναστήσονται οἱ νεκροί καὶ ἐγερθήσονται οἱ ἐν τοῖς μνημείοις καὶ εὐφρανθήσονται οἱ ἐν τῇ γῇ...βάδιζε λαός μου εἴσελθε εἰς τὰ ταμίειά σου ἀπόκλεισον τὴν θύραν σου ἀποκρύβηθι μικρὸν ὅσον ὅσον ἕως ἂν παρέλθῃ ἡ ὀργὴ κυρίου.

---

[26] Eisenman and Wise, "*The Dead Sea Scrolls Uncovered*, 58, reconstruct נאשם here written above line 6. What looks like a *mem* I believe is actually a *resh* with the top of a *lamed* extending from the line and touching the *resh*. I am not certain at all, based on the microfiche photo, that the letter preceding the *aleph* is a *nun*. It could just as easily be the top of a *lamed* from the line below. Hence I have reconstructed אשר here.

INDICES

INDEX OF ANCIENT SOURCES

1. BIBLE

5. Dead Sea Scrolls

6. Christian Authors and Works

7. Classical Literature

11. Targums and Other Translations

12. Medieval Jewish Authors and Works

13. Ancient and Supernatural Figures

14. Locations

INDEX OF MODERN AUTHORS

Westermann, C. 160
Wills, L. 125
Wilson, A. M. 125
Wise, M. O. 8, 14, 15, 19, 187, 193
Wright, B. G. 55, 117, 186
Wright, W. 78
Wynkoop, J. D. 34

Yadin, Y. 12, 14, 15, 121, 122, 124,
128, 175, 180
Yerushalmi, Y. H. 31

STUDIES ON THE TEXTS
OF THE DESERT OF JUDAH

1. WERNBERG MØLLER, P. *The Manual of Discipline*. Translated and Annotated, with an Introduction. 1957. ISBN 90 04 02195 7
2. PLOEG, J. VAN DER. *Le rouleau de la guerre*. Traduit et annoté, avec une introduction. 1959. ISBN 90 04 02196 5
3. MANSOOR, M. *The Thanksgiving Hymns*. Translated and Annotated with an Introduction. 1961. ISBN 90 04 02197 3
5. KOFFMAHN, E. *Die Doppelurkunden aus der Wüste Juda*. Recht und Praxis der jüdischen Papyri des 1. und 2. Jahrhunderts n. Chr. samt Übertragung der Texte und Deutscher Übersetzung. 1968. ISBN 90 04 03148 0
6. KUTSCHER, E.Y. *The Language and linguistic Background of the Isaiah Scroll (1 QIsaᵃ)*. Transl. from the first (1959) Hebrew ed. With an obituary by H.B. ROSÉN. 1974. ISBN 90 04 04019 6
6a. KUTSCHER, E.Y. *The Language and Linguistic Background of the Isaiah Scroll (1 QIsaᵃ)*. Indices and Corrections by E. QIMRON. Introduction by S. MORAG. 1979. ISBN 90 04 05974 1
7. JONGELING, B. *A Classified Bibliography of the Finds in the Desert of Judah, 1958-1969*. 1971. ISBN 90 04 02200 7
8. MERRILL, E.H. *Qumran and Predestination*. A Theological Study of the Thanksgiving Hymns. 1975. ISBN 90 04 042652
9. GARCÍA MARTÍNEZ, F. *Qumran and Apocalyptic*. Studies on the Aramaic Texts from Qumran. 1992. ISBN 90 04 09586 1
10. DIMANT, D. & U. RAPPAPORT (eds.). *The Dead Sea Scrolls*. Forty Years of research. 1992. ISBN 90 04 09679 5
11. TREBOLLE BARRERA, J. & L. VEGAS MONTANER (eds.). *The Madrid Qumran Congress*. Proceedings of the International Congress on the Dead Sea Scrolls, Madrid 18-21 March 1991. 2 vols. 1993. ISBN 90 04 09771 6 *set*
12. NITZAN, B. *Qumran Prayer and Religious Poetry* 1994. ISBN 90 04 09658 2
13. STEUDEL, A. *Der Midrasch zur Eschatologie aus der Qumrangemeinde (4QMidrEschatᵃ·ᵇ)*. Materielle Rekonstruktion, Textbestand, Gattung und traditionsgeschichtliche Einordnung des durch 4Q174 („Florilegium") und 4Q177 („Catena A") repräsentierten Werkes aus den Qumranfunden. 1994. ISBN 90 04 09763 5
14. SWANSON, D.D. *The Temple Scroll and the Bible*. The Methodology of 11QT. ISBN 90 04 09849 6
15. BROOKE, G.J. (ed.). *New Qumran Texts and Studies*. Proceedings of the First Meeting of the International Organization for Qumran Studies, Paris 1992. With F. García Martínez. 1994. ISBN 90 04 10093 8
16. DIMANT, D. & L.H. SCHIFFMAN. *Time to Prepare the Way in the Wilderness*. Papers on the Qumran Scrolls by Fellows of the Institute for Advanced Studies of the Hebrew University, Jerusalem, 1989-1990. 1995. ISBN 90 04 10225 6
17. FLINT, P.W. *The Dead Sea Psalms Scrolls and the Book of Psalms*. 1997. ISBN 90 04 10341 4
18. LANGE, A. *Weisheit und Prädestination*. Weisheitliche Urordnung und Prädestination in den Textfunden von Qumran. 1995. ISBN 90 04 10432 1

19. GARCÍA MARTÍNEZ, F. & D.W. PARRY. *A Bibliography of the Finds in the Desert of Judah 1970-95*. Arranged by Author with Citation and Subject Indexes. 1996. ISBN 90 04 10588 3

20. PARRY, D.W. & S.D. RICKS (eds.). *Current Research and Technological Developments on the Dead Sea Scrolls*. Conference on the Texts from the Judean Desert, Jerusalem, 30 April 1995. 1996. ISBN 90 04 10662 6

21. METSO, S. *The Textual Development of the Qumran Community Rule*. 1997. ISBN 90 04 10683 9

22. HERBERT, E.D. *Reconstructing Biblical Dead Sea Scrolls*. A New Method applied to the Reconstruction of 4QSamᵃ. 1997. ISBN 90 04 10684 7

23. BERNSTEIN, M., F. GARCÍA MARTÍNEZ & J. KAMPEN (eds.). *Legal texts and Legal Issues*. Proceedings of the Second Meeting of the International Organization for Qumran Studies, Cambridge 1995. Published in honour of Joseph M. Baumgarten. 1997. ISBN 90 04 10829 7

24. LEFKOVITS, J.K. *The Copper Scroll – 3Q15: A Reevaluation*. A new Reading, Translation, and Commentary. ISBN 90 04 10685 5 (In preparation)

25. GLEßMER, U. *Die Ideale Kultordnung*: 24 Priesterordnungen in den Chronikbüchern, kalendarischen Qumrantexten und in synagogalen Inschriften. ISBN 90 04 10837 8 (In preparation)

26. MURAOKA, T. & J.F. ELWOLDE (eds.). *The Hebrew of the Dead Sea Scrolls & Ben Sira*. Proceedings of a Symposium held at Leiden University, 11-14 December 1995. 1997. ISBN 90 04 10820 3

27. FALK, D.K. *Daily, Sabbath, and Festival Prayers in the Dead Sea Scrolls*. 1998. ISBN 90 04 10817 3

28. STONE, M.E. & E.G. CHAZON, (eds.). *Biblical Perspectives: Early Use and Interpretation of the Bible in Light of the Dead Sea Scrolls*. Proceedings of the First International Symposium of the Orion Center for the Study of the Dead Sea Scrolls and Associated Literature, 12-14 May, 1996. 1998. ISBN 90 04 10939 0

29. HEMPEL, C. *The Laws of the Damascus Document*. Sources, Tradition and Redaction. 1998. ISBN 90 04 11150 6

30. PARRY, D.W. & E. ULRICH (eds.) *The Provo International Conference on the Dead Sea Scrolls*. Technological Innovations, New Texts, and Reformulated Issues. 1999. ISBN 90 04 11155 7

31. CHAZON, E.G. & STONE, M. (eds.) *Pseudepigraphic Perspectives*. The Apocrypha and Pseudepigrapha in Light of the Dead Sea Scrolls. Proceedings of the International Symposium of the Orion Center for the Study of the Dead Sea Scrolls and Associated Literature, 12-14 January, 1997. 1999. ISBN 90 04 11164 6

32. PARRY, D.W. & QIMRON, E. (eds.) *The Great Isaiah Scroll (1QIsaᵃ)*. *A New Edition*. 1999. ISBN 90 04 11277 4